Luminos is the Open Access monograph publishing program from UC Press. Luminos provides a framework for preserving and reinvigorating monograph publishing for the future and increases the reach and visibility of important scholarly work. Titles published in the UC Press Luminos model are published with the same high standards for selection, peer review, production, and marketing as those in our traditional program. www.luminosoa.org

The author gratefully acknowledges the generous support of the Fellows at Independent Research Institutions program of the National Endowment for the Humanities.

NATIONAL ENDOWMENT FOR THE HUMANITIES

Any views, findings, conclusions, or recommendations expressed in this publication do not necessarily reflect those of the National Endowment for the Humanities.

Awarded the

Edward Cameron Dimock, Jr. Prize in the Indian Humanities

by the American Institute of Indian Studies and published with the Institute's generous support

AIIS Publication Committee

Sarah Lamb, Co-Chair
Anand A. Yang, Co-Chair
Sonal Khullar
Gabrielle Kruks-Wisner
Preeta Mani
Tulasi Srinivas

Rated A

FEMINIST MEDIA HISTORIES
Shelley Stamp, Series Editor

1. *Their Own Best Creations: Women Writers in Postwar Television*, by Annie Berke

2. *Violated Frames: Armando Bó and Isabel Sarli's Sexploits*, by Victoria Ruétalo

3. *Recollecting Lotte Eisner: Cinema, Exile, and the Archive*, by Naomi DeCelles

4. *A Queer Way of Feeling: Girl Fans and Personal Archives in Early Hollywood*, by Diana W. Anselmo

5. *Incomplete: The Feminist Possibilities of the Unfinished Film*, edited by Alix Beeston and Stefan Solomon

6. *Producing Feminism: Television Work in the Age of Women's Liberation*, by Jennifer S. Clark

7. *To Be an Actress: Labor and Performance in Anna May Wong's Cross-Media World*, by Yiman Wang

8. *Rated A: Soft-Porn Cinema and Mediations of Desire in India*, by Darshana Sreedhar Mini

Rated A

Soft-Porn Cinema and Mediations of Desire in India

Darshana Sreedhar Mini

UNIVERSITY OF CALIFORNIA PRESS

University of California Press
Oakland, California

© 2024 by Darshana Sreedhar Mini

This work is licensed under a Creative Commons (CC BY-NC-ND) license. To view a copy of the license, visit http://creativecommons.org/licenses.

Suggested citation: Mini, D. S. *Rated A: Soft-Porn Cinema and Mediations of Desire in India*. Oakland: University of California Press, 2024. DOI: https://doi.org/10.1525/luminos.195

Library of Congress Cataloging-in-Publication Data

Names: Mini, Darshana Sreedhar, author.
Title: Rated A : soft-porn cinema and mediations of desire in India / Darshana Sreedhar Mini.
Other titles: Feminist media histories (Series) ; 8.
Description: Oakland, California : University of California Press, [2024] | Series: Feminist media histories ; 8 | Includes bibliographical references and index.
Identifiers: LCCN 2023054323 (print) | LCCN 2023054324 (ebook) | ISBN 9780520397453 (paperback) | ISBN 9780520397460 (ebook)
Subjects: LCSH: Pornographic films—India—Kerala—20th century. | Pornographic film industry—India—Kerala—20th century.
Classification: LCC PN1995.9.S45 M56 2024 (print) | LCC PN1995.9.S45 (ebook) | DDC 791.43/6538—dc23/eng/20240111
LC record available at https://lccn.loc.gov/2023054323
LC ebook record available at https://lccn.loc.gov/2023054324

33 32 31 30 29 28 27 26 25 24
10 9 8 7 6 5 4 3 2 1

To Ammumma, *for your encouragement*

CONTENTS

Acknowledgments　　ix

Introduction: Soft-Porn 101　　1

1. *Madakarani*: The Screen Pleasures of the Sex Siren in Malayalam Cinema　　31
2. Waiting for Kodambakkam: Economies of Waiting and Labor in Tinsel Town　　60
3. Embodied Vulnerabilities: Precarity and Body Work　　87
4. The Alternative Transnational: Migration, Media, and Soft-Porn　　116
5. (Dis)Appearances: Digital Remediations of Soft-Porn in the Contemporary　　139

Conclusion: In Praise of Bad Women　　166

Notes　　173
Bibliography　　199
Index　　209

ACKNOWLEDGMENTS

Although books are written in relative loneliness, they are always marked by the kindness and generosity of many co-passengers. In writing this book, my heart and mind have been touched by many friends, family members, and mentors without whom I would not have completed it.

My dissertation chair Priya Jaikumar's support and encouragement over the years was crucial for this project. Her sharp thinking and meticulous organization shepherded me as I made my way through the maze of research. My committee members—Ellen Seiter, Nitin Govil, Kara Keeling, and Bhaskar Sarkar—guided and supported me to move beyond the conventional trappings of fieldwork and research. Ellen Seiter was more than just a committee member; her bounty of warmth kept me going even when there were significant challenges.

At USC, I want to thank Tara McPherson, J. D. Connor, Todd Boyd, Akira Lippit, Christine Acham, Bill Whittington, Michael Renov, Aniko Imre, Lan Duong, Laura Serna, Tania Modleski, Nancy Lutkehaus, Vanessa Schwartz, Sunyoung Park, Diana Blaine, Alicia Cornish, Maria Cheteboune, and Katherine Steinbach. Classes and conversations with Philana Payton, Şebnem Baran, Michael Turcious, Eszter Zimanyi, Emma Ben Ayoun, Sara Bakerman, Jake Bohrod, Darol Kay, and Ashley Young have made it an intellectually stimulating journey.

J. Devika's support and generosity was crucial for the completion of this project. The assurance that I could rely on her for critical input, as well as emotional support, was more than I could ask for. Priya Sangameswaran was always a strong advocate for me from my M.Phil. days and taught me how to combine academic rigor with humane values.

This book was first conceived as a dissertation at Jawaharlal Nehru University, New Delhi, and I remember with fondness the support of Ira Bhaskar, Y. S. Alone, Ranjani Mazumdar, Veena Hariharan, and Udaya Kumar. Scholarly work by C. S. Venkiteswaran, Ratheesh Radhakrishnan, Jenson Joseph, Navaneeta Mokkil, Bindu Menon, Meena T. Pillai, Mohammed Shafeek, Manju Edachira, Sujith Parayil, Dileep Raj, and others working on Malayalam cinema were also crucial in setting up my project.

At various points, this project received the support of the USC Graduate School, USC's Visual Studies Research Institute, the Social Science Research Council, the American Institute of Indian Studies, and the National Endowment for the Humanities. The AIIS Dissertation-to-Book workshop session facilitated by Jyoti Puri and Harleen Singh helped me with the initial drafting of the book proposal. I am thankful to my media studies cohort at the workshop, Swapnil Rai and Padma Chirumamilla, for their helpful comments. Support for this research was provided by the University of Wisconsin–Madison's Office of the Vice Chancellor for Research and Graduate Education, with funding from the Wisconsin Alumni Research Foundation. I am also thankful to the First Book Award granted by the Center for Humanities that supported the book workshop, and for the generous comments and suggestions by Monika Mehta, Mireille Miller-Young, Preeti Chopra, and Lindsay Palmer.

I am fortunate to work in UW–Madison's Department of Communication Arts, and would like to thank Kelley Conway, Eric Hoyt, Aaron Greer, Jeff Smith, Ben Singer, Jeremy Morris, Jonathan Gray, Derek Johnson, Lori Lopez, Catalina Toma, Lyn von Swol, Zhongdang Pan, Sara McKinnon, Rob Asen, Jenell Johnson, and Rob Howard for the intellectual comradeship that made this book possible. Lynn Malone, Clara Schanck, and Sophie Houghland helped keep me on track with the book work and my many research trips. I am also grateful to Mary Russa, Steffie Halverson, and Daniel Feuer for their wonderful company (and many a warm chat). A special shout-out to the "real, real executive committee"—Allison Prasch, Lillie Williamson, and Jason Lopez, who were the absolute best support group.

At the Center for South Asia, I want to thank Anthony Cerulli, Sarah Beckham, Preeti Chopra, Aparna Dharwadker, Mitra Sharafi, Todd Michelson-Ambelang, Mou Banerjee, Vinay Dharwadker, Priya Mukherjee, Venkat Mani, Viren Murthy, and Andrea Fowler. The warmth and generosity with which they welcomed me to Madison was a salve (especially since I moved to Madison during the pandemic). Thanks to Laurie Beth Clark, Sarah Wells, Paola S. Hernández, and Lori Diprette Brown for their comradeship.

My book owes its origin to the stimulating scholarship on adult media produced by a group of scholars, many of whom are part of the Adult Film History SIG at the Society of Cinema and Media Studies. As I was struggling to articulate why explicit media has to be studied on its own terms, I found an intellectual home among scholars who were able to support and mentor me. I am thankful to

Eric Schaefer, Constance Penley, Patrick Keilty, Elena Gorfinkel, Feona Attwood, Susanna Paasonen, Peter Alilunas, and Clarissa Smith, who have contributed to my thinking on pornography. Thanks to Brandon Arroyo, Finley Freibert, John Stadler, Rebecca Holt, Nikola Stepic, and Desirae Embree for their camaraderie. I also remember fondly the circle of South Asian scholars—Swarnavel Eswaran, Madhuja Mukherjee, Rashmi Sawney, Lotte Hoek, Pavitra Sundar, Tejaswini Ganti, Neepa Majumdar, Anuja Jain, Anupama Prabhala, Manishita Dass, Ravi Vasudevan, Kareem Khubchandani, Akshya Saxena, Monika Mehta, Sriram Mohan, Lia Wolock, and Pallavi Rao—who have enriched me with their insights.

As this work spanned a decade, I was fortunate to be supported by my respondents who went out of their way to open their personal archives and connect me with their networks to support my work. Sreekumar's generosity in connecting me with many distribution and exhibition agents in Kerala is fondly remembered. Special thanks to my Chennai-based respondents A. T. Joy, Thrikunnapuzha Sreekumar, Ponaiyan, P. Chandrakumar, Nagarajan, Kerala-based respondents Gladys, R. K. Prasad, and others who became an important part of this project's narrative. Mohsina Najeeb and Arathi M. R. helped me track down contacts and material. Thanks, Radhakrishan, for the wonderful illustrations that accompany this book. Thanks to Unnamati Syama Sundar, Sarat Chandran, Priyaranjan Lal, Ammar Al Attar, David Farris, Mini Richard and Rajeev for allowing me to use their images.

Family and friends have been a crucial part of this journey as well. My parents, N. Sreedharan and Mini Syamala, and my brother, Vivek, have been a constant source of support. Over the years, they supported me despite their initial misgivings on the porn aspects of the project. Anima Baishya, Amit Baishya, Andreea Marculescu, and Leon were key sources of inspiration and gave me the much-needed emotional anchoring. My grandparents, Gopinathan and Shyamala; my father-in-law, Dwipen Baishya; and my close friend Anushree passed away before I could complete this book, but I like to think that they would have been happy to see its completion.

During research trips in India, I was fortunate to be in the company of Srinivasans in Chennai, the Tambes in Bombay, and the Niroop family in Calicut. They have all opened their doors and homes to me, and facilitated my research with warm food, a comfortable bed, and most of all, great company. Library personnel at Kerala University Library (Kerala Studies section), AKG Center Library (Trivandrum), Center for Development Studies Library (Trivandrum), Appan Thampuran Library (Thrissur), Chittira Thirunal Grandashala (Trivandrum), National Film Archive of India (NFAI) Pune, Nehru Memorial Museum and Library (New Delhi), and *Mathrubhumi* archives (Calicut) were kind and helpful during my constant search for archival material. During the fieldwork in India, I was also lucky to be hosted by the Center for Development Studies (CDS) and Center for Cultural Studies, Institute of English. Individual collectors such as Gopan Sasthamangalam, Ethiran Kathiravan, and R. Gopalakrishnan have opened up their personal archives for me and enriched my work.

I would like to thank *Bioscope: South Asian Screen Studies*, *Feminist Media Histories*, and *Music, Sound and Moving Image* for granting me permission to reuse material that has been previously published.

A few friends deserve special mention—they not only facilitated my work but also served as emotional refuge. Spandan Bhattacharya has been a longtime friend, but as far as this book goes, was a crucial "field-agent." He was generous with his time during my Kolkata fieldwork by accompanying me to many theaters where I would not have gained entry as a single woman or able to communicate as a non-Bengali. I would also like to thank P. K. Sreenivasan who helped me with the Kodambakkam leg of the fieldwork, and for his continued support remotely. Samhita Sunya was always there for me to chat about work and life. I would like to think of her as one of the guardian angels of this book.

Thanks to Maneesh Narayanan and Remya Raj for connecting me with the respondents, and for their support of this project. N. P. Sajeesh, Aparna Eswaran, Subin Menon, Anargha Niroop, Aswathy Sivaram, Priyanka H. S., Mehboob and Dipti Tambe are close friends who were there for me when I needed them. Without their constant support and their patience with my constant chattering about work, I may not have survived the writing process. Sarah O'Brien generously helped me with the flow of the arguments and how to make it a better read.

At UC Press, I want to thank Shelley Stamp for the support she offered to feature the book in the Feminist Media History series. Special thanks to Raina Polivka's meticulous streamlining and advice that helped me with the timeline for the book. Sam Warren and Susan Larsen were a pleasure to work with, and I appreciate their advice and support.

Finally, I would like to thank Anirban, who has supported me throughout. His insights have been crucial in helping me develop my thinking and writing. He was my sounding board when I was wading through raw ideas. He has supported my scholarship in more ways than one, including of course, his legendary skills in the kitchen. This book might not have seen the light if not for his unconditional support.

Introduction

Soft-Porn 101

I grew up in the Malayalam-speaking state of Kerala in the southwestern tip of India, where gendered expectations dictated everyday social interactions—from the kind of clothes women could wear to how they should behave within the remit of heteronormative femininity. Modern Kerala's history has been marked by social reform movements, the impact of Christian missionaries, and left-leaning activism initiated by the first democratically elected government in 1957. Over time, Kerala has come to be known for its matrilineal past, seen in some communities like the Nairs and Ezhavas, and for its famous "development model," which emphasized progressive social development through high levels of literacy, longer life expectancy, low mortality, and higher rates of fertility. But the fruits of such development did not translate equally for marginalized groups, including women, Dalits (caste-oppressed communities), queer people, and tribal communities whose claims to public resources fell outside the neat matrixes of developmentalist discourse.[1] Feminist critiques exposed the rhetorical conceit of selective "development," which imposed expectations of idealized sexuality and behavior on women, thereby limiting their chances to fruitfully participate in public and political life.[2] Critical interventions offered by autonomous women's movements and civil society activism exposed the heteropatriarchal strongholds that underlined family and workspaces.[3] While developmentalist feminism and political decentralization brought gender discourses to the mainstream and increased women's representation in local self-governance, such mainstreaming also diluted the oppositional power of feminism when state interventions co-opted women's empowerment through the figure of the gender expert.[4] Amid such developments, social norms and gender relations continued to be fraught, and the state saw several high-profile cases of sexual abuse, casteist discriminations, and homophobic attacks that reflected the violence in everyday social exchanges. Such interventions mobilized public opinion in critically important ways and fortified oppositional civil society by organizing marginalized groups such as sex workers and the queer community.[5] Even against this background, young women like myself found ways of exploring our sexuality and discovering that the erotic spectrum of the world was far wider than what heteropatriarchal norms would allow.

During my time in high school in the early 2000s, I would look forward with much anticipation to assisting my father in his convenience store after school. Situated at an intersection between two schools (one for boys, the other for girls) and two hospitals, and adjacent to the Government Secretariat, our shop catered to a varied constituency of patrons and was a sociosexual assemblage in its own right. A vending machine for condoms and a private phone booth-type cubicle stood amid stacks of sensational magazines like *Fire* and *Crime* in full view of our customers, providing me with a chance—while playing the good daughter helping with chores—to observe the innocuous ways customers would indicate their interest in such publications. These magazines—carrying confessional narratives and stories about teenagers; sensational accounts of political scandals; and daring, attention-grabbing covers—were bought by men and women alike, and the placement of women's magazines, such as *Vanita* and *Grihalakshmi*, next to *Fire* and *Crime* incentivized combo offers. As Shobha, one of the fifty respondents I interviewed for this book between 2011 and 2022 explained: "Seeing women purchasing these magazines was seen as an opportunity by men, who took it as sign to ask us out or imagine a free-sex companion in us, while for suburban working women like myself, this provided a space for liberation."[6]

Though it was a run-of-the-mill establishment, many variants of which can be found all over India, our shop was the space where I first began to think about the social and spatial configurations that informed public discourses about and private attitudes toward sex in Kerala. My first brush with Malayalam "soft-porn" as an analytical object came a little later when I conducted research on sex education policy in Kerala in 2010. As I soon found out during focus group discussions for this research, soft-porn films were considered "sex education" material by teenage boys. The state government's sex education program was shelved in 2007, when conservative teachers' associations disagreed with the safe-sex practices outlined in sex education booklets and demanded morally conservative content to promote "healthy citizenship."[7] This move was rooted in debates about the kind of material that could be used by young people to scientifically understand safe-sex practices. Anti-sex education lobbyists flagged as a major concern the influx of *ikkili* (titillating) material that was packaged as sex education and marketed as scientific tracts compiled under the supervision of medical doctors.[8] For the young men I spoke to in my research, soft-porn became an unlikely sexual supplement that filled the lacuna created by these developments. In breakout group discussions about how they encountered explicit material, my respondents referred to "Shakeela films" (referring to the name of a popular actress), "soft-porn," *thundu katha* (vernacular erotic stories), and internet porn as sources of their sexual education. Following up on their comments, I visited the proprietors of shops that sold CDs (compact discs) in Thampanoor and Beemapally (both in the capital city of Trivandrum, the latter an erstwhile hub for pirated CDs), and they confirmed that they were popular with teenagers and middle-aged men who bought the soft-porn films they stocked. In the process, I became aware of the gendered matrices that shaped consumption patterns, as the very same erotic material available for teenage boys who were my age was denied to girls due to codes of ideal feminine values. Seeking out these videos in the CD-turned-DVD shops as a woman was considered taboo, and there were a handful of instances when I was asked to return later because I offended the sensibilities of the "middle-class family customers." Such gendered discrepancies were built into the way industrial apparatuses of adult media were ingeniously accommodated within quotidian spaces. My interest in such discrepancies was the kernel from which this book has grown.

In *Rated A*, I examine how soft-porn films have shaped media publics in India by improvising industrial models and reshaping representational idioms. These films have been at the center of debates about sex education, censorship, and gender nonconformity. All films in India screened in public spaces must be certified by the Central Board of Film Certification (CBFC), the body constituted according to the provisions laid out by the Cinematograph Act of 1952. The films are rated "U," "UA," "A," and "S" to denote which audiences can attend such screenings: "U" means unrestricted public exhibition; "UA" indicates "unrestricted public exhibition," with the caution that parental discretion is required for children under twelve years of age; and "S" is "restricted for any special class of persons." Films rated "A" are meant for adults (18 years and over). They consist of a mix of themes and genres that requires careful and mature handling of images of sex and violence. As per the Cinematograph (Amendment) Act of 2023, the cabinet has approved UA 7+, UA 13+, and UA 16+ ratings based on age to replace the UA labels.[9] The new ratings are a result of the expansion of internet-distributed television, which demands uniformity of categorization across different platforms. The "A" or "Adult" category was initially used only for foreign films; it was applied to Indian films for the first time in 1978 as part of the revised censorship guidelines, whereby contemporary standards were to be taken as a rule of thumb. Accordingly, the censor board was given permission to judge the film in terms of overall impact, as opposed to individual scenes.[10] Over time, the "A" rating has come to be associated with pornographic content in the collective consciousness. Malayalam soft-porn films are perhaps the most notorious and the most popular constituent of this territory rated A.

Over the years, India's relationship to pornography has been fraught because of multiple and often conflicting notions of permissibility and obscenity. Charu Gupta has shown that laws and regulations proscribing pornography find their origin in nineteenth-century colonial India, when obscenity laws first began to appear. Sections 292, 293, and 294 of the Indian Penal Code made punishable "any form of obscenity . . . any visual or written material that was 'lascivious or appealed to the prurient interest' or which had the 'effect of depraving or corrupting persons exposed to it.'"[11] In 1920, examining and certifying boards were instituted in Madras, Bombay, Calcutta, and Rangoon with jurisdiction over films exhibited in all of British India, including British Balochistan (in 1927, a censor board was set up in Lahore as well). After independence, the regional censors were absorbed into the Bombay Board of Film Censors. The Cinematograph Act of 1952 made it the Central Board of Film Censors, and it was made the Central Board of Film Certification in 1983. Periodicals like *filmindia* also performed para-censorial work, demanding uniformity in censorship operations and thereby vying for the cleansing of objectionable materials that were considered inimical to public morality.[12]

In her historical work on the emergence of cinematic publics in India, Manishita Dass identifies the segmentation of class as a crucial feature, hinting at the classed and gendered exclusions that underlie the functioning of media publics.[13] This exclusionary logic shapes the imagination of cinematic publics as hierarchically organized, creating the category of a "lower-class mass" that is vulnerable to moral corruption from "offending" cinematic representations. In this imagined mass exhibition culture, the spectators' immersive, visceral experience manifests through hooting and whistling in the cinema as they watch these films. William Mazzarella alludes to this though his metaphor of the "pissing man"—the abstract, unruly mass "incapable of the kind of critical reflexivity that was the sine qua non of coolly deliberative public reason."[14]

A similar anxiety peppers discourses that support censorship regulations. The 1980s and 1990s were marked by debates about the role of regulatory bodies and the implementation of the cuts recommended by the censor board.[15] The backdrop of Indian cinema's larger censorial climate becomes important in the case of Malayalam soft-porn, as it forms the basis for much of the genre's reception in the public imagination. In the 1980s, reports in the national press singled out Malayalam cinema as the harbinger of "sex films." In such reports, soft-porn film was featured as a constantly mutating, manipulable text because of *thundu*, the splicing of extra reels (usually sexually explicit, but not always) during the projection.[16] Distributors provided English-language titles of Malayalam films that differed significantly from their literal translations—for instance, *Raudy Ramu* (dir. M. Krishnan Nair, 1978) became *Rape Rape Rape*, *Eeta* (Parsimony; dir. I. V. Sasi, 1978) became *Thirst for Love*, and *Kutumbam Ena Swargam* (Family is heaven; dir. N. Sankaran Nair, 1984) became *Wine and Women* (Fig. 1).

FIGURE 1. Lobby card of *Kutumbam Ena Swargam* showing both Malayalam and English titles, along with the "A" for adult rating. Author's personal collection.

Activist groups, in turn, rallied against Malayalam soft-porn armed with arguments similar to the anti-pornography camp of Catharine Mackinnon and Andrea Dworkin that equated pornography with women's subordination to patriarchal power.[17] In his discussion of the anti-obscenity campaigns of the 1980s, S. V. Srinivas writes about the "Asleelata Pratighatana Vedika" (Anti-Obscenity Forum) that ran a magazine carrying lists of offending sex films. The forum alleged that obscene posters in public places embarrassed "'ladies' and 'families,'" and argued that women's presence or absence in the cinema hall could be used as evidence for a film's status as clean or obscene, as good women would avoid frequenting obscene films.[18] In 1981, Janwadi Mahila Samiti, a committee of working women, and Jan Sanskriti, a civil society group, organized protests outside Plaza Cinema in Delhi against a Malayalam film that was advertised as *Sexy Girl*.[19] The protest was led by the Janata Party leader and Member of Parliament Pramila Dandavate, under the auspices of the "Committee on [*sic*] portrayal of women in media," who demanded restrictions be placed on the screening of "dubbed films," which allegedly flouted censorship regulations by inserting pornographic sequences.[20] In the 1980s, the Delhi Media Group organized demonstrations outside a theater that was purportedly exhibiting what they alleged to be "pornographic Malayalam films," while the Forum Against Vulgar Posters advocated for legislative measures against explicit posters and titles and organized protests to raise awareness about dubbed "pornographic" films from South India.[21] Vimal Balasubramanyam writes that the issue amounted to a "parochial attack by North Indians on South Indian movies."[22] Nina Kapoor, a member of the group, wrote, "None of us could have imagined that protesting porn, whether it came from West, East, North or South could have cause so much communal passion."[23] These protests provoked the Malayalam Film Society in Delhi to counter the attack on Malayalam cinema by organizing a seminar on "Sex and Violence."

With the advent of new technologies, such as satellite television, and cyber culture, the changing mediascape of the 1990s brought to the fore a new set of anxieties around the threat of obscene representations, with soft-porn often at the center of debates. A recommendation proposed by the CBFC chairperson Vijay Anand much later in 2002 reflected some of the same tensions from the 1980s. In his review of the Cinematograph Act of 1952, Anand suggested introducing a new category, "XA," to regularize the exhibition of soft-porn films in adult-only theaters and thereby stem the tide of covert operations.[24] Following a disagreement with the government, he resigned from his post in the first year of his three-year term. Interestingly, after his resignation, he stated: "All I said was that there was a suggestion from Kerala to have designated theatres showing adult films. This is a state which makes over 200 films every year. A substantial chunk of it is pornographic films that are shown without certification."[25] Thus, even in the suggestion for a new category of certification and separate adult-only cinemas, Kerala's exceptional situation of soft-porn film production was pitched as the reason why a policy change at the national level would have to take regional cinemas into account. In 2006, Sharmila Tagore, then chairperson of the CBFC, also mentioned exploring options of "A+" or "X" rating for films so they need not be censored for explicit language or actions. However, she also added that she would not support the screening of pornographic films, which "Indian people" were not ready for due to cultural difference.[26]

The rift between the pro- and the anti-censorship lobbies reverberated in the film industry. Indeed, filmmakers attempted to use the medium of film as a subversive political tool to resist intolerant attitudes to difference. This was true of soft-porn filmmakers, as they often experimented with the formal aesthetics of film to allude to and comment on contemporary political scandals. Despite working in a seemingly "low" cultural form, soft-porn filmmakers managed to comment on issues such as corruption, the criminalization of politics, and sex scandals. This aligns with the anti-censorship lobby's claim that a relaxed censorial climate could

FIGURE 2. Artist's impression of a soft-porn shooting floor based on my interviews with industry personnel. Image courtesy S. Radhakrishnan.

allow for multiple viewpoints and diverse forms of representation.[27] Thus, taking stock of Malayalam soft-porn's nuanced negotiation of issues of gender, film production and distribution, labor practices, and the intricacies of the soft-porn imaginary in Kerala and India's social fabric requires moving beyond narrow and simplistic accounts of moral decay.

Tracing the informal transactions, precarious labor practices, and fluid regimes of visuality inaugurated by the indigenous production of soft-pornography in India, I explore how soft-porn's emergence as an industrial form is tied equally to the professional aspirations of the lower rungs of production units and to questions of sexual representation and shifting gender relationships. Given its hierarchical and exclusionary structure, the film industry does not offer opportunities for social mobility to below-the-line personnel. Workers in soft-porn acted on their desire to produce films independent of this hierarchy by turning to trust-based and informal labor arrangements. Such arrangements veered away from contractual agreements and solidified an ethical relationality that was built around the identity of "cine-workers"—a term I use to refer to anyone who has been part of the filmmaking apparatus in various stages and schedules—preproduction, production, or postproduction phases, as well as the distribution and exhibition of the films (Fig. 2).

Most filmmakers and technicians who worked in soft-porn migrated from the mainstream Malayalam film industry when it faced a huge financial crisis in the 1990s. The pseudonym-driven nature of the soft-porn industry allowed them to use their creative labor to produce low-budget films that allowed some room for representing nonnormative sexual practices on-screen, sometimes by gaming the censorship machine. The growth and sustenance of the soft-porn film industry was facilitated by revenue-sharing models that gave distributors and exhibitors a chance to negotiate deals based on speculative capital with the cast and crew—a system that relied more on trust and individual contacts than legally binding contracts. I combine a study of the regulatory practices and alternative financial circuits that motivated the soft-porn industry with a reading of the aesthetic lineage and social spaces of its form. Countering popular accounts that tell us that soft-porn films were either mired in questionable casting practices or had degraded aesthetic values, I attend to the negotiations and strategic working relationships that production personnel forged as they worked through questions of representation, female desire, and sexuality.

As a cultural form, Malayalam soft-porn is enmeshed in narratives of struggle and the precarious labor of its workers, especially the women—starlets who dreamed of becoming part of the glamorous world associated with cinema. In adopting a historical lens, I take seriously Arvind Rajagopal's assertion that we need to be "attentive to the historicity of mediatic form and the collision of different temporalities as multiple communication technologies overlap and interact with each other."[28] Although it is located in Kerala and flourished as an industrial genre only in the 1990s and early 2000s, Malayalam soft-porn exists on a continuum with earlier forms. Sexually charged print material, both from Kerala and elsewhere in India, provided a repertoire of visual and narrative codes for soft-porn, forming part of an assemblage that Sanjay Srivastava refers to as "footpath pornography."[29] The genre also drew inspiration from American exploitation cinema, which was imported to India in the 1970s and 1980s. Malayalam soft-porn is characterized by the desire to explore the lurid underpinnings behind sexual desire as it moves beyond private spaces and is framed for a voyeuristic audience—something it shares with sensational magazines. Important sources of influence on soft-porn include *kambikathakal* (combining *kambi* [erect penis] and *kathakal* [stories]), a genre of vernacular erotic literature featuring graphic descriptions of experiential sexual encounters that circulated among male readers from the 1970s onward. Another offshoot was *rathikathakal* (*rathi* [sex]), confessional columns that appeared in many popular magazines featuring stories of the sex lives of unnamed women. Although many stories were purportedly written by men using female pseudonyms, some featured soft-porn actresses such as Shakeela, Reshma, and Maria, and can be seen as connective links that cross-reference the transactions between soft-porn films and sex work. Soft-porn films also drew from sensational pulp fiction known as *painkili*, penned by writers like Pamman, Ayyaneth, and Rajan Chinankath, among others. These mostly appeared in serialized form in literary magazines, as well as in film magazines like *Nana, Film*, and *Chitrabhumi*. In addition to vivid descriptive metaphors, *painkili* was popular for the line drawings and illustrations that accompanied the stories. *Painkili* and soft-porn cinema were thus imbricated in larger cross-media conversations, with soft-porn films often drawing on *painkili* narratives for their choice of character types and narrative patterning. The "inter-textual relay" between soft-porn cinema and vernacular pornographic literature allowed these films to circumvent established visual and narrative cues.[30] Many *painkili* writers had to publicly face questions about their tacit support of *ashleela sahityam* (obscene literature). As the writer Pamman says, "I have never treated sex as *ashleelam* [obscene]. In my works, I have written with a controlled and restricted treatment of sexuality. I have tried to make *sringaram* [eroticism] enjoyable, not to make it *abhasam* [obscene]."[31] The resulting generic hybridity of soft-porn appealed to the many different imaginations of desire that are culturally encoded in the psyche of the Malayali male audience, the most enthusiastic patrons of these films.

Tracing the history of soft-porn requires, then, simultaneously examining films, magazines, and other popular accounts that circulated in public discourse—what, following Warwick Mules, I call "media publics."[32] Media publics are assemblages of infrastructures, audiences, and meaning-making apparatuses that condition the way discourses operate and define who can legitimately put their claim before others. This encompasses consumers of newspapers, radio, television, internet, cinema, and other mass culture forms. Media publics are constituted by the relationships, formations, and exchanges that media facilitate and that contribute to the organization of everyday life. While Mules broadly defines media publics as the "discursive constitution of the public through media discourse," his focus, ultimately, is on the shape of democratic societies when media impacts the constitution of public opinion.[33] But what does a media public mean for something like a popular (even, low) cultural form like soft-porn cinema? To account for this question, I conceptualize media publics as event-centric formations that accommodate contradictory viewpoints and opinions, including speculative claims and gossip; their conflictual nature offers us productive opportunities to interrogate codes of sexual and gender normativity that have kept women and other minorities out of public spaces.

I address two forms of media publics in this book: publics formed around events that are reported or represented in and by media; and collectivities formed around certain media forms and practices such as cinema (the *cinematic* public) and literature (the *reading* public). Given the extent to which mass-media forms are overwhelmingly present in the conduct of everyday life and the highly mediatized nature of public affairs, the term *media public* at this historical juncture overlaps with the public sphere. This conceptualization challenges Jürgen Habermas's condemnation of mass-media publics as "false" public spheres that limit the formation of authentic public opinions by focusing on specific objects and discourses.[34] Critics of Habermas, including Craig Calhoun, Nancy Fraser, and Joan Landes, push against the putative "truthfulness" that he associates with print media compared to newer mass media such as television, as well as his argument that the public sphere offers a level playing field, irrespective of differences in class, gender, and race.[35] Other scholars, including Geoff Eley and Michael Warner, have suggested that not only can the total "public sphere" imagined by Habermas be exclusionary, but many publics and competing counterpublics can coexist at any time within a given society.[36] Warner's distinction between "*the* public" and "*a* public" is instructive here: "the public" is the social totality, and "a public" is a collective that is spatially and temporally bounded and comes into being as it interacts with an event or an object.[37] If one considers the diversity of media forms, their varied target audiences, and the myriad ways in which they use media, we can begin to talk of "*a* media public" in relation to specific media objects and issues. Although "media publics" can refer to a totalizing "the" ingrained in Warner's definition of "the public," speaking about specific objects such as soft-porn necessitates thinking in terms of "a public."

In the context of South Asia, scholars such as Thomas Blom Hansen, Sudipta Kaviraj, and Sandria B. Freitag have addressed the various manifestations of public spaces and the multiple publics that have coexisted, contested dominant and popular forms, and unsettled efforts to universalize a singular public.[38] To conceptualize a "public sphere" in the South Asian context, one must attend to the messiness and conflicting publics that have historically coexisted in the region. Aligning with this approach, I draw on Arjun Appadurai and Carol A. Breckenridge's conception that public culture forms a "*zone* of cultural debate . . . where other types, forms and domains of culture are encountering, interrogating and contesting each other in new and unexpected ways."[39] My conceptualization of soft-porn's "media publics" in Kerala is indebted to this understanding of forms that encounter and contest each other. In conceptualizing a "media public" in relation to soft-porn in Kerala, one cannot simply speak of an isolated cinematic audience. Instead, various media forms, including pulp fiction, erotic literature, yellow magazines, television news, and the cinema, and their corresponding policies, moralities, and ethicalities collide, contest, and negotiate with each other in this assemblage. In this, media publics are by nature what Aravind Rajagopal calls a "split public."[40] Rajagopal envisages this as "a heuristic in thinking about an incomplete modern polity, standing for the relationship between the configuration of political society desired by modernizing elites and its actual historical forms."[41] Although Rajagopal's specific focus is on the role of English and Hindi print media in the rise of Hindu nationalism in the 1980s and 1990s, as a heuristic it offers us ways to think about the sexual-popular and how the imagination of chaste sexuality (seen in censorship mechanisms, for example), can contrast with the realities of lived sexual experiences and non-normative representations.

MEDIA PUBLICS, SCANDALS, AND THE POLITICS OF EXPOSURE

In the context of modern Kerala, the public sphere solidified in the second half of the nineteenth century when newspapers and journals began intervening in matters that were of "public interest" to the community.[42] Udaya Kumar identifies newspapers' direct address to the people as a performative element that brings into existence *pothujanam*—*pothu*, meaning "the common," and *janam*, "the people"—the public whose opinions it claims to represent.[43] Thus, the public sphere is perceived as constituted by common people who engage with issues that are of shared interest to the community—the commons is delineated as an area of shared responsibility between the media and the society it represents. This idea of "the common" is also central to the proliferation of gossip, rumor, and scandals that are often pitched as publicizing private spaces and affairs—what J. Devika has called "scandal publics."[44] In scandal publics, intrusion into the private realm is legitimized under the guise of collective responsibility. An instance that showcases the media's intrusive gaze can be seen in the footage of a young couple hugging in the Kairali People news channel's coverage of a 2008 protest supporting a land struggle at Chengara, organized by Dalits and Adivasis to demand ownership of cultivable land. Including this footage was aimed not only at delegitimizing the protests against the government but also at dictating what kinds of bodies and interactions could be scrutinized in a protest space. The very fact that it was a night vigil was used against the couple for having transgressed the codes of protest. After this footage was aired, the women's wing of Kerala's left party organized a cleansing ritual against the alleged sexual indiscipline at the event.[45]

Often, as the examples in this book will show, scandal publics overlap with media publics and fold representational and social spaces into each other. The figure of the prostitute connects scandal- and media publics, as the need to control women's sexuality was the fulcrum around which these debates took shape. An early instance of this enfolding can be seen in the history of the Trivandrum-based daily *Thaniniram* (True color), started by Kalanilayam Krishnan Nair in the 1950s, which soon expanded to include *Thaniniram Film Entertainment Magazine*. The magazine's logo featured a monkey looking intently at its reflection in a mirror, a symbolic image that refers to the motto of the publisher—"to reveal the true color," without any dilution of facts. *Thaniniram* framed its exposure narratives as empowering citizens to keep abreast of the latest happenings around them, be they political scandal, crime, marital infidelity, or corruption. Using the phrase *thurannu parachil* (exposure/ confession), which refers to the total revelation of information, *Thaniniram* gave confessional accounts a wide currency. It featured catchy headlines that stirred the reader's curiosity, and its reporters included a somewhat loose category of "citizen journalists" or stringers, collectively referred to as "the Gestapo" (the "touring Gestapo" and "Madras Gestapo"), who exposed the latest gossip about prominent people's bedroom secrets.[46] By borrowing the name of the Nazi secret police, *Thaniniram* guarded the identities of the stringers who collected such information while preventing possible defamation suits against them. *Thaniniram* was unofficially "banned" in most family-oriented domestic spaces because of its concentration on salacious news, but it circulated widely in male-dominated public spaces such as salons and teashops. Its accounts spun narrative threads aimed at delaying closure by continuously revealing new potential factors that needed to be accounted for in the context of a crime or scandal, and this signature style sustained *Thaniniram*'s readership. This strategy of deferral would later be replicated in obituaries for female stars and starlets in film and yellow magazines, which I explore in the first chapter of this book. *Thaniniram*'s content included columns on illicit relationships and prostitution, confessions by film actresses, and erotic stories. It also featured advertisements for sex magazines, extracts from and advertisements for forthcoming sex-related books (e.g., *Seduction Science, The Surprising Secret in the Sex World, The Sex Plays of Malayali Girls, Prostitute's Dairy, Nameless Prostitute,* and *Prostitute's Daughter*),[47] and advertisements for collector's editions of nude photo albums like the one by "Music Book Stall, Kottayam," which featured "bedroom photographs" of young women and men and women engaging in sex acts.[48]

Exceeding the genre of film-based reporting or evening tabloid reportage, such content set the stage for the kind of mix that later films and sensational reportage would feature. Further, the practice of inserting photographs sourced from film shoots alongside content with erotic undertones prefigured soft-porn's culture of splicing in explicit bits during film exhibition. This mixture reveals a field of exchange among politics, news, and cinema in terms of narrative and rhetorical structure. The "media public" in this context is not necessarily created by the media event or object, but already exists in relation to it. In this case, *pothu* is generated at the interstices of common concerns and shared responsibilities, although the language of "responsibility" often disguises voyeuristic formations and erotic sensationalism. This is a key point, because it is impossible to separate debates around soft-porn from wider discourses on obscenity and voyeurism in Kerala.

The Malayalam words *ashleelatha* (obscenity) or *ashleelam* (obscene) point to coarse, vulgar, or indecorous behavior that violates societal proscriptions. Discussions of obscenity in Kerala have a long history in literature in the writings of authors such as Sanjayan (M. R. Nair), Kutti Krishna Marar, Thakazhi Sivasankara Pillai, and Vaikom Muhammad Basheer, who were part of the progressive literature movement, and in art, as seen in public debates about Kanayi Kunhiraman's 30-foot-tall nude female sculpture *Yakshi* (1969). Rajeev Kumaramkandath notes that debates on obscenity were at the forefront of the regulation of literary publics in Kerala in the 1940s.[49] For instance, Basheer's novella *Sabdangal* (Voices, 1947) caused an uproar in Kerala because the author attempted to deal with themes such as homosexuality and prostitution. Written in the form of a confessional narrative, the novel features an encounter between the author and an unnamed soldier who is discharged from the army. The soldier says: "During my time in the army, my lover was the photograph of an actress. For many bachelors like me, she was our shared lover. The picture had eyes, breasts, navels and thighs and we had our own imaginations . . . kisses, embrace and masturbation."[50] M. S. Devadas, a communist ideologue, delivered a scathing attack of *Sabdangal* for its explicit sexual referencing. For Devadas, the book imitated the cheap novels from the West that revel in "sexual anarchy."[51] In 1957, the Kerala school curriculum board's inclusion of a short novel *Nteuppuppaykkoranendarnnu* (My grandfather had an elephant, 1951) by Basheer also had to be recalled at the last minute in the wake of protests against obscenity.[52]

Crucially for our understanding of soft-porn, such obscenity debates also extend to the sphere of politics, manifesting in a series of political scandals that have centered the figure of the sexualized woman. This includes a 1963 case in which newspapers reported that State Home Minister P. T. Chacko was having an affair with a mysterious, unidentified woman;[53] the notorious Suryanelli case of 1996, in which a sixteen-year-old girl was raped by forty-five men in different locations over forty days;[54] and the 1995 Indian Space Research Organization (ISRO) case that charged Mariam Rasheeda, a Maldivian woman, as a *charasundari* (beautiful spy) who was allegedly a CIA agent planted to prevent India's deal with Russia to acquire cryogenic technology.[55] In each of these cases, women as either victims or conspirators were rhetorically centered as uncontrollable, unreliable, or dangerous agents whose unbridled sexuality was the main driver of the unfolding events. In the Suryanelli case, for instance, the High Court deemed the survivor an untrustworthy witness because of "her past conduct of squandering the amount given by her parents for remitting hostel fees and even daring . . . to pledge her ornaments."[56] In the Chacko case, newspapers compared the incident with the Profumo affair, the British scandal over the Secretary of State for War John Profumo's affair with Christine Keeler, an aspiring model—"Who's Kerala's Christine Keeler?" ran one of the headlines in a Malayalam daily.[57] In the ISRO case, Rasheeda was portrayed as a femme fatale who portended disaster to everyone around her. Other newspapers picked up *Thaniniram*'s description of Rasheeda as "Kerala's Mata Hari" and the *Mangalam* newspaper likened Rasheeda to "a tuna in bed" in reference to her purported sexual skills. Such reportage and the ensuing public perceptions laid the groundwork for the cinematic rendering of the *madakarani* (sex siren) as a site of danger and illicit pleasures.

FROM *ASHLEELATHA* TO SOFT-PORN

In the realm of film, the first major debates about obscene representation emerged in the case of *Avalude Ravukal* (Her nights; dir. I. V. Sasi), a 1978 film that is often (and erroneously) cited as the origin of soft-porn.[58] *Avalude Ravukal* depicted the life of a sex worker, Raji (played by Seema), and her subsequent reintegration into a bourgeoisie middle-class household. Despite the narrative's underlying social realist impulse, the sensational publicity mechanisms used to promote the film, including a shot of the heroine in silhouette suggesting an erotic premise, gave it the reputation of a "sex film" (Fig. 3). With four daily shows at Besant (Chembur), Capitol Cinema, and Jaihind Cinema, *Her Nights* was advertised in the Bombay edition of *The Times of India* as a "Sexplosive Malayalam Film for Adults" and "Sex-citing hit for Adults only."[59] Similar journalistic usage—"Sexplosive film"—recurs in *The Indian Express* coverage of the film as well, where the writer wonders "how certain bathing scenes of Seema got through censor's scissors."[60] Some of the publicity posters had catchy text like "Sex needs no language" and "Tells all! Shows all!," which added to the film's public reputation. A widely publicized poster for *Avalude Ravukal* shows a young woman in a flimsy, clinging white shirt examining a scratch on her thigh. At right, a man with thick-framed glasses—his gaze away from the camera—seethes with conflicted desire for the woman. At the bottom of the poster is a silhouette of a reclining girl, her leg outstretched. The poster also features the title in bold type, with the letter "A" being formed by the legs of the silhouette.

The poster's designer improvised this clever strategy to foreground the "adult content" in response to the film's problems with the censor board. The scene of Seema examining her thigh divided the members of the examining committee. Although the majority of the members voted to remove this scene, the sole woman member, Konniyur Meenakshi Amma, insisted on retaining it, arguing that it had narrative logic. As one film critic recounted to me, the very fact that Raji's dialogue reveals that the scratch was caused by an iron railing and is not a "love bite" speaks to the unadulterated love she has for the hero.[61]

A different publicity image for *Avalude Ravukal*, published on the back cover of the magazine *Film*, places a shot from the film in a small circle inset above the much larger image of the actress and her bare back. The text reads, "The story of sleepless nights and dreamful days of a girl who was forced to sacrifice her body in the dark rooms in the hotels, like a burnt sandalwood stick."[62] The reference to the hotel as a site where Raji was meeting the clients in the film also led to litigation. The Kozhikode Second Additional Subjudge ordered the producer and distributor to pay a compensation of 25,000 rupees (approx. $3,052) to the owners of the Beach Hotel, Kozhikode, and directed them to exhibit the film after removing the parts

FIGURE 3. Poster of *Avalude Ravukal*. Image courtesy National Film Archive of India.

objected to by the hotel owners, who claimed that the film featuring prostitution was shot in the hotel without their permission and caused them disrepute.[63] The CBFC temporarily canceled the film's certification after allegations that film prints distributed outside Kerala featured objectionable scenes. In fact, prints of the film exhibited in a theater in Annamalai, Madras, were seized by the police for incorporating uncensored scenes.[64] In its ruling on December 6, 1978, the Madras civil court declared that the film "may be screened in Kerala, but not in other areas."[65] This verdict was taken up at the government level to emphasize that censorship mechanisms should also curb the unauthorized interpolation of reels. It also made it compulsory for the film board to retain a copy of the censored version, along with instructions to film labs that no copies of the film other than the one to be censored should be made until they were furnished with the certificate.[66]

In 1984, *Her Nights* ran for six months at Plaza Cinema in Delhi's Connaught Place. Bhrigupati Singh quotes Munni Raj, who was known as the "porn pasha" (porn king) of Delhi, stating that the morning show became a prominent presence with *Her Night*'s circulation in 1984. Interestingly, for a film released in 1978, its popularity only increased after its troubles with censorship.[67] *Avalude Ravukal* was remade into Kannada as *Kamala* (dir. C. V. Rajendran, 1979) and in Hindi as *Patita* (dir. I. V. Sasi, 1980). The controversy around *Avalude Ravukal* also coincided with the revision of censorship guidelines, and the then Minister of Information and Broadcasting L. K. Advani used the controversy to argue for stricter censorship regulations.[68]

Journalistic accounts also pointed to the "daring baring exposure" of Malayalam films as leading to the uncontrolled proliferation of soft-porn films.[69] In 1978, the Kerala-based state awards committee that reviewed the submissions spoke at length about the Malayalam cinema industry's need to devise mechanisms of self-review to discourage the use of sex as a catalyst for experimentation.[70] Excerpts of the censor certificate and suggested cuts of *Her Nights* later made their way into the documentary *Censor* (dir. Vinod Ganatra, 2002) made by the state-funded film unit, Films Division, as a part of the mandate to make viewers aware of the regulatory function of the CBFC. The images of the censor certificate show recommendations for suggested cuts. The final recommendation states, "The film deals with adult theme of prostitution and there are many visuals of adult nature; hence recommended for 'A' certificate."

These instances demonstrate the mutual imbrication of the female body and social taboos in *ashleelatha* discourses. Paying attention to this backdrop is a crucial part of *Rated A*, because soft-porn filmmakers incorporated contemporary political controversies, sex scandals, and sensational news items as a part of their films' narratives. *Kalluvathukkal Kathreena* (dir. A. T. Joy, 2000), a soft-porn film starring Shakeela, is a particularly good example of such overlaps between news and sensational film narratives (Fig. 4). The film drew its narrative elements from a tragedy that occurred in 2000 in Kalluvathukkal, a village in southern Kerala, in which forty-one people died and many others lost their eyesight after consuming bootleg liquor made in a hooch den owned by a Muslim woman named Hyrunnisa. The backdrop to the film is a mine that employs daily-wage workers, and the happenings are orchestrated by the liquor don Mathachan to reap profits and build his establishment. The film begins with a sequence in a toddy shop run by Kathreena (Shakeela), Mathachan's business partner, who has a wide network of connections. Prioritizing business interests, Kathreena advises him how to influence government officials by bringing police- and excise officers onto their payrolls to ensure there is no government intervention in their business. Kathreena's range of operations also includes offering and arranging sexual services to officials to get them to agree to her business propositions. Kathreena's toddy shop caters both to mine workers looking for affordable options and richer folk who are served on the first

FIGURE 4. Newspaper cutting of the advertisement of *Kalluvathukkal Kathreena*. Text reads: "Shakeela and Sajini cast together for the first time. The Shakeela film that has broken collection records." Image courtesy Sarat Chandran.

floor. From the outset the film establishes Kathreena's and Mathachan's class differences from the regular consumers. Kathreena moves easily between the lower-class patrons and those with money, and her change of costumes from a *veshti* (an unstitched cloth wrapped around the lower part of the body) and blouse to a *sari* as she welcomes government officials indicates the malleability of her social position.

Overlapping storylines make Kathreena's path cross with the other lead heroine, Sophie (played by Sajini). Sophie's father, Joseph, dies after consuming adulterated toddy in Kathreena's den, and her sister is sexually abused by Mathachan's son Johnny, pushing her to suicide. Sophie takes a job in Mathachan's firm and uses her sexual charms to lure both father and son. After killing Mathachan and Johnny, Sophie and her lover Sahadevan leave Kathreena to a violent mob of women who have lost loved ones in the toddy tragedy. Sophie stabs Kathreena, and she and Sahadevan are arrested by the police.

This narrative structure is important insofar it signposts the use of revenge narratives as a common trope in soft-porn films. The film pits Kathreena, who is considered as a collaborator of a morally corrupt social order, against Sophie, who wants to take up the system by eliminating the people responsible for the disintegration of her family. The film also brings together Shakeela and Sajini as co-stars, indicated in the poster as a novelty—a trend that soft-porn films regularly used in promoting multistar productions. The film also has some metatextual moments that foreground Shakeela's presence as an actress. One of these is the relationship she shares with Johnny, in which he calls her "aunty" (in English), a term used to refer to some variants of the *madakarani* in soft-porn films. Another metatextual moment is Johnny's comment to Kathreena that she is "very popular among old men"—a reference to the popularity of soft-porn films among different age groups of male viewers. Although the Muslim identity of the real Hyrunnisa was obscured by the use of a Christian-identifying name (Kathreena) for Shakeela's character, the film's references to the real tragedy were substantial enough for the audience to identify it.

Such examples of representational exchanges and thematic commonalities point to the shared space that exists between audiences, media forms (including soft-porn), and the public sphere. Media publics form when audiences, events, and media forms come together, as in the case of *Kalluvathukkal Kathreena*. Conceptualizing soft-porn as a part of this "media public" consolidates a layered understanding of the public and allows us to think beyond simply film texts or current events or audience demands. Malayalam soft-porn's resonances in the news and elsewhere, and soft-porn films' real-world references, elicit a zone of contact in which a public as a totality is awakened to issues, themes, and concerns that are historically and spatially specific. The "media public" as it pertains to soft-porn then forms a "force-field, an intersubjective realm in and by which sexual desire is variously aroused, blocked, or violated."[71]

AN ECONOMY OF "SOFTNESS": THEMATICS, PRODUCTION, DISTRIBUTION, AND EXHIBITION

Soft-porn films marked themselves as distinct from hardcore pornography in a variety of ways. The narratives incorporated "softness" in direct opposition to "hardcore" porn. Focusing on female sexual desire, soft-porn films used visual and aural tropes to work through the power of suggestion, often avoiding any direct exposure of genitalia.[72] The softness in soft-porn is defined by the deflection of female sexual pleasure to body parts such as thighs or cleavage. This deflection is a crucial deviation from hardcore pornography, which, as Linda Williams discusses, relies on the phallocentric climax of the hardcore "money shot" (cum shot).[73] In his work on soft-core films, David Andrews argues that soft-core emerged as a self-conscious genre steeped in negation. He defines it as "any feature length narrative whose diegesis is punctuated by periodic moments . . . of simulated, non-explicit sexual spectacle [and] leans on standardized forms of pornographic spectacles such as striptease numbers, tub or shower sequences, modeling scenes, voyeur numbers, girl-girl segments, threesomes, orgies and the like."[74] "Spectacle" here serves a visual and affective purpose, with the female breast and thighs emerging as crucial visual signifiers. In Malayalam soft-porn, one encounters most of these features but with certain differences. For instance, the female breast is often (but not always) deflected to an image of cleavage that connotes (often unattainable) sexual desire. Similarly, the thighs assume the role of maximum visibility possible in soft-porn films, as most of these films steer away from showing female genitals as part of the main narrative, although *thundu* were sometimes sexually explicit.

By incorporating sexually charged moments into the storyline and using extended shots of cleavage and thighs, soft-porn films highlighted female orgasm as their main organizational logic. Williams argues that in pornography, female orgasm cannot be visibly demonstrated like the male orgasm, and "sounds of pleasure . . . seem to out the realist function of anchoring body to image, halfway becoming aural fetishes of the female pleasures we cannot see."[75] Eithne Johnson expands William's idea of female auralization to capture how "sound effects texturize the aural space as a surface of vibrations as if to spatialize the text itself as a responsive 'body.'"[76] Soft-porn films, for example, texturize the sonic space by using dubbed-over moaning to convey affective registers that align with the viewer's expectation of soft-porn as a body-genre. As John Corbett and Terri Kapsalis argue, "female pleasure is better thought in terms of a 'frenzy of the audible' than that of the visual."[77] The evidentiary proof provided by the aurality of female orgasm to some extent transcends the visual demonstration of male sexual pleasure that is prominently featured through money shots in hardcore films. Here, the melodic fragments used as background music in intimate scenes and during the insertion of "bits" unfold as four-bar phrases, which become eight-bar periods, and develop through an accretion of melodic and harmonic repetition and variation. Such patterning is distinct from American and European film music, which has formal properties that are very irregular, with frequent shifts of tempo and time signature. Not only do the instrumental timbres tend to be on the lighter side, but they are also designed to accommodate the aurality of sexual union. A typical characteristic of contemporary pop music is that a producer creates rhythmic patterns in the arrangement's bottom end and then asks another artist to "topline" it by adding a melody. In the soft-porn films I examine here, the "topline" is primarily sexual. The instruments seem to float over a rhythmic groove beneath it, with the woman's moaning forming the most important sonic layer in this arrangement.[78] Thus, soft-porn films gave female characters ample screen space, as well as aural centrality to assert their agency.

The absence of graphically depicted on-screen sex necessitates a careful arrangement of the mise-en-scène to capture female sexual pleasure. This extended to allowing seemingly radical narrative choices, such as depicting, for example, a heroine's preference for masturbation over heterosexual coitus,[79] in the process reflecting what Laura Kipnis characterizes as "the oppositional political form" of pornography, which is its power to become "a home for those narratives exiled from sanctioned speech and mainstream political discourse."[80]

While anti-pornography feminists have also used "softness" as an oppositional term to refer to erotica and to signal its distinction from graphic phallic pornography,[81] Malayalam soft-porn filmmakers have used "soft" to refer to acts of foreplay that can allow them to work without facing legal penalties for depicting graphic sex. Filmmakers strategically used "soft" to define the genre against the injunctions laid out both by the anti-porn brigade and by the censor board certification clauses, which were becoming increasingly stringent to weed out the spread of sexually explicit content. Soft-porn films not only facilitated a flourishing alternative production and distribution economy, but they also allowed filmmakers to work around the codes of censorship regulations. In her study of censorship in Indian cinema, Monika Mehta examines the diffused networks through which different stakeholders tease out the "productive effects" that censorship can entail.[82] Malayalam soft-porn is the manifestation of such productive effects; soft-porn as we know it today exists precisely because censorship regulations forced filmmakers to resort to specific visual, narrative, and aural strategies. Thus, the existence of soft-porn points to the loopholes in India's censorship mechanisms that enabled filmmakers to think creatively and incorporate sequences of masturbation, bathing, and foreplay without drawing too much attention to the censor script.

In addition to the localized vernacular idioms that it borrowed from the threads of *kambikathakal*, *rathikathakal*, and *painkili*, Malayalam soft-porn aligns itself with a larger history of exploitation films. American exploitation films exerted a strong influence on Malayalam soft-porn films when they were imported to India in the 1980s. India's censorship policies made it necessary for filmmakers to find ways of slipping through the cracks in the system, and "softness" became as much a method of making and distributing these films as a generic indicator. This took different forms, such as bypassing censor-mandated cuts and creating alternative scripts. Filmmakers often employed *randam-ezhuthukar* (second writers) to generate alternate "censor scripts" that would be submitted to the CBFC. As I discuss in chapter 3, second writers knew how to save scripts from being butchered indiscriminately by the censor. Their primary goal was to follow censor regulations in all seriousness and even to think *like* a censor. They flagged possible objections on the script so that the director could strategize about how to circumvent potential problems. Given the riskiness of second writers' tasks, an unwritten code existed that only the most essential production details of a film would openly circulate. Second writers also produced alternate scripts that were variations of the ones submitted to the censor board. My respondents referred to these as "Plan B and C, in case there are more roadblocks while getting the censoring done."[83] Many of these writers were hopefuls who came to Madras in search of opportunities to write film scripts, but, when life became difficult, they moved to other occupations; some became "mentors" who helped submit scripts for censor certification. Those who were good at handling two languages became script writers for films that were dubbed from other languages. Censor script writers were adept at skimming through scripts and marking parts that were likely to be contentious, and they could even write new scripts that were cleansed of all "impurities." This group was distinct from "ghost writers," who wrote film scripts without being credited.

Thus, as much as genre and aesthetics, infrastructures of film production and sites of theatrical exhibition were a significant component of how the soft-porn field negotiated censorship mechanisms. Gaming the censoring machine also included tactics such as using personal contacts to facilitate filming and certification to border towns and the neighboring states of Tamil Nadu, Karnataka, and Andhra Pradesh, which fell under the jurisdiction of different regional censor boards. Some filmmakers also used the government-owned Kerala State Film Development Corporation's (KSFDC) Chitranjali Studio to avail themselves of the subsidies and facilities that were meant to aid the production of films in the state. According to the package scheme of KSFDC, any film project that could furnish a surety of five lakh rupees ($6,109) as bank guarantee, would be eligible for availing ten lakh rupees ($12,218) as financial support from KSFDC, which included a four lakh rupee ($4,887) government subsidy. This put a lot of pressure on KSFDC, and the chair, P. Govinda Pillai, had to respond to the allegation that the government facilities were used to fund blue films—the phrase used to refer to erotica. Pillai said, "The films have become blue between production and censor certification" and hence KSFDC "cannot be blamed if the films ended up as blue films."[84]

The success of soft-porn films hinged on the role played by single-screen B- and C-circuit theaters that usually perform the bare function of film exhibition and cater to semi-urban and less affluent audiences.[85] The demarcation of A, B, and C circuits in the exhibition of films in India reflects different scales of manageability that are premised on the location of theaters; ability to procure prints from distributors by paying advance for booking; and amenities provided for patrons, including air conditioning, car parking, snack bars, and reservation provisions. Ticket prices in B- and C-center theaters were comparatively lower due to lower tax rates, allowing exhibitors to negotiate different models of profit sharing with distributors and to make informal transactions that never existed on paper. Whereas B- and C-center theaters had to wait to screen new releases until they had finished their first runs at the A centers, soft-porn films were released at all centers at once. In some ways, this model catered to audiences in the outskirts who wanted to see the film on the "first day, first show." The runaway success of soft-porn films thus unsettled long-standing distribution patterns that restricted new releases to A-center theaters and thereby demarcated B- and C-center theaters as zones that merely added revenue.

For their part, distributors used ingenious marketing strategies that foregrounded adult content by emblazoning posters with the "A" (for "adult") and accompanying text that promised viewers that the ticket price was well worth it. Poster text sometime even included details about what the censor had recommended be cut. Phrases from newspaper reports such as "sexplosive" and "saucy" often doubled as publicity.[86] Soft-porn films used gendered language not only to address their audience but also to identify the narrative importance that these films granted female characters, which was one of their central generic features.

They were often publicized as "gents' films," because they were aimed exclusively at adult male audiences, and they were screened in theaters that were all-male spaces. The narrative prominence of the actresses made these films distinct but also alienated the male actors who worked in them. Actresses in soft-porn films used their relative advantage to dictate their sense of comfort in shooting scenes that involved intimacy, and male actors saw that as eating into the availability of screen time and full-fledged roles for them.[87] Rather than appreciating the narrative prominence of female characters, popular discourse often viewed it as resulting from a power play between actors and actresses, and from actors' inability to negotiate their own interests.

In addition to availing themselves of the services of second writers, soft-porn filmmakers also avoided the censors' gaze by splicing in extra reels in the form of *thundu* that were edited out of the original censor print or lifted from completely different source material. Although most of these explicit bits featured relatively new actors, images of identifiable actresses appeared in some footage. Projectionists added these bits during screenings to titillating effect, and each screening was different in the way they were added to the reels. In some instances, projectionists followed directions for which specific bits to add in at specific moments, but in most cases, it was left to the projectionist to add the most effective combination for the desired effect. The "uncontrollable" B-circuit audience, it was imagined, would come to theaters for these kinds of erupting pleasures, a sensibility associated with Tom Gunning's theorization of "cinema of attractions" in the context of early cinema—"a cinema that displays its visibility, willing to rupture a self-enclosed fictional world for a chance to solicit the attention of the spectator."[88] B-circuit cinema's exhibition strategies frame the film-text as an unstable signifier that is constantly reinterpreted based on audience configuration.

Thundu share their organizing logic with "cut-pieces"—"short strips of locally made, uncertified celluloid containing sexual or violent imagery that appeared and disappeared abruptly from the reels of Bangladeshi action films," as defined by Lotte Hoek.[89] The cut-piece as "unstable celluloid" thus points to the world spilling outside of the space of the screen.[90] In Hoek's reading, the "collective viewing of sexually explicit imagery can destabilize the operation of genre."[91] In a sense, soft-porn film often *becomes* soft-porn in the process of active exhibition, and softness thus also refers to a malleability and adaptability that is central to this form. Hoek describes cut-pieces as oscillating between temporary availability and invisibility insofar as they are able to bring the dissonance of the social to the attention of the audience. They thus encapsulate many contradictory impulses and hint at the disintegration of the Bangladeshi polity and its filmmaking traditions.[92] Bits in Malayalam soft-porn share this temporary visibility with cut-pieces in Bangladeshi action cinema.

However, whereas Hoek's cut-pieces are always explicitly about sex, *thundu* in Malayalam cinema encompass a wider array of cultural insertions. They might include fragments of footage that were shot separately, featuring female masturbation, lesbian sex, and, in rare instances, shots of male homosociality (not necessarily homosexuality). Sometimes, *thundu* insertion also cashed in on the currency of sensational news and viewers' familiarity with such events. In some instances, news items were used as *thundu* that simulated the titillation offered by sexually explicit sequences.[93] Sensational news stories from visual and print media were inserted into soft-porn films to evoke the erotic potential embedded in the collective imagination of the taboo, which ties it very closely to scandal publics and the politics of exposure. One prominent case of this that many of my respondents mentioned was the incorporation of references in many cut-piece eruptions to a 1997 sex scandal involving a state minister that was popularly known as the "ice-cream parlor sex scandal" because it was tied to an ice-cream parlor that doubled as a brothel.[94] By elevating the viewers as respondents who are entitled to make their stances public, such sensational overtures invited them to become interlocutors in unraveling the mysteries and speculative possibilities laid out before them.

Whereas soft-porn films were processed at prominent labs such as Gemini or Prasad Labs in Chennai, *thundu* were processed separately at Vasant Color Lab or R. K. Labs in Bangalore. My respondents explained that processing the bits in smaller labs allowed more options, especially with coverage shots (the process of filming multiple angles, shots, and performances of a scene), and even access to the lab's library, where they could source additional footage if needed. Additionally, agents in Bangalore mediated deals for "extra footage" (as they were referred to among brokers) between the distributors and the lab for a certain percentage of the cut from both parties. During my interview with field representatives who used to accompany the boxes carrying film prints, some recalled how they assisted projectionists in synchronizing the bits with the "gap"—a term signifying probable sequences that could precede and succeed the cut-piece.[95] Gaps were physically marked on the celluloid with chalk to enable the projectionist to find the exact points to insert *thundu*. There were also times when they reported ignoring these marks and picking other places for insertion. The addition of bits was in itself a collective, creative act with room for improvisation and spontaneity.

Thundu with recognizable actors were used because viewers could relate to them, but their inclusion raised questions about how such footage was procured and if it had been shot with the consent of the actors. Some bits were video footage of print material about sensational political scandals, and they now function as a kind of temporal stamp that can reveal hidden layers of production history. Footage from Hollywood and European films, referred to as "English bits," also appeared in soft-porn films as an interlude to the sexual scenes, and their usually sudden emergence provided a fetishistic eruption of white female skin amid the localized version of buxom women who were the lead heroines in these films. These cuts suggested intimacy in bedroom, shower, or massage sequences, or with reference to contemporary political and sex scandals. They had a disruptive logic, especially as they were often inserted at points that did not have a direct narrative connection. "Leaked" content came from various sources, including clips excerpted from "foreign XXX videos" that came from the Gulf. Projectionists were given creative license in exhibiting films, and they would sometimes "edit over" the film by splicing in extra reels with film glue, thereby inserting new narrative threads that were not in the censor's cut. In fact, the genre's specificity lay in the act of splicing in *thundu*. This means that even films that did not easily qualify as soft-porn in terms of look or formal qualities could adopt a soft-porn mode simply because the cut-piece functions as a completing appendage to the narrative's jigsaw.

Indeed, many films that were popularly known as or are now remembered as "soft-porn" could qualify as sexually suggestive melodramas or thrillers. For instance, *Aa Oru Nimisham* (That Moment; dir. U. C. Roshan, 2001) starring Shakeela, Roshni, and Devika, explores the story of love set in the backdrop of a revenge drama. Shakeela (whose character is unnamed in the film) is the stepmother of two teenagers, Deepa and Sudhi; her husband (Pratapachandran) is relatively older, and the age gap is evident in the way the children address her as *cheriyamma* (mother's sister). Things start to go haywire when Sudhi's friend Sushil comes to their house for a vacation. Shakeela's character, the stepmother (henceforth Shakeela), is upset on seeing the interactions between Sushil and her daughter and is quick to warn her husband about the inappropriate behavior she witnesses. While Shakeela tries to stop the marriage alliance between the two, Deepa overhears a conversation between Shakeela and Sushil that reveals Shakeela's backstory, and the ulterior motives behind Sushil's attempt to get closer to her becomes evident. It is revealed that in the past, Sushil tried to get a security guard to rape Shakeela, and when Shakeela stabbed the guard, Sushil begins blackmailing her. The film ends with Sushil's death, Deepa—the daughter—confessing to the murder, and Shakeela committing suicide. The trope of the guest who overstays and takes advantage of the hospitality shown to him, and ultimately Sushil's murder, signals a moral victory that makes the film a melodrama of sorts. Even though Shakeela kills herself at the end of the story, her death provides moral compensation for her brief affair with Sushil in the past. Through her death and Deepa's realization of Sushil's real nature, the film reunites the family members, who realize Shakeela's dedication to their well-being.

The narrative's melodramatic overtures are important as they often repeat across the genre of soft-porn and point toward another mode of "revision" that took place when the certifying committee would assign a "thematic classification" to the films.[96] Although most soft-porn films were categorized under the theme of "melodrama," the logic of classification remained nebulous. For instance, some of the members who were part of the certifying committee referred to their definition of melodrama as a clash between good and evil, leading to the victory of moral values over desires of the flesh.[97] This is a crucial reference, as the question of melodramatic closure places the burden of "evil" on unbridled sexuality. Although soft-porn films purportedly centered around an autonomous female figure, the tendency of melodramatic closure enforced the reinstatement of patriarchal structures within the narrative. Thus, despite the apparent sexual autonomy of the female figure, these films often conclude by showing her as regretting her wayward life, being given a second lease on life by cleansing her past, or sacrificing her life to amend her sins—all ways of containing her sexuality that align with Elena Gorfinkel's conceptualization of a moralistic tone or "guilty expenditure" that showcases the woman regretting or being punished for her wayward life.[98]

In the case of *Aa Oru Nimisham*, we can also identify the marginal role played by male characters in terms of screen- and narrative space. Crucially, Prathapachandran's role as an older partner who cannot satisfy the sexual needs of a relatively younger wife (often the catalyst for the sexual adventures of the *madakarani*) reappears in other soft-porn films as well. A mainstream actor who primarily played supporting roles, Prathapachandran took up such roles in soft-porn films during the last stage of his career. Although this was met with a lot of surprise by his co-actors, it also shows the liminal status of the soft-porn form as it blended the mainstream and the underground circuits, as well as provided alternate employment opportunities to a vast spectrum of film workers. In sum, the "liberatory" potentials of soft-porn films varied when it came to narrative and had more to do with their modes of production. These films exerted a counter-hegemonic pressure off-screen, as seen in the repeated assertions of both directors and actresses that the soft-porn industry functioned on an economy of trust, rather than exploitation—that is, based on the crews' and the actors' openness and accessibility during the making of the films.[99]

A NOTE ON (IMPURE) METHODS

In conceptualizing Malayalam soft-porn in this way, I align myself with sex- and porn-positive feminists who affirm the need to create inclusive approaches to studying pornographic practices and representations by accounting for the production and labor involved in making pornography.[100] This runs counter to traditional feminist approaches that link pornography to violence in toto, which also stymie efforts to critically study pornography.[101] More importantly, these approaches also dismiss the agency of women who live and work in the pornographic industry, projecting them as mute subjects who are exploitatively represented on-screen and who must be redeemed through representation in certain kinds of feminist work. In contrast, feminist porn scholars have asserted the need to remap the terrain of feminism by attending to labor, agency, pleasure, and desire. For instance, Mireille Miller-Young's scholarship on African American women who work in the porn industry recognizes that they do so for a variety of reasons, including economic sustenance and taking control of their own sexual images.[102] In a similar vein, Jennifer C. Nash's work on race and pleasure also pushes us to look at the "paradoxes of pleasures" and spectatorship, thereby shifting the lens to pleasure and desire rather than fixating on "the injuries that racialized pornography engenders."[103] Drawing inspiration from such approaches, I postulate that any understanding of Malayalam soft-porn's underground circuits of production and distribution, and its dependence on trust-based interpersonal networks, necessitates moving out of an "exploitation only" narrative and studying collaborative practices.

Malayalam soft-porn itself does not have a defined feminist politics nor is it necessarily oriented toward gender parity. But a feminist study of its production practices allows us to braid together the ground realities involved in its informal modes of recruiting and sustaining labor such as trust-based and ethical collaborative approaches. The bonds that sustained me during this research were mediated by a trust economy that works on an informal level. I was invited to the domestic spaces of many of my informants who worked in soft-porn, primarily to introduce me to their family members, who they feared would be worried that they were spending time with a female researcher. These invitations always came with a rejoinder that I was not to reveal my *real* research but rather couch it as an interest in "film production." While I was keen to follow the object of soft-porn as it was being produced, circulated, and exhibited, I was also interested in the social relations, labor, domesticity, and informal exchanges forged between people, institutions, and piracy networks as they partook in this travel. In other words, my work required tapping into the relational networks that defined soft-porn.

The feminist locus of this work is invested in the *madakarani*, the voluptuous lead female character at the center of soft-porn films. While *madakarani* is a colloquial term for a woman who exercises her sexual autonomy and activates a sense of fleeting (male, voyeuristic) sexual pleasure, it also invites an examination of how gendered demarcations, patriarchal mores, and implacable desires enter the space of the cinema. I use the term to imply such noncompliant sex-siren–like figures as well as a discursive concept to examine how many women strategically used their sexual agency to unsettle power relations and advance their own social mobility. In so doing, *Rated A* traces how the *madakarani* becomes more than a filmic trope and consistently emerges in media publics by disrupting normative expectations. Further, not only is the *madakarani* a site of nonnormative femininity, it is also a battleground of caste and body aesthetics. As I demonstrate through the figure of Silk Smitha in chapter 1, caste identity conditions how certain women are more readily read, and their images circulated, as *madakarani*. Caste is an ancient system of social hierarchy on the basis of birth—those born into a particular caste live their entire lives as members of that caste with no possibility of upward mobility. It is a marker of social status and shapes the opportunities they receive on the merit of their birth into a specific caste group. A complex and often hidden category that is made invisible for those who come from upper-caste or *savarna* backgrounds, this identity impacts the lower castes very differently by shaping their social existence. Not all of the actresses who played *madakarani* were of caste-oppressed backgrounds, and not all *madakarani* characters are explicitly coded as lower caste. However, it is through this filmic trope and figure that caste enters the field of cinema in Kerala (other than the social realist art cinema tradition). As Vijeta Kumar writes, such bodies are a "a site to perform 'perversions' that won't be performed on a 'purer/fairer' body or an opportunity to rescue a 'poor, hypersexualized, lower-caste woman' who might not know better."[104] In that sense, this book aligns with the work of scholars such as Jenny Rowena, Manju Edachira, Shyma P., and others who foreground caste as both as issue of representation on screen, as well as something that conditions the structure of the film industry itself.[105]

In addition to feminist porn studies, *Rated A* contributes directly to scholarship on production cultures and on South Asian film. Production and industry studies scholars such as Tejaswini Ganti and Clare M. Wilkinson have shown how film personnel negotiate their career prospects in the media and entertainment industries.[106] In *Rated A*, I extend this focus to veritably "illegitimate" media practices that impact how cine-workers navigate work and life. I move away from the landscape of A-list film stars, production sites, and practices that has generally been the focus of production studies and focus instead on B-list films and B- and C-circuit exhibition practices. With a focus on porous industry practices, gendered precarious labor, and adult media forms, *Rated A* locates forms of cine-labor that are largely invisible. The use of fictional names in soft-porn film credits was an effect of the devalued nature of the form—many who worked in this industry also doubled as cine-workers in the mainstream industry. I track the real people behind the fictitious credits often found in soft-porn films to unravel the economic necessities and inequalities that separate above- and below-the-line labor in media industries. This division—one of the very reasons why many below-the-line cine-workers tried their hand at soft-porn films—is theorized by Vicki Mayer as a convention that manifests itself physically and socially. "The line," as Mayer points out, has "indexed the scarcity or surplus of so-called creativity and professionalism, two competing resources for labor value in industrial capitalism since the late 1800s."[107] Malayalam soft-porn likewise is structured around an invisible organizing line between the mainstream and the underground that demarcates "professional" above-the-line personnel from ostensibly less creative (even deviant) below-the-line workers.

There is rich scholarship on stardom in South Asia, and scholars such as Neepa Majumdar, Kiranmayi Indraganti, and Usha Iyer have expanded the horizons by including singers and dancers, their voices, and their bodies as forms of labor and stardom.[108] In *Rated A*, I invite readers to think about stardom in the B-list and adult media circuits as forms of embodied, precarious labor. Much of this happens through my focus on the soft-porn star Shakeela. In mainstream Indian cinema, A-list actresses such as Madhuri Dixit were able to undo the vamp/heroine dichotomy in the 1990s, paving the way for more sexually charged dance sequences to later become part of the regular offerings of the Hindi film industry.[109] This did not hamper Dixit's fame and she remained a major figure whose stardom was not equated only with her sexuality. In contrast, soft-porn actresses such as Shakeela enjoyed a transient stardom—her branding as a poster girl of soft-porn cinema simultaneously symbolized her as the lasting image of the degrading quality of cinema and the unethical practices in the shadow economy of the film industry.

The dispersed nature of this book's cultural objects as well as their malleability across time—from the 1970s to the first decade of the 2000s—necessitated the use of mixed methods, including ethnographic vignettes, archival research, sociological observations, and textual and discourse analysis. Historiographically, *Rated A* moves away from dominant narratives of Indian cinema by focusing on failed schemes and underground practices—topics about which personnel in state institutions such as the CBFC and the National Film Development Corporation (NFDC) are not keen to disclose many details. My work focuses on the tensions that mark such state institutions, which even when they worked under the mandate of the government were invested in very different focus areas. The 1990s has been associated in Indian cinema with globalization, economic liberalization, family films, and diasporic narratives of return to tradition. However, *Rated A* presents a slightly different slice of that decade, focusing on aspects of liberalization and global flows that run underneath these mainstream narratives, showing how aspirations and desire blossom in the shadow of global flows and policies in the 1990s and early 2000s. I show not only how this impacts forms of cinematic labor, but also how desire and pleasure travel through clandestine global routes, as, for example, in the traffic in Malayalam soft-porn among Indian workers in the Middle East. Observations gleaned from visits to pirate CD markets, theaters exclusively meant for soft-porn exhibition in various parts of India, DVD markets meant for Gulf audiences, and makeshift cinema tents that cater to migrant labor camps inform this investigation. Expanding the scope of South Asian pornographies, *Rated A* uncovers the inclusions and exclusions that take place in the cultural imaginary when Malayalam soft-porn enters the Middle East and comes to coexist with a range of pornographic media, including Bangladeshi cut-piece films and Pakistani *mujra* (a form of sexually suggestive and expressive dance) videos.

As opposed to conventional ethnographies that focus on the present to map the complex currents of everyday life, my project looks at a form that had petered out of circulation in the first decade of the 2000s and is thus oriented toward tracing memories, informal transactions, and production and exhibition patterns that facilitated the proliferation of soft-porn films. As Purnima Mankekar writes, "Ethnographies of mass media require us to expand our repertoire of methodologies and combine participant observation and repeated in-depth interviews with policy analysis, archival research and textual analysis."[110] In effect, I had to treat this project like an investigative piece in which I worked as an industry insider, taking inspiration from Amy Flowers's work on phone sex workers in the United States.[111] I tried finding jobs, first as an aspiring dubbing artist and later as a production assistant (both between 2010 and 2013, prior to writing this book—both failed attempts, at least partially) in order to decode how the industry operated under the shadow of the fictional identities of my subjects. Part historian, part ethnographer, I had to move, physically and epistemologically, within the minute channels of communication and exchanges within the field, treating people and their memories or accounts as part of the historical archive (and perhaps, for lack of a better term, we can call this a form of ethnographic historiography).

As scholars of adult media have pointed out, in the absence of official archives that preserve such material, adult film historians end up trawling through and collating an array of materials to arrive at conclusions and eventually construct their own personal archives.[112] Peter Alilunas describes this as "trace historiography . . . a method to locate evidence where it seemingly no longer exists" by following the smoke rather than fire.[113] Similar to the under-the-radar circulation of soft-core in the American context studied by David Andrews, the distribution and exhibition of soft-porn films in India is marked by a recalcitrance toward bookkeeping.[114] In the absence of industry data, we are left with censor scripts held at archives that are cleansed of all "impurities," newspaper reports or scripts, and ancillary material. Often such material is owned by the filmmakers and personal collectors who collate newspaper cuttings and film weeklies because of their passion for film ephemera. The absence of official archives also enforces a turn to oral narratives and fragmented archival records that include center spreads, announcements about film titles, and production news in the industry weeklies and newspapers. Rummaging through materials left at the scrap dealers and secondhand booksellers, I found lobby cards, film posters, lab receipts, shooting-house booking forms, and continuity albums. A large part of this project is geared toward understanding how audiences engaged with spaces of soft-porn exhibition, how cast and crew negotiated the realities of production, and what role personal recollections and subjective experiences have in recounting the history of Malayalam soft-porn. Drawing on material such as diaries, court cases, novels, letters, news items, videos, and testimonies by and about artists and technicians, I trace soft-porn from its heyday in the late 1990s to its steep decline in the first decade of the 2000s, focusing on its transnational circulation, its local and global aesthetic influences, and the professional and personal networks that powered its production and distribution circuits.

A form such as Malayalam soft-porn thus encourages us to think about what counts as evidence and to acknowledge that evidentiary claims tend to elude the contingent formations that structure the way knowledge systems hierarchize and produce social claims.[115] My approach in *Rated A* resonates with what Jane Gaines describes as a speculative "What If?" way of doing feminist historiography. Gaines posits the counterfactual as a way of moving beyond empirical facts as the only anchor of historical narrative. More than merely filling in gaps, counterfactual speculation demands the historian's and reader's willingness to believe in the plausibility of what may have happened in a "What If?" situation. By 2012, the soft-porn industry had fizzled out completely and the personnel associated with this form had been cast aside as failures. As one of my respondents put it, "We were too early for the sexual revolution which Kerala was not yet ready for. Look at the cammers (online erotic performers) and phone sex folks who are able to make a living taking from what we did earlier. If society was willing to give us a chance, perhaps people would have appreciated the labor and effort that went into the making of these films, than rubbish it as just sex films."[116] Like Gaines, I wonder what possibly could have happened if soft-porn films had been able to withstand this industry shift, and if filmmakers and actors who were associated with this form had been able to continue working without having to face the consequences of their alleged moral lapses.

1

Madakarani

The Screen Pleasures of the Sex Siren in Malayalam Cinema

In an iconic sequence from Milan Luthria's 2011 Bollywood film *The Dirty Picture*, the male lead, Surya Kant, berates the female lead, an actress named Reshma (who is later given the screen name Silk), calling her a "dirty secret." The fictional character of Reshma/Silk, played by Vidya Balan, was based on the real-life actress Silk Smitha, a popular South Indian dancer-turned-actress of the 1980s who died by suicide in 1996. Silk Smitha was a prominent presence in South Indian films made in the Kannada, Tamil, Telugu, and Malayalam film industries, and many of her films were also dubbed into Hindi. *The Dirty Picture* fictionalizes the life of this actress—a central figure in this book. In the scene described here, Surya Kant questions her status as an actress and attributes her popularity only to her sex appeal: "They all know you are not one of us . . . you are our nocturnal secret which no one will acknowledge in broad daylight." Handing her an award for the best actress, he whispers to Silk that she, too, will disappear like others who have aspired to stardom, and the audience will soon forget her. In using this exchange to sow the seeds of suspicion in Silk about her own career prospects, *The Dirty Picture* pronounces her active sexual life and ambition as the reason for her professional failure. Casting Silk as a sex siren by collating sensational fragments of gossip and speculative news, the film deviates from the historical accuracy expected of a biopic and marks her as a figure of corporeal excess and moral decline—the archetypal imagination of a soft-porn star.[1] *The Dirty Picture* demonstrates how the sex siren in Indian cinema also doubles as a discourse about a moral and professional decline in the film industry, especially with the influx of women from lower caste and class backgrounds who pushed the boundaries of middle-class social mores. The figure of the "extra"—women who ended up on film sets as background actors—began appearing in mainstream Hindi films like *Kaagaz Ke Phool* (dir. Guru Dutt, 1959), *Khamosh* (dir. Vidhu Vinod Chopra, 1985), *Rangeela* (dir. Ram Gopal Verma, 1995), and *Om Shanti Om* (dir. Farah Khan, 2007). What is inevitably left out of such narratives of extras is the impact that caste and class have on opportunities in an industry and a social context in which the normative precondition for a woman's success is fair skin. By organizing female extras into different types and classes based on their looks, and accordingly assigning different wage scales (a practice that continues to this day), those at the lowest level are often deprived of opportunities. The industry practice for dark-skinned characters is to darken the face of fair-skinned actors rather than cast actors who are dark-skinned. Categorizing female extras based on looks aligns with the premium placed on fair skin as a marker of social capital. This system is complicated by suppliers and contractors who play a mediating role in procuring on-screen labor, as they often demand unreasonably high commissions from meagerly paid extras.[2]

The history of Indian cinema is peppered with stories of gendered exclusion. Even in the silent film era, women in cinema were looked down upon with suspicion. Their absence in early cinema was tied to restrictions on women's participation in social life, as caste order and purity dictated their honor and respectability, and upper-caste women were subjected to the moral panic that demanded unconditional obedience to uphold caste purity.[3] In the field of cinema, this exclusion can be seen in several instances, such as the Parsi community's discomfort with Bombay Talkies' employment of Parsi actresses in the 1930s; the physical and social violence against the Malayalam actress Rajamma, a.k.a. P. K. Rosy—who acted in the first Malayalam silent film, *Vigatakumaran* (dir. J. C. Daniel, 1928)—because of her lower-caste status; and the social boycott of Aideu Handique, the first woman to act in an Assamese film (*Joymoti*, dir. Jyotiprasad Agarwala, 1935), who lived most of her life in a hut until she was recognized in her old age by the government for her contribution to Assamese cinema.[4] In this early period, women's aspirations for career mobility were viewed with suspicion. Women from courtesan backgrounds like Begum Akhtar, Jaddan Bai, and Fatima Begum were part of Bombay cinema and used their interest in music and dance to build their careers.[5] Starlets, who come much later in this chronology, marshal long-standing anxieties about women's participation in the film industry and the moral uprightness that the industry demands from actresses as a precondition for their entry into it. In turn, popular discourse has presented the film industry as a morally suspect sphere in which quick profits matter more than ethical and artistic concerns. A 1988 article focused on starlets in *The Times of India* outlines the varying intensities within which male and female starlets are narrativized in Hindi cinema:

> [An] aspiring woman star is always a butt of ridicule, fuel for the limitless libido, a perfect target of exploitation. The male on the other hand is pristine, he can do no wrong. His struggle to make it is even glorified. The tales of those boys who slept

on the pavement, ate *channa* for dinner, travelled ticketless in the local train are never-ending. If a starlet has to survive in a hole in the wall, she's as bad as sin.[6]

Discussions about women's entry into professional acting often conflated film work and prostitution. Even early on, film trade magazines reported the difficulty of finding actresses from "respectable" families, citing the influx of courtesans and *nautch* girls (temple dancers dedicated to a deity) from red-light districts as tarnishing the industry's reputation. Madhuja Mukherjee captures one such narrative in the singer Rattan Bai's exchange with the publicity manager of New Theatres Kolkata. When she confronted the studio about removing four of her song sequences from *Karwan-e-Hyat* (dir. Premankur Atorthy, 1935), the manager alluded to her erstwhile status as a performer in Calcutta's red-light district. Bai responds by outlining the history of performers from other red-light districts who participated in the film industry to counter the manager's suggestion that she was of an inferior status.[7] The manager's remarks about Bai's background resonate with the delineation of different categories of prostitutes in Nripendra Kumar Basu and S. N. Sinha's 1933 book *The History of Prostitution*, outlined in Durba Mitra's history of Indian sexuality—*paricharika*, a maid who could possibly have a secret relationship with the male member of the family; *Kulata*, a married woman who secretly courts lovers to satisfy her lust; *Svairini*, who snubs her husband and entertains her lovers; and *Nati*, who lives by dancing and music, and entertains people of her choice for earning "extra."[8] Thus, actresses were already perceived as part of the taxonomical categorization of "clandestine prostitutes" who navigate illicit sexual practices by their willingness to step outside strictly monogamous partnerships.

Such anxieties around the scandalous private lives of actresses diluting the respectability of the film industry find their match in the way the term *madakarani* encapsulated the tensions around women's sexual autonomy. *Madakarani* is used in the Malayalam language to describe a woman whose frank sexuality and readiness to use her body mark her as an unstable social figure. Derived from the Sanskrit root words *madam* or *madakatvam*, *madakarani* refers to unbridled desires that unsettle social mores and conventional expectations. As opposed to the Sanskrit loan word *premam* (love), a feeling that is associated with individuation and interiority, *madakatvam* ascribes a transitory and ephemeral nature to a relationship in which emotional intimacy and respect toward the female lover are lacking. Thus, the popular perception of the *madakarani* is pitched at the margins of heteronormative conjugality, framing her as a public woman over whose life the readers/viewers can lay claim.

In Malayalam soft-porn cinema of the 1990s, female leads were cast as *madakarani*, a label that symbolized both their narrative role and their professional distinction as second-tier contract laborers (as distinct from A-list female actors in mainstream cinema). Tied to the desire for upward mobility, the *madakarani*'s sexual labor renders her desirable as a sexual body and, simultaneously, an object of social derision because of her perceived moral depravity and availability. The image of *madakarani* that was stamped on these women resonates with the term *veshya*, the Malayalam equivalent for prostitute (also found in many other Indian languages). The use of the term *madakarani* in relation to film actresses also imposed normative heterosexual standards on all women in the film business. Thus, the discursive construction of the *madakarani* is tied to visual and narrative practices that exceeded the films they acted in and constantly threatened the social codes of respectability.

This othering of the bodies of sex sirens is prominent in film journalism across time and space within India, some of which provides historical precedent for discourses around female actresses in the soft-porn industry. Although such film weeklies can be seen as engaging in a protracted effort to legitimize these actresses' contributions by highlighting the embodied risks they took, they also became machineries of normative control. In Malayalam film magazines of the 1940s, such as *Cinemavarika* and *Cinemamasika*, sensational news reports about actresses' moral decay and legal troubles often ran alongside short-form fiction narrated by an actress about her experience navigating the space of cinema. These included snippets of the compromises they had to make to maintain their career prospects. One news report that was published under the heading "Cinemalokam" (Cinema world) in *Cinemamasika* reports the arrest of an actress in Bombay who was pimped by her stepfather for a day and her arrest by Bombay secret police under the Prostitution Prohibition Act.[9] Film magazines often reported such perils they faced in the film industry through the discourse of prostitution and voiced concerns about whether the right kind of women were being accepted into it.[10] The pressure on actresses to be recognized was amplified because of the presumed *veshyathvam* (sexual profligacy or "sluttiness") stamped on their public presence. *Cinemamasika*'s 1946 column on the secret lives of cinema stars compiled the divorce, marriage, and affairs of actresses in an effort to expose their unconventional lifestyles.[11] A 1948 report in *filmindia* detailed the case of an extra who was arrested by the Bombay Vigilance Police at a hotel in Juhu and the proceedings of a press conference convened by the secretary of the Indian Motion Picture Producers' Association to clear the air, as sex workers identifying as extras were seen as bad for the industry's reputation.[12] Speculating on the various means by which sex workers may have allegedly infiltrated the film industry, the report recommends that talent agencies follow transparent practices to filter out women with "doubtful credentials" to preserve the sanctity of acting as a profession.[13] Such reports about desperate extras served as a warning to mainstream actresses (emblems of middle-class values) to avoid controversy.

We can imagine a gendered genealogy between these early cinema discourses and current attitudes toward *madakarani*. For instance, when the former soft-porn actress Shakeela was the featured guest at the launch for the mainstream film *Nalla Samayam* (Good time; dir. Omar Lulu, 2022), a mall in Kozhikode denied permission for the event on the grounds of "public safety," because another actress had been subjected to sexual misbehavior by some men in the mall in the past, and the mall authorities wanted to have additional layers of security.[14] Although wrapped in a veneer of protocol, the operating rationale was to rein in the public visibility of Shakeela's former soft-porn status by invoking women's safety as a general principle. Thus, over the years, the *madakarani* has become a symbolic marker of a morally dubious woman who can potentially endanger other, more "respectable" (usually middle-class, *savarna*) women. In this framing, the *madakarani* is a destroyer of heteronormativity—a gender-betrayer or a marriage-breaker. To some extent, the *madakarani*'s dangerous presence in such discourses rehearses the argument made against prostitution—the figure of the prostitute could spark men's sexual desire so much that any woman on the street could be subjected to sexual violence by being mistaken for one, or so the rhetoric goes.

Despite the soft-porn industry's hyper-visualization of actresses as symbols of sexual liberation, historical accounts documenting these women's lives and narratives are scarce. For a film historian tracing the conditions under which these women worked, this paucity of historical sources is a major problem. Dominant journalistic accounts and popular film writings are quick to dismiss their film work as an extension of sex work conditioned by economic hardships, a rhetoric that aligns with some feminist groups that refer to all sex workers as "trafficked women."[15] For instance, the film magazine *Nana* published a series titled "Those Trapped in Redlight Streets," compiling testimonies of women who migrated to Kodambakkam in search of acting careers and ended up as sex workers.[16] Anjali Arondekar's idea of abundance "that does not replace paucity with overflow, but rather unravels a set of questions that are fertile ground for producing and contesting our attachments to history writing" offers a heuristic for critically examining loss, marginality, and disenfranchisement as core ideas in the study of sexuality. Pursuing a similarly inspired idea of abundance, I turn to pages in film weeklies to attend to "both the efflorescence of the past and to attend to its strategic and active mobilization within the politics of the present."[17] Through such materials, I trace the invisible labor of the women who participated in these films as extras, body doubles, and heroines in sexualized roles. Film weeklies catered to readers who saw these print materials as accessories to sexual thrills mediated via gossip columns, center spreads, and off-screen information about actresses. At the same time, these weeklies used an unenthusiastic and flat tone in detailing the production details of soft-porn films, which rarely went beyond the bare outlines. Thus, while the films were delegitimized as low grade and uncinematic in dominant film narratives, such shooting-floor reports paradoxically placed them as a significant, even legitimate part of the film industry. A 1989 article in *Film Mirror* alleged, for instance, that more than "mere acting" is demanded of extra actresses.[18] In an industry marked by precarity, aspiring actresses often agree to unpaid opportunities in the form of initial acting commitments and photo shoots, with the hope that real work with remuneration will come with more experience and visibility. The gray zone where unpaid work coexists with informal casting routines makes the film industry rife with exploitation and unsafe gendered labor arrangements that pressure aspiring actresses to "compromise." In this space, the figure of the sex siren is more than a narrative presence on the film screen; she is a social manifestation of the complex relationships between gender and labor.

To examine such phenomena, I train a feminist historiographic lens on a body of films starring actresses who did not necessarily identify as feminist and tease out how being cast as *madakarani* limited their opportunities, and how debates on cine-labor address the repetitive bodily labor contributed by these actresses, extras, and background artists.[19] A feminist approach to the *madakarani* necessitates looking critically at the mechanisms whereby these women *became madakarani*. These mechanisms are structured through what I call "screen pleasures"—a sociosexual arrangement that denotes the gendered value-economy of the film industry, where aspirational mobility to cross class lines and caste origins is mediated by sexuality. As they animate the cinematic experience of fantasy, screen pleasures go beyond the representational dynamics captured on the physical screen and transpose them onto noncinematic contexts. They exceed the screen's capabilities and become part of an extratextual fantasy that sparks desire even as the screen shields viewers from excess. As embodiments of screen pleasures, actresses who played *madakarani* and performed nonnormative sexual roles were consumed as fragmented rather than iconic images associated with "professional" actresses who managed to negotiate life and work without losing their social status.

Film magazines often bracketed the lives and careers of *madakarani* between the climaxes of screen pleasure and their sudden death by suicide or murder. In their reportage of *madakarani*'s deaths, film magazines rendered the actresses' corpses and the audience's posthumous memory of these actresses as objects of a forensic gaze. I look closely at the obituaries of three actresses—Vijayasree, Rani Padmini, and Silk Smitha—who were perceived as sex sirens in their time (although Vijayasree was a mainstream actress) and whose deaths were as contentious as their on-screen lives. Examining varied sources such as studio histories, film journalism, and yellow magazines (sensational or sexually suggestive magazines), I argue that the discourse of obscenity emerges as a larger framing device in film reportage that fixes the *madakarani* in cyclical narratives of visibility and decline. In fact, the very factors that contribute to the making of the figure of the *madakarani* were also seen to be the cause of her decline; these magazines foreground sex and sexuality not just as sources of pleasure but also as forces that threatened the previous "good standing" of these women when they entered the field of erotic films. In publicizing starlets' identities through centerfolds and introductory columns, film journalists applauded them for their enterprising judgment while simultaneously deriding them and pronouncing verdicts on their careers. In time, such reportage led to a perception of the *madakarani* as not only an unacceptable form of the hetero-feminine but a symbol of an entire region's "degenerate" film culture.

The Dirty Picture is a prime example of how the local image of the *madakarani* was mainstreamed by character stereotyping, as well as an entire form of cinematic practice that deviated from the seemingly "national" model of Bollywood. Following a formulaic Bollywood blueprint that includes song-and-dance sequences, a rags-to-riches plot of a small-town girl pursuing her dreams, and a narrative of heterosexual romance, *The Dirty Picture* brought great success to Vidya Balan, whose decision to play Silk Smitha was seen as a radical step, as other prominent actresses had refused to take the role. Not only did Balan win the National Film Award, but rave reviews also praised her performance, for example, as "an ode to cinema and the liberating power of sexuality. . . . As the two stories merge, one realizes it is the legend of Vidya Balan that is being created on-screen, as she takes the Silk-route to reinventing herself."[20]

The Dirty Picture was initially publicized in preproduction as a biopic of Smitha, but the production house, Balaji Telefilms, retracted the biopic elements it had used in publicity after Smitha's family sued the filmmakers for defaming her memory and reducing her life to a series of sexualized images.[21] Consequently, Luthria repitched the film, sidelining its biographical elements by saying that it was inspired by multiple actresses, including Smitha and starlets such as Disco Shanti and Polyester Padmini, who were a sensation in the 1980s Tamil cinema.[22] Luthria's justification that the film drew on the lives of the "breed of dusky women," who, despite money and fame, led a "lonely life," reinforced the stereotypical depiction of actresses who are cast in erotic roles as incapable of sustaining familial connections with lasting emotional bonds, and whose inability to maintain professional commitments in turn challenges their status as actresses.[23] The film's reference to "South India" as a hotbed of erotic films led to debates about how Bollywood film appropriated regional cinemas and sensationalized Smitha as a starry-eyed dancer whose rise and fall made her an emblem not only for erotic films but for the region from which she hailed. Ashish Rajadhyaksha points to Bollywood's centrality and industry dominance through the phrase "'Bollywoodization' of Hindi Cinema," where "Bollywood" is used as an umbrella term to refer to the whole of Indian cinema, diluting the complexities of the country's diverse linguistic and regional groups, which all have their own cinematic traditions.[24] The South Indian film fraternity alleged that Bollywood had co-opted the tragic life of a South Indian actress for commercial gain and reduced their film culture to stereotypes to suit the tastes and expectations of a national audience. Many South Indian film personalities who worked closely with Smitha expressed their disappointment with the Bollywood version, and some even went on to portray an "alternative" narrative of Smitha through films that drew inspiration from her life.[25] Vinu Chakravarthy, who cast Smitha in her debut film *Vandichakkaram* (1982), felt that Vidya Balan was miscast in *The Dirty Picture*, and he got into a public spat with Ekta Kapoor (the film's producer of) about the narrative's authenticity.[26]

FIGURE 5. Cartoon by Unnamati Syama Sundar (2011) that exposes the silencing of caste in *The Dirty Picture*. Image courtesy Syama Sundar.

In her interrogation of caste and gender in India's film culture, Jenny Rowena argues that the real Silk Smitha's lower-caste status energized the vamp roles she enacted on-screen. Rowena sees the lack of attention to questions of caste within larger discourses about *The Dirty Picture* as normalizing *savarna* (upper-caste) aesthetics. She writes that it "allows the fair-skinned Tamil Brahmin (Vidya Balan), located within the Hindi film industry, to make use of the image of the dark-skinned South Indian actress. By silencing the caste issues involved, it helps her build her upper-caste heroine self over the subaltern vamphood of Silk Smitha."[27] A cartoon by Unnamati Syama Sundar themed on *The Dirty Picture*, which was shared on Facebook and later formed part of Rowena's article in *Dalit Web*, conveys this whitewashing of Dalit experiences.[28] Syama Sundar's cartoons emerge from Ambedkarite politics and are critical of the left *savarna* complicity in sidelining Dalit concerns. Syama Sundar highlights the problematic formulation of women's sexual liberation in *The Dirty Picture*, which dilutes the social context of Dalit experiences and flattens variations in women's experiences and struggles (Fig. 5).

The Indian film industry does not, as *The Dirty Picture* presents it, function devoid of caste—a fact highlighted by Ambedkarite filmmakers such as Pa Ranjith, Mari Selvaraj, and Nagraj Manjule, who simultaneously denounce casteist images and use anti-caste aesthetics. Read alongside the politically mobilized art made by filmmakers conjoining the prisms of "justice with aesthetics," in which the caste body becomes a locus of power and resistance, Syama Sundar's sharp strokes from the Dalit-Bahujan perspective reveal the entitlement and endowments that structure the nexus of cultural and social capital.[29] *Bahujan*, meaning "the majority of the people," is used here to emphasize that caste is not solely a Dalit issue, and caste-bound practices abound in the day-to-day practices that affect the majority of the population.[30] Resonating with these politics, Syama Sundar's cartoon exposes the flip side to the liberal humanist take on the film by pointing to the complicity of *savarna* interests in framing it as a narrative of individual liberation.

In explicitly drawing the viewer's attention to the dehumanization of Dalit women implied in the reference to the "skinless" chicken that is hung in a meat shop, Syama Sundar's cartoon makes us aware of the problematics in the liberal narratives around women's sexual empowerment. In the panel, skinless chicken is a specialized product that is rated higher than the chicken with skin. If skin refers to a caste body, the "skinless" (casteless) body of Vidya Balan is rendered malleable enough to take up a variety of roles. Making a comparison with Smitha's presence in the industry, which has been relegated to "skin show," Syama Sundar's cartoon points toward the capitalist logic of filmmaking, which creates specialized cultural forms like cabaret but refuses to give respect and dignity to the women who perform these roles by casting them as threats to bourgeoise respectability. The power relationship between Balan and Smitha within the economy of the National Award is unequal. This unequal relationship—between an upper-caste (read casteless) body, and a caste-marked body whose status is erased in the space of cinematic narrative is analogous to Susan Gubar's characterization of masquerade and impersonation in American culture. Gubar writes: "Racial impersonation and masquerading are a destiny imposed on colonized black people who must wear the white mask—of customs and values, of norms and languages, of aesthetic standards and religious ideologies—created and enforced by an alien civilization."[31] In this social hierarchy *some* bodies can legitimately masquerade as the "other" with little impact (white, in Gubar's analysis, *savarna* in the Indian case), while any masquerade on the part of the oppressed is always a necessity for survival.

Vidya Balan enacted the life of Smitha, a lower-caste woman. Although Smitha's "dusky skin" featured prominently in journalistic write-ups when she was alive, her caste origins never found space in these columns. Instead, the write-ups discussed her dance sequences through stereotyping and oversexualizing her body. But this marking of Smitha as a "casteless" body in cinematic and journalistic discourse is in corollary, the very condition that tills the ground for her consumption as a sexual fetish. (This kind of caste erasure is not casteless in the abolitionist sense but an extension of the caste prison.) In her discussion of *tamasha*, a traditional Dalit cultural performance branded as *ashlil* (vulgar) by Brahminical society, Shailaja Paik writes about the "sex-gender-caste complex" that conditions *tamasha* performers through a prism of surplus and sexual excess. This double detraction of value makes them bear the burden of being lowly, immoral, and dishonorable women who can never gain entry to respectable social position. Paik's discussion of *manuski* (humanity or dignity) is relevant in our discussion of *madakarani* as well. What allows the disposability of sex sirens as immoral and flippant is their reification as social subjects irremediably unworthy of humanity. Their very existence as "brazen, reckless, and rebellious—a desirable and dangerous woman on the loose" is conditioned by a sexual excess and surplus that make them sexually available and negated as the other.[32] Smitha's marginalization must be read in this light. Enacting eroticized dance sequences as a secondary artist further relegated her embodied labor to the status of inessential component for artistic value. Even in the discussions around the making of *The Dirty Picture*, Silk Smitha was less of a subject than a fetish-object to be molded to the needs of the box-office economy. Likewise, the film offers no inkling of the experiential or lived accounts of lower-caste actors struggling in a system in which caste-class nexus and contact networks create opportunities.

Thus, Smitha's image has been posthumously co-opted and improvised to fit various narratives that emerge from the unequal terms that actresses must negotiate within a deeply patriarchal industry. It is ironic that in today's digital proliferation of Malayalam film clips, Smitha's name finds mention mostly as a sex siren or a "porn star" alongside later soft-porn actresses such as Shakeela, Reshma, Sindhu, and Maria, who came to the limelight well after Smitha's death in 1996. The retrospective construction of Smitha as a soft-porn actress participates in and is produced by the same sociocultural dynamics that contribute to the construction of the *madakarani*. The figure of the sexualized woman with her unapologetic diva image has often countered the normative values and sexual mores that constitute the Indian middle-class value system.

THEORIZING THE FIGURE OF *MADAKARANI*

In her work on Bombay cinema, Ranjani Mazumdar describes "vamps" as symbols of wanton sexuality who occupy public spaces such as the nightclub or bar.[33] The *madakarani* is relatively distinct from this hypersexual, westernized imagination of the vamp. Instead, the *madakarani* encompasses a gamut of roles and relationships that defines the possibilities for sexual transgression within public imaginaries of sex. This includes situations that allow women to explore sexual refashioning and engage in open and candid relations with the opposite sex, or situations that suggest the possibility of intergenerational desire. In some instances, the use of exotic locations, such as the wilderness, or cabaret sequences racialize desire through access to othered bodies that rely on sexual pleasure. Whereas the vamp stands in stark contrast to the virtuous woman, the *madakarani* is a morally liminal figure whose very existence is marked by a replaceability that makes her an extension of the sex worker in the public imagination. A transactional value animates the *madakarani*'s exchanges, especially in the way she uses her identity as a public woman to convey her concerns and visibility. Her alliances are often temporary and her efforts to negotiate with the heteropatriarchy involve calculated moves to use the system to her advantage. The *madakarani* upsets social norms not through selfishness or rampant individualism; rather, her actions break open the nexus of caste, class, and heterosexual structures that underlies patriarchy. Thus, the *madakarani* becomes an image, a posture, and a representational trope, and some of these functions find reflection in soft-porn films even at the level of production. In a film industry in which wage gaps and unsafe working conditions persist, making gender equity impossible, the resistant force emblematized by the fictional *madakarani* offers us an entry point to explore the complex terrain of gender relations that envelop this figure's depiction in Malayalam soft-porn cinema.

One early literary approach in Malayalam to incorporate erotic descriptions is the *manipravala sahityam* (a syncretic tradition of Sanskrit and Malayalam), which involved the penning of *achi charitam* (history of woman) through the description of the heroine's physical beauty, often interlaced with erotic undertones.[34] Thus, there is a prehistory to the *madakarani*, but the term as it is used in film magazine discourses encompasses an ensemble of imaginative strands associated with women and sexuality drawn from genres as diverse as *painkili* (sensational pulp fiction), *kambikathakal* (erotic stories circulated among male readers), and *rathikathakal* (write-ups in which anonymous women share their bedroom secrets). In some instances, the *madakarani* also emerges as a metonym for the film world and as a vital link connecting the textual worlds of *kambikathakal* and *rathikathakal*, both of which use a first-person narrative to share sexual experiences. Line drawings and illustrations detailing erotic encounters elucidate the narrative, while scene descriptions contribute to outlining the *madakarani*'s visual imagination. The illustrations that appeared as part of erotic stories were sometimes culled and reassembled as part of pornographic books. For instance, the illustrations that came with the *Chitrakarthika* had visually captivating line drawings that became the fulcrum around which the erotic stories were written (Fig. 6).

The circulation of *madakarani* in different genres manifests in public interest about the intimate lives of actresses verging on voyeurism, expressed in letters to the editor written by readers of film weeklies. Using vocabularies of consumption, these readers demand that magazines divulge the actresses' personal details to expose their purported double lives. In these accounts, actresses emerge as fragmented images alienated from their subjectivity, agency, and labor. The film industry generates commercial gain by galvanizing audiences' special rights over the film product (whether as song booklets sold during film screenings or other merchandise, such as posters), and viewers in turn extend their consumer privileges by commanding rights over images of and narratives about actresses as if they were themselves film paraphernalia. An extractive logic of getting the maximum benefit operates in this value-for-money argument, such that the spectator becomes the ultimate arbitrator of celebrity culture by acquiring a part, or the derivative (song booklet, merchandise), that is taken for the whole product, while the actresses are perceived as belonging to the public domain insofar as their film careers and market values rest on the support offered by viewers.

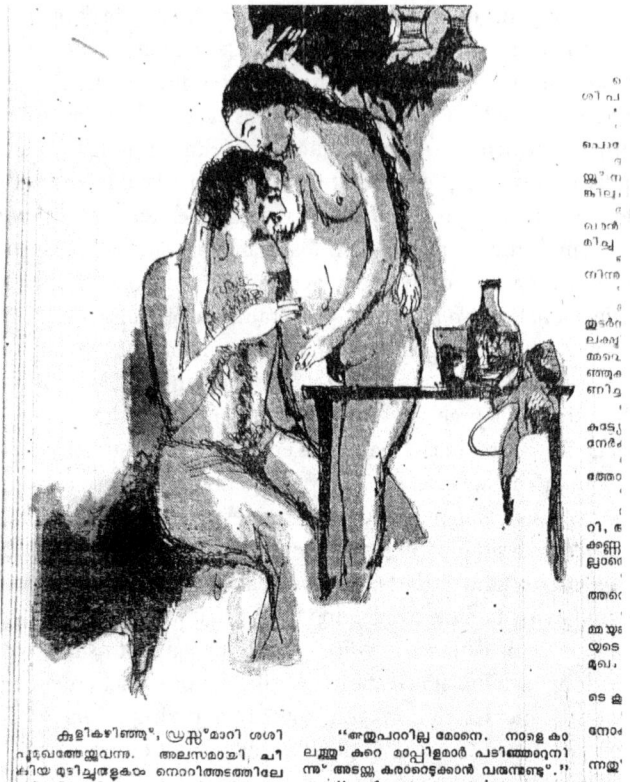

FIGURE 6. An illustration that appeared as a part of "Papathinte Sambalam" (The wages of sin) by Ekalavyan, in *Chitrakarthika*, April 1974, 36. Image courtesy Appan Thampuran Library.

The *madakarani* also emerges as essential to erotic fiction in yellow magazines, pulp fiction, and later, soft-porn films. Such erotic narratives frame the female subject in an interstitial space that reflects a tension between three recurrent strategies of representation. First, the magazines represent these actresses as devoid of any interiority, and they flit past the reader without any intimation of their own desires, intentions, hopes, and aspirations. The label of *madakarani* obliterates their individuality, such that sexuality becomes the only prism through which their history is unveiled before the reader/viewer. The second representative mode depicts the woman as an initially reluctant participant who subsequently pretends to enjoy the sexual act, only to use this as a ploy to avenge the male partner through emasculation. This mode is used by soft-porn films in vendetta narratives in which the actress avenges an injustice by mutilating the villain through her sexual ploys. Third, men's magazines such as *Kochu Sita, Muttuchippi, Mathalasa, Lolitha, Seemanthini, Sandhya, Sakhi, Geetha, Fire, Mini Fire,* and *Crime* use confessional narratives that showcase women as keepers of secrets and spinners of mysteries, whose desires can be channeled for erotic spectacles. The narratives are simulated as having been written by women who are willing to share their sexual experiences with the reader, such that the columns make readers privy to the "deep desires and passions" that underlie their revelations.[35] The columns also feature confessional accounts that are assigned to fictitious sex workers. As opposed to the lack of interiority that animates other articles, these accounts use the sex workers' experiences with different clients to reveal complex power dynamics, pleasure, and varying modes of public posturing.

Men's magazines assume a moralistic register by foregrounding men as guardians and caretakers who are responsible for exposing skewed social realities. *Fire*, for instance, describes its journalistic function as emerging out of its need to intervene in "exposing atrocities against women, children & also men."[36] Using exposure as its main organizing principle, *Fire* incorporates crime stories, erotic fiction, and centerfolds, placing women and their sexual pleasure as the cornerstone of its revelations.[37] Such popular discourse created a relay between the realm of screen pleasures and the audiences who consumed them, circulating not just through the space of the film theater but also in a peripheral network of print media such as gossip columns, yellow magazines, and centerfolds that kept the gendered mechanics of the film machinery at work outside the theater. The image of the *madakarani* was popularized not only by film actresses but also a multitude of aspiring young women who wanted to be on the screen. Print magazines and film weeklies became important dealers in this economy of screen pleasures, performing as an interface between Malayalam cinema's diegetic and nondiegetic worlds.

FILM JOURNALISTS AS CAREER DEALERS

In the 1960s and 1970s, Kodambakkam was a bustling film production base for the South Indian language industries of Tamil, Telugu, Kannada, and Malayalam. Kodambakkam is in the city of Chennai (formerly Madras), the capital of the state of Tamil Nadu.[38] It is where South Indian film production began in the 1920s with R. Nadaraja Mudaliar's establishment of the India Film Company. With the relocation of Telugu, Kannada, and Malayalam films to their regional bases in Hyderabad, Bangalore, and Trivandrum, respectively, in the 1980s and 1990s, Kodambakkam became a hub for glamour films and subsequently soft-porn production, while it simultaneously continued to serve mainstream Tamil cinema. In addition to large studios like A. V. M., Vijaya Vauhini, Gemini, and L. V. Prasad, a string of small studios like Kalpakam, Sarada, Uma, and Prakash catered to different clientele based on budget and shooting needs. The settlement around Kodambakkam, including the adjoining area of Saligramam, was dotted with one-room houses rented out to aspiring film artists at comparatively cheap rates. Production managers and agents supplying junior artists regularly visited these tenements in search of new faces. Freelance journalists who contributed stories to film magazines like *Nana, Chitrabhumi, Cinerama, Cinemamasika,* and *Film* had minor celebrity clout among the film aspirants who came from various parts of South India looking for their big break.

Most of the Malayalam film-based magazines were centered in Kerala. They employed Madras correspondents who freelanced and procured photographers from shooting locations. Beginning in the late 1970s, these film magazines and their reporters began to change how they mediated narratives from Kodambakkam and increasingly used fictitious names. In the 1980s, columns in *Chithrabhumi* such as "Gossips Out" and "Karuppum Veluppam" (Black and white) recounted the latest news from production units in the form of caricatures and memorable quotations. The column "Nanaji Kanda Lokam" (The world Nanaji saw) in *Nana* was immensely popular, as it laid out the latest gossip from outdoor shooting units and details of private lives with little discretion. More than film-related news, the lives of artists and technicians who had come to Kodambakkam took center stage in these magazines. The magazines' bargaining power grew so immense that some freelance reporters doubled as publicity agents and took on public relations work for production companies.[39] Many others who stuck to journalism strengthened their columns and became prime fixers in the industry by providing formulas for success to new entrants. The verdicts they offered in predicting actresses' futures in their columns could make or break a newcomer's career. In its October 1986 issue, *Nana* issued a call for submissions from aspiring actresses to be featured in the column "Puthumukham" (The new face), with an advertisement titled "Grab the opportunity that beckons you":

> If you have come to Madras with dreams to build a career in films, here is a golden opportunity for you. No one has made it big in Kodambakkam without the support of a helping hand or two. *Nana* is becoming a pioneer in the publishing front by extending its readers opportunities to live their dreams. Be the selected few to feature your profile in the newly launched column *Puthumukham* and change your destiny forever.[40]

Being featured in this two-page profile promised to jump-start the career of a struggling actress. Alongside a full-page photograph, the feature would carry a page-length interview in which the actress could talk openly about her interests, even her willingness to act in roles that would involve intimacy. Photoshoots using contrasting images to showcase the range of roles the actresses were capable of portraying were integral to these columns. The informality and mundane ordinariness of these photographs undercut the authoritative voice of the journalist in the accompanying write-ups.[41] While the aesthetic quality of these photographs varied, they were valued for their context-specific social function. For instance, *Nana*'s introductory article about an aspiring actress named Sreekala (Fig. 7) features two photographs accompanying the write-up. The hard lighting and strong shadows in these two images indicate that they were not taken in ideal studio conditions. The traces of domesticity that involuntarily make their way into the

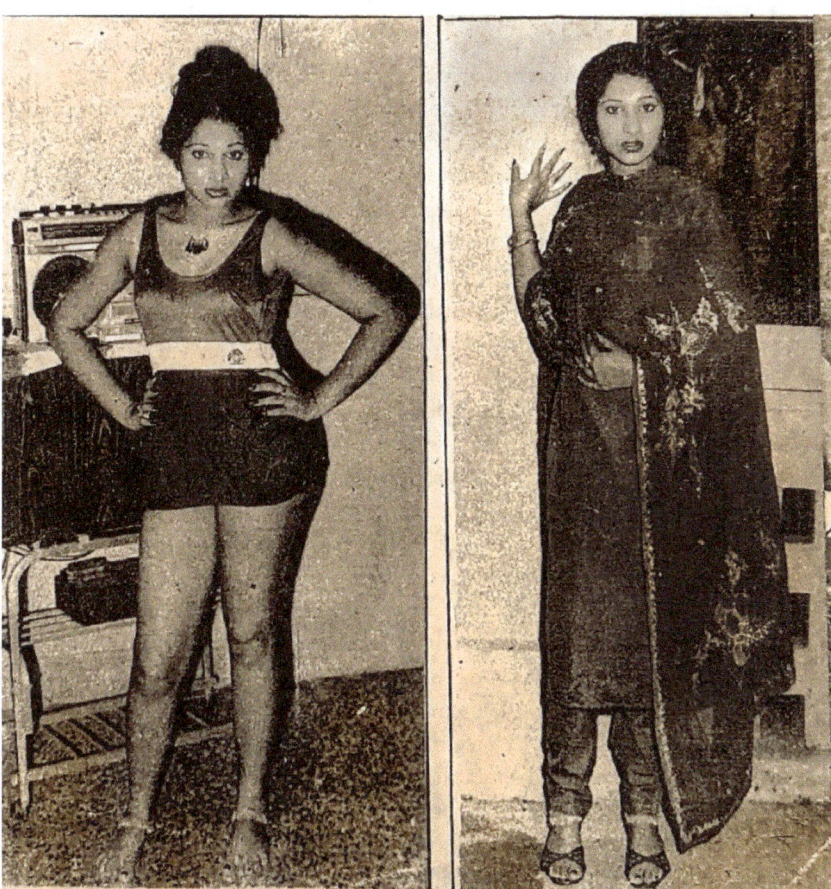

FIGURE 7. Aspiring actress Sreekala in "Cinema Bhagyam Thedi Oru Nadi" (An actress in search of luck in films), *Nana* 8, no. 3 (1986): 13. Image courtesy Appan Thampuran Library.

frame—the actress's frontal gaze, a cassette player, hard shadows—open the images up to varied interpretations that escape the photographer's intent.[42] In the first image, Sreekala has a relatively modern look in a swimsuit, an often-used strategy to showcase an actress's willingness to take up "bold" roles that deviate from the traditional look that many of these women were used to in their relatively modest upbringings. In contrast, in the second image, Sreekala appears in a traditional outfit that imbues her with middle-class respectability.

Centerfolds in the film magazines showcased actresses in skimpy outfits, often showing off bare midriffs or exposed thighs and cleavage. Avid film enthusiasts collected and displayed them. These center spreads did not always carry the names of the models, yet their appearance nevertheless provides a glimpse into their brief fame. For instance, one collector named Rarichan—a film buff in his late seventies—told me that center spreads hold a special place in his personal archive. Referring to the collection he had amassed since the 1980s, Rarichan recounts: "I used to wonder what might have happened to these women who were featured in the centerfolds. Did any of them make it to the industry? Possibly not. I call these centerfolds 'death warrants' (*maranapatram*)—the last traces of their short-stints in the industry."[43] Despite Rarichan's suggestion that actresses introduced through tabloid columns like "Puthumukham" uniformly failed, not all of them ended up playing sexually charged roles. Although most of them could not make inroads in the industry, some managed to land supporting roles in average and low-budget films. Rarichan's use of the phrase "death warrants" to signify the failed aspirations hidden in these center spreads draws our attention to how these actresses were irremediably relegated to the dustbin of history.

Given this emphasis on death, attention to the form of the obituary and the forensic gaze is productive. In fact, obituaries played a crucial role among the various genres that film magazines and weeklies used to showcase the lives of *madakarani*. One of my respondents who specialized in writing them explained, "Obituaries are not always eulogistic accounts; it can also be a move toward making the lost connections that were never uttered but was within the ambit of the known."[44] Malayalam film magazines inventively used reportage of unnatural deaths to revisit the life and contributions of the deceased. Frequently, entire issues of a film weekly were dedicated to the memory of the person concerned and included remembrance columns written by technicians, actors, and crew members and stories that had gone unreported when the subject was alive.[45] The sensationalism of tabloid journalism focused intensely on the untimely deaths of the subjects. These "exclusive" columns were gleaned from gossip that made the rounds during the person's life but had been screened from circulating as news stories. When the person died, these earlier protocols and informal agreements could be laid to rest. The ostensibly chaste genre of the obituary was used to fill in the gaps and fissures in the narrative of the person's life. Their deaths were opportunities to entangle and air out their hitherto clandestine backroom dealings. Most of these obituaries reported natural deaths, except for the three actresses I examine in the next section: Rani Padmini, who was murdered in 1986, and Vijayasree and Silk Smitha, who committed suicide in 1974 and 1996, respectively.

THE OBITUARY GAZE

As a genre of biographical writing, obituaries, known as "obits" in the journalistic register, include industry insiders' reminiscences about the deceased written immediately after the death of the subject. Obits are narratives, heavily drawing from the dead person's life and contributions written for anyone who might not have much inkling about the subject's personal life. They differ from "death notices," which are short factual announcements of a death. Early obituaries often included graphic descriptions of the death and obsessively recounted the circumstances surrounding it, reflecting a postmortem sensibility. The form of the obituary was refined over time, culminating in what Alden Whitman, a reporter for the *New York Times*, described as a "lively expression of personality and character [and] a well-focused snapshot, the fuller the length the better."[46] Malayalam film reportage about the deaths of *madakarani* is firmly rooted in the obituary's primal scene and revels in the exposition of sensational, gory, and illicit details. The deaths of actresses such as Rani Padmini, Vijayasree, and Silk Smitha exemplify this kind of reportage and its activation of the field of screen pleasures. Although the specific details of the actresses' personal circumstances and deaths differ widely, they are bound in this intentional construction of these women as *madakarani*—something that molded their public images in both life and death.

The murder of Rani Padmini and her mother, Indira, in Chennai on October 15, 1986, set off a slew of reports couched in the language of evidence probing and forensics. Padmini debuted in *Katha Ariyathe* (dir. Mohan, 1981) and went on to act in almost fifty films across the Malayalam, Tamil, and Telugu film industries. A rape sequence in *Sangharsham* (dir. P. G. Vishwambharan, 1981) launched her into the league of sex sirens and, after a point, she was typecast. Although Padmini had also acted in more "serious" films like *Parankimala* (dir. Bharatan, 1981) and *Thusharam* (dir. I. V. Sasi, 1981), posthumous reports almost completely neglected this work while focusing on allegations that she had acted in many "sex films." Reports of the murder in these magazines ask the reader to partake in the task of solving the puzzle. Details of the developing investigation, twists and turns in witness testimonies, and photographs of police personnel working at the crime scene appeared in film magazines and newspapers alongside accounts of the actress's backstory as she initially struggled to make her mark in the industry. While the reports in *Chitrabhumi* speculated on the mother-daughter duo's means of amassing wealth, the issue of *Nana* devoted to the case carried a separate section outlining the possible implications of the actress's off-screen life.

An article in *Chitrabhumi* carried photographs of Padmini, picked randomly from her photo shoots, and a detailed sketch of her house with the dimensions of the crime scene measured and marked out.[47] Other photographs captured policemen posing with the partially disintegrated bodies wrapped in palm mats, a close-up of the kitchen area from which the bodies were retrieved four days after the murder, the prime suspect as he was arrested in his hometown, and a list of objects recorded by the police. The article also carried details about the number of cuts on the victims' bodies, the angle of the blows they received, the possible weapon, and a speculative sequence of events leading up to the murder, gathered from the investigation desk.

Another article in *Chitrabhumi* reconstructed the plausible chain of events preceding the murder by culling testimony from one of the suspects, Jabharaj, who was Padmini's former driver.[48] The article states that Padmini was so secretive that drivers, maids, and watchmen were never employed for more than three months at a stretch.[49] The article hinted at the secrecy involved in Padmini's interactions and that no one, including the broker who finalized the purchase of the house, had any knowledge that Padmini was an actress.[50] If *Chitrabhumi* reported only one version of the narrative given by Jabharaj, *Nana* went a step further, placing two versions of his story side by side and asking readers to draw their own conclusions from the "evidence" before them. *Nana* dedicated its November 1986 issue to unraveling the nuances and tying up the loose threads of the mysterious "case history" of Rani Padmini.[51] The dissection of details included a brief biographic sketch of Padmini's mother Indira, an aspiring actress who had eloped when she was seventeen and who, according to this account, worked as a dubbing artist after acting prospects vanished.

By placing clues before the reading public, such magazines invited readers to be party to a metaphorical stripping, offering them the vicarious pleasures of voyeurism in solving the mystery. In conventions familiar to readers of pulp fiction, the columns were written like a detective story, with investigators assembling the clues. The obituary mode presented Rani Padmini as living a life of compromises, taking part in casting-couch practices in which sexual favors were traded for roles. The articles cast doubt on how Padmini amassed wealth, subtly suggesting that she could have been involved in sex work. Some of the articles in *Chitrabhumi* stressed that the men who supported female artists—managers, secretaries, or even distant relatives—protected them from life-threatening situations, thereby reiterating that such figures required paternalistic control.[52]

The corpses were kept in the hospital for more than ten days after the autopsy, because no family member came forward to claim them, possibly because they feared being incriminated in the case. A crowd of onlookers thronged outside the window of the autopsy room in hopes of seeing Padmini's bare body, while only five people turned up for her funeral—members of the Malayalam Chalachitra Parishad, an actors' forum based in Madras, who were obligated to act in a "responsible" manner. The obsession with the sight of the dead body conjoins Rani Padmini's death with that of two other actresses, Vijayasree and Silk Smitha, as photographs of their corpses were also featured in film magazines, making them part of the social memory of their death.

Whereas Padmini's death was mired in conspiracy theories about her murder, Vijayasree's suicide and its subsequent reportage were entangled in a larger fight between two studios (Fig. 8). One of the leading Malayalam actresses of the 1970s, Vijayasree's sex appeal was exploited in almost all the films in which she acted. "Vijayashree's thighs were a favorite among audience; her presence in the poster meant that there would be rape sequences in the film," writes Kakkanadan from Abu Dhabi in a column in *Nana*.[53] Vijayasree debuted in Malayalam cinema in the 1969 film *Pooja Pushpam* (dir. Thikkurissi Sukumaran Nair), and by her third year of acting she averaged one movie release per month. Her suicide on March

THE DEATH OF AN ACTRESS
Was South Indian star Vijayashree poisoned or did she commit suicide?
Report filed from Madras by Selvi

ON March 17, the brilliant career of a beautiful 22-year-old promising Malayalee actress was cut short. Mystery surrounds the death of Vijayashree, who consumed insecticide at her residence. Small news items in the city dailies mentioned the event in a casual manner. It seemed as though she was too insignificant to be given any importance. But today the event has assumed sinister nuances, involving many people. Meanwhile, the city is rocked by rumours. It was believed that the rivalry between two studio owners in Kerala had created tension in Vijayashree's life.

She entered the film world when she was 16. Her first movie was *Sity*, and her last film was ironically titled *Jeevikan Marannu Poya Stree* (The woman who forgot to live). She played an excellent supporting role in this picture.

For the past few months the actress was troubled and frustrated. Professional jealousy and rivalry between film makers had entrapped her. There had been rivalry between the Kunchakko group and Merryland Subramaniam. She had acted for both. When Kunchakko's group warned her not to accept

FIGURE 8. A newspaper report on Vijayasree's death. Image courtesy National Film Archive of India.

17, 1974, came during a turbulent phase after she emerged as a controversial figure due to her trouble with the management of Udaya Studios, which the director-producer Kunchacko established as the first production studio in Kerala in 1947. Her departure from Udaya in 1973 to work with its rival Merryland Studios, owned by P. Subramanian, sparked negative publicity. The rivalry between Udaya and Merryland created open alliances and camps, dividing the allegiances of artists and technicians. In an exclusive interview for *Nana* in December 1973, Vijayasree let loose a tirade against Udaya's typecasting of her as a *madakarani*.[54] The scripts of Udaya productions, she alleged, incorporated erotic sequences with the sole purpose of bodily exposure, regardless of whether or not the narrative required them. Vijayasree accused Udaya of allowing shots of a wardrobe malfunction that occurred on the set of *Ponnapuramkotta* (dir. Kunchacko, 1973) to be used in the film's final cut without her permission. In a sequence shot near the waterfall, a zoom lens captured her bare body in tantalizing detail without her knowledge, and she only discovered the existence of this footage when someone told her they had seen it during the editing of the film in the lab.

Udaya initially ignored her appeal to remove the shots but was forced to delete them when the censor board raised objections. However, by then, multiple versions of the cut sequences had begun circulating as *thundu* in India and the Gulf. In an effort to silence Vijayasree, Udaya enlisted her co-stars, including the actor Prem Nazir, to dissuade her from making public statements; these negotiations failed, however, and a public spat between the two stars ensued. Udaya then filed a defamation suit against Vijayasree and the senior staff of *Nana*, alleging that she made her claims against the studio for personal gain.[55] Udaya contended that *Nana* interfered on behalf of Vijayasree to tarnish its reputation and benefit its rival studio, Merryland, with whom they alleged *Nana* had maintained "more than cordial relations."[56] The skirmishes between *Nana* and Udaya stemmed from the magazine's unflattering reviews of *Ponnapuramkotta*, which openly critiqued the film's display of sex and violence; rebuked Udaya for diluting the historical facts of the *Vadakkan Pattukal* (Northern ballads) on which the film was based; and stated, "rather than making trash like *Ponnapuramkotta*, it was better to engage in toddy business or prostitution."[57] Enthusiastic film buffs produced a shot-by-shot analysis detailing bestiality in the film, where a chimpanzee (played by an actor in a chimp suit) was shown raping the supporting actress Vijayanirmala.[58]

Amid this back-and-forth it became evident that reels had been inserted during the film's exhibition, and this tampering with the prints blatantly violated censorship rules. The censor board deployed squads to theaters, mostly in the B-circuit, to identify any open display of the cut scenes, and action was taken against exhibitors for screening the extra reels and hefty fines were imposed on Udaya for misleading exhibitors into believing that the reels had been censored.[59] What was initially perceived as a one-off incident involving exhibitors inserting *thundu* to bolster Vijayasree's sexual appeal soon catapulted into a debate about the studio's unethical stance and lack of accountability when confronted with a leak of images that had been shot without the actress's consent. When Vijayasree went public with her allegations, Udaya painted her as an ambitious go-getter who had problems adhering to the studio's instructions and working with a team. As things spun out of control, Vijayasree had no choice but to agree to the conditions set by Udaya and retract her allegations. Vijayasree's death came immediately after this, and the police's haste in closing the case as a suicide roused suspicion of a murder cover-up. Vijayasree's last letter was posthumously published in *Nana* in memory of her unyielding defiance. In it, she blames her inability to wear the *mulakkacha* (traditional Malayali corset) in the song sequence in *Ponnapuramkotta* on her "outsider" status as a "Madrasi" (someone hailing from Madras, the capital of the neighboring state of Tamil Nadu).[60] The popular press gave a different twist to the "outsider" status Vijayasree mobilized to justify her innocence, framing it as her tacit acceptance of her status as a *madakarani* and of the popular image of the *madakarani* as a transient figure who comes from "elsewhere," has a short stint in the industry, and disappears. Whereas some of the readers' letters published in *Nana* applauded Vijayasree for registering her grievances against Udaya, others blamed her for biting the hand that fed her, pointing to the support the actors Prem Nazi and K. P. Kottarakara had offered to help build her career. "If she has an allergy with clothes, why should the readers be subjected to the mess that comes out of it?," wrote one such reader, Jayaraj from Bombay.[61] In sum, the letters found fault with Vijayasree for asserting her rights to the image and her demands that the shots of her wardrobe malfunction be removed from circulation. Although Vijayasree was a mainstream actress and performed extensively before the soft-porn boom, this narrative strand links her to other actresses like Smitha and Shakeela who covertly and overtly exposed the duplicity of a system that castigated their excess but also shaped their career trajectory.

The last interview Vijayasree gave before her death was to *Nana* in December 1973. It is unclear whether her death was a result of the revelations published in this interview. By and large, the interview ended up as a premature obituary, laying the basic groundwork for what was to follow. It resembled the framing device used by obituary writers to use the backstory of the subject as a dress rehearsal for the writing of the real obituary. *Nana* took varied stances in its coverage of Vijayasree, mainly to reinforce its position as a vanguard film publication. Initially, the magazine stood by Vijayasree and actively mobilized support in her fight against a stronger opponent. At the same time, *Nana* was harsh in its criticism of the erotic sequences in *Ponnapuramkotta*. By taking a moral high ground, they presented her as a lost sheep that had to be brought back into the fold. This is evident in a cartoon of Vijayasree that appeared in *Nana* in 1973, after she recanted her initial statements. The cartoon taunted Vijayasree for refusing to take responsibility for her revelations. Showcasing a woman in underwear holding up a piece of cloth, the cartoon ran with the caption: "What do you want? An interview or a confession?"[62] Although the cloth she was holding was seen as a reference to the *Ponnapuramkotta* controversy, *Nana*'s duplicitous stance is hard to miss, as for them she ultimately became a sex symbol because she allowed herself to be cast in such roles.

In this cartoon and in other texts, *Nana* peddled the notion that Vijayasree was a sex siren whose body played a transactional role in the visual economy of Malayalam cinema. This became clear in an autobiographical column by *Nana*'s chief editor, K. V. S. Elayath, published in 1987. The article's opening lines referred to Vijayasree with the epithets *madakathidambu* (sexy siren) and "sex-bomb" (in English) and said she had cast a spell on young men.[63] The article spurned Udaya's strategies of spinning off megahits by exposing Vijayasree's buxom figure in salacious detail in bath and cabaret sequences. Elayath's column presented Vijayasree's sequences as superfluous shots included to ensure minimum returns even for badly made films. It also censured distributors who were ready to give large advances to book the films, even in the preproduction phase, if they could be assured that Vijayasree had signed the contract. Thus, despite the support she was able to get from film publications, it ultimately boiled down to Vijayasree's need to rescue her image when faced with the explicit images. This conditioned the way Vijayasree is remembered even after her death only as a *madakarani*, and her protest against the inclusion of these images are scarcely discussed, even in accounts by those who seemingly wrote on her behalf.

The circumstances around Vijayasree's death are markedly similar to those of Silk Smitha, another "outsider" actress whose bodily presence was of value to film producers and who would become the subject of *The Dirty Picture*. Born into a Telugu family as Vijayalakshmi, Smitha entered the film industry as an assistant to a makeup artist. She made her debut in the role of a sex worker in the Malayalam film *Inayathedi* (In search of a partner; dir. Anthony Eastman, 1980). Inspired by Smita Patil, an actress prominent in the art cinema circuit, Anthony Eastman, the film's director, gave her the screen name "Smitha." She went on to act in more than 350 films across the South Indian film industries in the next seventeen years. According to several reports, Smitha had the most releases in the whole of South India in the years 1980 to 1985.[64] Her dance numbers were so popular that film tabloids celebrated her as the "South Indian Helen," referring to Helen, a Burma-born Indian actress famous in 1970s' Hindi cinema for her cabaret performances. Reminiscing on Smitha's popularity, film critic Paul Zacharia states that demand for Smitha's dance numbers was so high that the release of nearly completed films sometimes had to be delayed while filmmakers waited for her to become available to shoot dance sequences, and at other times films that had been shelved for want of distributors were released and became successful by incorporating a few Silk Smitha dance sequences.[65]

In Malayalam cinema, Smitha's presence was not limited to dance numbers, and she had supporting roles in films starring prominent stars such as Mohanlal (*Spadikam* [Crystal], dir. Bhadran, 1995), Mammootty (*Adharvam* [The fourth Veda], dir. Dennis Joseph, 1989), and Suresh Gopi (*Miss Pamela*, dir. Chellappan, 1989). But many of the roles that Smitha played were variations on the *madakarani*, be it the sexually liberated women outside the heteronormative moral universe in films like *Rathilayam* (dir. P. Chandrakumar, 1983) and *Karimbana* (dir. I. V. Sasi, 1980), or the widowed woman looking for sexual pleasure elsewhere (*Layanam*, dir. Thulasidas, 1989) (Fig. 9). *Layanam* is a particularly important example for the kind of afterlife it has had as a "soft-porn" film and its repeated resurfacing in Indian public culture even now (see chapter 5). Directed by Thulasidas and co-produced by R. B. Choudary's Super Good Films and R. Mohan's GoodKnight Films in 1989, *Layanam* was a low-budget film made well before the soft-porn wave of the 1990s and the first decade of the 2000s, but became successful as a soft-porn film later on. Smitha was not a soft-porn actress per se, but the later soft-porn wave allowed

FIGURE 9. Publicity poster for the Hindi-dubbed version of *Layanam*, titled *Reshma Ki Jawani* (Reshma's story). Image courtesy National Film Archive of India.

her bold acting choices to be recast as soft-porn performances. In fact, both Das and Choudhary became prominent in the mainstream film fraternity, and *Layanam*'s soft-porn status did not impact their ability to make other films.

Layanam explores the blossoming intimacy between Archana (Smitha), a young widow, and Nandu (Prince), who is taken in to help her with the house. The film captures the hardships she has to navigate when her neighbors either make assumptions about her sexual availability or think of her sexual agency as something dangerous enough to unsettle familial stability. The casting of a relatively young hero as a sexual interest in the film broke with societal mores that held that sex must be between partners of relatively similar age range—used in other mainstream Malayalam films like *Rathinirvedam* (dir. Bharatan, 1978). On being asked what he told the neighbors who ask him about Archana's image, Nandu replies: "I told them that I am twenty-eight and you are eighteen," reversing their real ages in an attempt to subscribe to the societal expectations. Archana's poised appearance as a confident woman who must battle unwanted attention yet at the same time also look for a companion with whom she can share her dreams and desires is one of Smitha's best roles.

The film uses fantasy sequences as an expression of intimacy and courtship rituals, and the sequence ends with the viewers, intimating that it was a dream. One of the songs features an actor in blackface with a fair-skin dancer, highlighting the racialized imagination and fascination of white skin that colors the sexual imagination in India. As opposed to the perceived expectation of soft-porn film as solely being about female desire, *Layanam* offers a backstory to situate Nandu's narrative of how he became homeless when he was falsely implicated for attempting to molest a distant relative, which led to his perpetual fear whenever he is courted by an older woman. In response, Archana says: "Not all women are like this." Anxieties about their age difference and the unconventionality of their relationship nevertheless recur throughout their interactions. Archana bursts into anger when Nandu jokingly refers to him wanting to settle down with a woman for a "normal family," and Nandu feels insecure when Archana's supposedly dead husband comes back after being released by the enemy during the war. The film ends with Nandu killing himself, while Archana dies when she accidentally falls from the stairs and is killed by a sharp spear-like object. This narrative of desire culminating in death mirrors the public perceptions about such intense feeling, which are encapsulated in the figure of the *madakarani*, in particular, and illicit love, in general.

During Silk Smitha's lifetime, writing about her was scarce, apart from tabloid columns reveling in gossip and columns accompanying centerfolds. Smitha was curt in her responses to journalists' questions and her outspoken demeanor irked columnists, who ensured that there were plenty of sensational reports about her in the tabloids. Many tales circulated about Smitha's bold comments about how the film industry discriminated against actresses who were labeled sex sirens by placing them on a lower rung of the hierarchy and separating them from other actresses, particularly leading ladies. However, by early 1995, the success formulas, including inserting erotic dances in films that had previously reaped profits, started to show diminishing returns. When leading ladies themselves took on roles as dancers, the market began to dwindle for the likes of Smitha. The fatal blow was dealt by Smitha's decision to try her luck in film production, which proved to be a disaster. By then, she was deep in debt, having borrowed money from film financiers at high interest rates. It is generally believed that Smitha's suicide in 1996 resulted from such financial and professional turmoil.[66]

Responses to Smitha's death primarily took the form of remembrance columns that framed her death as an opportunity to look back at her life and career. *Chitrabhumi* published a special issue on Smitha, collating articles from various magazines about her rags-to-riches story and final exit from the scene. Smitha's death was also remembered in the 1997 publication of an anthology of poems titled *Vishudha Smitha* (Virtuous Smitha), edited by Shivakumar Kankol. The collection brought together nine poems that had appeared in different magazines in the wake of Smitha's death. Kankol frames his own poem, "A Post-Suicide Note," as Smitha's posthumous thoughts as her corpse awaits dissection on the postmortem table.[67] Here the poet takes on Smitha's persona and narrates her thoughts as a crowd swarms the mortuary to see her corpse. The refrain "But, still I do not hate anyone" acts as Smitha's gesture of reconciliation. The poem is signed "Smitha Chechi," the way Smitha's memory would be recounted by her fans in the years to come. *Chechi* translates as elder sister, but here the word is used in a colloquial sense to mean an older woman to whom young men are sexually attracted.

The marketing of *The Dirty Picture*, though, cast Smitha's death in a different light, framing it as a biopic to authenticate Vidya Balan's makeover as Silk, as well as render it an homage to Smitha by timing the film's release to coincide with her birthday on December 2. By using Vidya Balan as a stand-in for the leading lady who can push against the hero-centric stardom that dictated Bollywood success, the film capitalized on Balan's willingness to take on the role of Smitha, which many top actresses had declined. Even in this early phase, every detail about Balan was publicized with great enthusiasm, from her selection for the lead role to her responses to the wardrobe (which included plunging necklines, midriff-baring tops, and butt pads), to her decision to put on more than twenty-six pounds to do justice to the role. But it was not a smooth ride for her; Balan was charged with obscenity for appearing in sexually suggestive poses in publicity banners. Newspapers ran columns with catchy headlines like "Silk Smitha of *The Dirty Picture* Booked for Obscenity," conflating her screen image with her actress persona.[68] Nampally Criminal Court in the state of Telangana ordered police to book Balan for posing in indecent photographs for the film posters and promotions for *The Dirty Picture*. Anti-obscenity protests overtook the film's release in many parts of Andhra Pradesh and Tamil Nadu. Thus, the film triggered interest in the lives of sex sirens, as demonstrated by the creation of fake Facebook profiles in the name of Silk Smitha. While some of these profiles remembered Smitha's life through her photographs and dance sequences, others became performative spaces in which Smitha competed with trendy new dancers like Katrina Kaif, Mallika Sherawat, and Malaika Arora Khan.

The commercial success of *The Dirty Picture* led to other films about Smitha's life that invited viewers to reinterpret it and the lives of other *madakarani*. Films based on Smitha's life that came in the wake of *The Dirty Picture* include the Kannada-language film titled *Dirty Picture: Silk Sakkath Maga* (dir. Trishul, Kannada, 2013) featuring Pakistani-origin actress Veena Malik; *Climax* (dir. Anil Kumar, Malayalam, 2013), which was also dubbed into Tamil as *Oru Nadigaiyin Diary* (An actress's diary); and *Gajjala Gurram* (dir. Anil Kumar, Telugu, 2013). Sana Khan, who starred in *Climax* as Supriya (the filmic equivalent of Smitha), had appeared in a controversial advertisement for a men's underwear brand that was banned by the government and provoked protests from women's organizations. The film's title nodded intertextually to the advertisement's narrative suggestion of a moment of orgasmic climax, reinforcing the designation of Smitha's presence in mainstream films as a sex symbol. In addition to using an actress associated with controversial depictions of sexuality, *Climax* paratextually foregrounded the personal relationship that Smitha had with the scriptwriter, Anthony Eastman, and dialogue writer, Kaloor Dennis. When Kaloor Dennis was asked whether *Climax* can be seen as a part of the trend inaugurated by *The Dirty Picture*, he responded that it was in fact made to make amends to the injustice done to Smitha's image in *The Dirty Picture*.[69]

The trailer of *Climax* interspersed images of Silk Smitha with shots from the film, accompanied by a female nondiegetic voiceover comparing Smitha to a firefly that has died prematurely. Although the subtitle announces the film to be "the true heart-rending story of an actress," it portrays Smitha's decision to end her life as the last resort of someone who has found that her calculations have been proven wrong, mostly due to her own bad decisions. The urge to "reveal" the "real Smitha" is apparent in the opening shot, which shows Supriya's dead body being removed from its grave.

The excavation of the corpse in *Climax* resonates with the forensic gaze underlying the obituaries of Smitha and Rani Padmini, as well as the photographs of their dead bodies that appeared in film journals. The deaths of these three actresses are marked by an obituary gaze—a postmortem sensibility that informs reporting on their deaths, as well as a narrative mode that fixes the memory of these actresses within a thanatological frame.[70] This specific sensibility and narrative mode insists that these actresses can only be remembered for their sensational deaths. As a process, a postmortem examination is distinct from the forensic one in that it records the history of the dead subject from the traces left behind on the corpse. Drawing from the information gathered from the crime scene investigation, forensic examination works through plausible scenarios that can elucidate what happened on the day of death. The penetrating gaze to capture the crime scene in these obituaries finds its inspiration in "the exchange principle" posited by the French forensic scientist Edmond Locard: "At every crime site the criminal takes something away and leaves something behind."[71] Obituaries conjoin these two modes to narrate the evidence left by the dead body—what Christopher Hamlin characterizes as the urge to locate "recoverable signal among the noise."[72]

This reading of clues is doubly complicated for actresses who enact sexual roles or who are cast as *madakarani*, as the sexual excesses of their on-screen life spill into public interest in their corpses. In this drama, the body of the *madakarani* becomes a mute object stripped of subjectivity and personhood. Images of her living and dead body overlap in a morbid yet sensual assemblage. This postmortem visuality brings together death, vision, and sexual excess in varying ways in the cases of Padmini, Vijayasree, and Smitha. For instance, Padmini's body had started to disintegrate by the time it was found four days after she was killed, but even that did not stop the photographer from capturing her remains, which were wrapped in a palm mat.

In her reading of autopsies as models for early cinema and a male gaze aimed at dead women, Giuliana Bruno posits an "epistemological relation between the cinematic eye and the anatomist's eye," in which the anatomical-analytical gaze "provides a model of perception, proleptically pointing towards film's visuality."

Bruno argues how the epistemology of the "visible invisible" lies at the basis of the language of film, which also doubles as a fascination for the woman's body. This is seen in the way women were featured in medical representations of anatomy lessons, in which the cadaver functioned as a key to anatomical mysteries. Bruno concludes that this desire for female anatomy can be compared to how "film language develops as a form of anatomical 'writing,'" whereby "cinema embodies the detective apparatus of dissection, the 'cutting' up and montage of parts, 'the construction of the female body, the ideal object of desire, . . . synthesized by the viewer, as if inevitably, from the juxtaposition of part objects.'" Thus, autopsies offered to film "a visual model of disclosure, enabling the possession of the female body and an uncovering of its secrets by way of unveiling."[73]

In line with this reasoning, the photograph of Vijayasree 's body, clad in a white cloth on the postmortem table, circulated as a memento mori, appearing on *Nana*'s front cover as a keepsake with which to remember her. It was widely reported that a rush of onlookers thronged Smitha's house as her dead body was taken to Vijaya hospital. The postmortem sensibility of these obituary gazes laid these actresses' bodies bare for public consumption. *Madakarani* like Padmini, Vijayasree, and Smitha remain in our memory as embodiments of sensuality. Their sensual roles define their lasting image. For these *madakarani*, death abruptly cut short their eventful lives, which were then recounted through the cold facts of forensics. This reportage portrays their sudden deaths as the only sensible, predictable outcome that these women could have expected in light of the lives they lived.

CONCLUSION

Whereas Padmini, Vijayasree, and Smitha were high-profile actresses, starlets who debuted and remained only briefly in the film industry before disappearing into oblivion were the focus of most write-ups and columns in Malayalam film magazines of the 1990s. Columns featuring disappeared starlets also produced a nostalgic thought process, in which writers in film magazines discussed unsuccessful attempts to experiment with film production in terms of themes, casting, and aesthetics. Phrases like *nirashajanakam* (hopelessness) and *nirbhagyam* (unfortunate) appeared as epitaphs for the deceased person. So-called remembrance columns included "Arangozhinja Tharangal" (The actresses who have left the stage), a column in *Chitrabhumi* by O. Rajagopal, as well as "Classic Malayalam Films," which detailed the production histories of these films. These articles used the evocative term "disappearance" (*apratyaksham, adrishyam,* or *maranju povuka*) to interrogate the actresses' uncertain courses. The beginning of their publication in the 1990s coincided with a transitory phase in Malayalam cinema, when male superstars and their personas started to dictate box-office success.[74] The male star emerged as an independent producer of meaning, who by virtue of his image mobilized the ingredients that would reap theatrical success. The rise of the male star affected the prospects of many films that did not feature renowned actors. The criteria used to grade theaters also affected film distributors, as they had to vie with each other to get their films into A-circuit theaters before they were exhibited at B- and C-center theaters.

The release of *The Dirty Picture* in 2011 triggered a similar boom in remembering starlets who, despite their efforts to succeed in the industry, had fallen off the grid. Columns like "Ormayile Nayikamar" (The actresses who are remembered) by Shijesh Naduvanoor in *Rashtradeepika Cinema* film weekly and "Malayalathile Classic Rathi Chitrangal" (Classic sex films in Malayalam) by K. N. Shaji Kumar in *Cinemamangalam* film weekly attempted to bring starlets back into the limelight. These columns take on the genre of the obituary to underline the failures of starlets in their professional and personal lives. These attempts to incorporate starlets into the dominant narrative of Malayalam cinema were facilitated by films like *Naayika* (dir. Jayaraj, 2011), *Celluloid* (dir. Kamal, 2013), and *Vellaripravinte Changathi* (dir. Akku Akbar, 2011) that addressed the idea of "loss" (lost narratives, figures, objects).[75]

The Malayalam film industry regularly saw influxes of actresses from other language industries—for instance, Swapna from Punjab and Poonam Das Gupta from Maharashtra, who had short but intense stints as *madakarani* in Malayalam cinema. Many of these starlets were abandoned in the cutting room and the only evidence of their existence seems to be limited to the columns of the film magazines, continuity albums, and center spreads. A prime example is Madhuri, who rose to fame with the 1984 film *Pavam Krooran* (dir. Rajasenan), in which she played Nimmy, a teenager who entices Damu, a sexually frustrated middle-aged servant, in a saga of sexual explorations. When her interest in Damu wanes, she refuses his advances to continue the relationship. Considering this a betrayal, Damu turns into a psychopath who murders sixteen-year-old girls. *Pavam Krooran* was a hit and dubbed into many languages. The Tamil version, *Kamini* (Attractive woman), circulated mostly as a soft-porn film, with liberal insertion of *thundu*. *Kamini*'s suggestive poster pulled crowds into theaters. In a 2013 column in *Rastradeepika Cinema*, Madhuri is described as someone whose repeated attempts to return to "good films" are marred by her debut, a debacle from which she never recovered.[76]

The list of such starlets is endless and names such as Sharmila, Babita, Usha Rani, Surya, Satyakala, Kanaga Durga, Sreekala, Prameela, and Suparna are part of this obscure pantheon of actresses who could never break into successful mainstream films after their stint in sexualized roles. Like all categorizations, the label "starlet" is delimiting and marked by a selective inclusion. Accounts of Malayalam cinema rely on narratives about starlets' unrealized aspirations and their lasting impression as failed actresses who withdrew before the right opportunity came along. The figure of the starlet has been framed in film journalism as someone so desperate to make it that they can resort to exchanging favors, using their bodies as "their gambling ticket," as one report puts it.[77] In Kodambakkam, stories of disappearance run alongside stories of resilience and other informal modes of making do—waiting for work, waiting for a break, and other informal trust-based arrangements. These modes of organizing life in the soft-porn industry arguably have older cinematic precedents, and Kodambakkam's history, its spatial arrangements, and social life are important nodes in the history of the soft-porn genre.

2

Waiting for Kodambakkam

Economies of Waiting and Labor in Tinsel Town

The tendency of starlets of Malayalam cinema to drop off the cinematic map after short stints was a product of the film industry's structure. Informal labor practices, which extended to all levels of the cast and crew, and especially to newcomers and below-the-line labor, shaped the lives of these actresses and their aspirational mobility. Waiting for a break in the industry—what I conceptualize as "cinematic wait-time"—became part and parcel of the affective economy of labor in the Malayalam film industry. Cinematic wait-time is spatially organized and incorporated in the industrial practices in Kodambakkam, a neighborhood in the city of Chennai. Cinematic wait-time refers neither to the time expended in the making, distribution, and exhibition of a film nor to representations of waiting or suspended temporality in film narratives. Most crucially, cinematic wait-time is *not* a "waste of time" in the "political economy of waiting."[1] Rather, it is the time spent waiting to enter the film industry—time that must be invested for future returns and opportunities to be employed in film production. In this, cinematic wait-time also involves what Debashree Mukherjee, writing about filmmaking in colonial Bombay, refers to as the "hustle"—"a form of speculative action, a gamble from a site of immediate precarity."[2] Wait-time does not always involve participation in the labor force, but it is a form of invisible labor that is nonremunerative and involves efforts to make oneself marketable through uncredited work and apprenticeship. Many of my respondents who were aspiring actors and professionals used the idea of wait-time to mean "experience" that counts in a labor market that highly values learning on the job. The political economy of Kodambakkam's production, distribution, and exhibition pathways incorporate waiting as a constitutive part of the system. While waiting for work is not uncommon in mainstream commercial cinema as well, it takes on distinct contours in the case of soft-porn. For instance, for a still photographer or makeup artist wanting to work as a director making creative choices, advancing through the system was an uphill battle. In most departments, there would be other "waiters"—for instance, associates and assistants under the cinematographer, who were waiting their turn. Soft-porn "hacked" this waiting game; many film personnel could moonlight as soft-porn cine-workers in departments other than their own, while in the process bringing the dwindling audience back to the theaters.

Wait-time is also incorporated into the language of Kodambakkam's grooming centers or acting prep schools, which promote the idea that waiting is an integral part of a successful career and a sign of sincerity. In my interviews with many film hopefuls who were receiving training in acting schools, there was a recurrent narrative of how being acknowledged for their talent after a long period of struggle is what defines a successful stint; *payatti theliyuka*—to excel after a series of ups and downs—was how one of the members of a grooming school referred to the process of waiting. Ghassan Hage calls this an "endurance test . . . that is referred to in common language as 'waiting it out.'"[3] Yet whereas Hage refers to waiting out a crisis, wait-time in Kodambakkam's film circuits has more of an everyday feel to it. Hopefuls waited, but not necessarily through a storm or a crisis. Their waiting was more akin to an athlete's training during the offseason. It is not passive, but strategic—an "explicit expression of agency" that filters the investment of time through hope.[4] I use the term "wait-time" to account for such informal labor practices that are otherwise ignored within filmmaking's transactional economy. Due to the premium placed on the commodity's exchange value, wait-time remains under-theorized in most studies of the political economy of film production.[5] But wait-time is an integral mode of operation in informal and fringe cinematic practices, where above- and below-the-line costs do not exist as distinct foolproof categories.

Accounts of the deaths and disappearances of starlets were the starting point of my investigation, yet many other surprises awaited me as I began to explore the references that led me to Kodambakkam. I entered Chennai following the trails of the brief careers of many aspiring actors and technicians, some who built workable professional relationships and some who left their careers midway. These were not anomalies—rather, disappearing was part of the process of transiting between aspirational dreams and losing hope of finding footing in the industry. The industry's regulated flow of production was seldom interrupted by such individual hurdles and pitfalls. A constant flow of aspirants was ready to replace actors who departed in these interstitial periods. Cinematic wait-time is a by-product of this demand for labor and the incessant entries and exits of aspiring actors to fill that demand and achieve their own goals.

Cinematic wait-time involves *waiting for* a break as well as *waiting in* anticipation of gigs and job opportunities. Through these two modalities, I track how temporal notions and practices of waiting become central to the imagination of a "tinsel town" and how wait-time etches itself into cinematic history itself. This mapping requires an ethnographic lens, as waiting can only be mapped by *waiting with*. By waiting with my respondents (conceptually and physically), I map the space of Kodambakkam and untangle different layers of remembrances and temporal invocations that connect it to the history of Malayalam cinema. In so doing, I locate diverse cinematic practices that are endemic to low-budget cinemas in southern India. I use the term "tinsel town" to refer to the struggle of the actors and technicians to establish their careers and the contingencies that accompany this process of waiting. The word "tinsel" plays into the imagination of a glitzy, Christmassy artificiality, as well as a datedness, in terms of the studio-based film productions that were produced from different centers in India from the colonial period.

Kodambakkam as a tinsel town highlights the spatiotemporal specificities that define regional cinematic processes. Kodambakkam is arguably the ur-scene for many of the South Indian film industries and later became the center of soft-porn production. Aspiring film actors who came to Madras in the 1960s and 1970s saw Kodambakkam as a hub for potential jobs. Although Tamil Nadu and Kerala are separate states, historically the various southern Indian film industries have overlapped since the silent cinema era. The intersection of these multiple temporalities and regionalities crystallize within Kodambakkam's heterotopic space and govern its cinematic practice.[6] In her spatial conceptualization of film historiography, Priya Jaikumar explains that separate "physical, mental and social" spaces govern films and filmmaking and their contingent historical processes.[7] Jaikumar refers to cinema's spatiality as "artifactual," drawing attention to the craft, labor, art, and politics that help further technology's mimetic and plastic capacities.[8] I likewise approach my study of Kodambakkam as a search for artifactual histories of film-industrial culture. While the historicity of Kodambakkam is specific to South Indian cinema, my larger theoretical intervention is to think about space *through time*—that is, to consider time not only as the chronological unraveling of historical events and facts, but also as it is lived, managed, and practiced within the film industry. This approach accounts for the ways in which memory, nostalgia, and unremunerated labor contribute to the construction of a tinsel town. As a product of consumption and exchange, cinema involves processes of labor and negotiation that remain unseen in the finished film product. Paying attention to waiting allows us to understand the tension between tangible and more invisible forms of labor. Malayalam soft-porn is marked by informal modes of production and distribution, and the roots of its transactional practices can be traced back to older forms of waiting and aspirational economies that were already at work in Kodambakkam's cinematic ecology.

In examining Kodambakkam as a tinsel town, my intentions are twofold. First, I historicize the forging of regional affinities in South Indian cinema and the emergence of Kodambakkam as a site of affective encounters that mark the experience of living and working in a tinsel town. Second, I untangle the heterogeneous temporalities that are embedded in this notion of the tinsel town. The terms "tinsel town" and "cinema city" foreground the multiple industrial practices that cinema facilitates. At the same time, they can hide the different experiences of time that go into the making of such spaces. Subjective experiences of time as either fast or slow allow for equally subjective experiences of space to emerge. Thus, to examine the embodied practices associated with Kodambakkam as a space of mnemonic cultural production, I argue for a "sense of space" rather than an idea of fixed, unchanging space. This sense of space is deeply rooted in psycho-geographies of movement in which the act of navigating city-space creates an alternative "itinerary of emotions" that is distinct from the official cartographic representation of places signified through landmarks.[9]

This chapter is divided into three sections. The first, historical in focus, situates Kodambakkam as the base of film production for Tamil, Malayalam, Kannada, and Telugu films from the 1950s to today. Kodambakkam's journey from "studio city" (that housed the major film studios of its time) to a site of B-movie production exposes the contradictory impulses that undergird our present understanding of both Kodambakkam and the rise in the late 1970s of "glamour" films—low-budget movies that dealt with sensationalized and sexualized themes and imagery. Informed by my experiences of observing a production manager in the low-budget film industry in Chennai, the second section examines the labor structures that position the production manager as the fulcrum of film production. The third section focuses on two filmmakers, K. S. Gopalakrishnan and P. Chandrakumar, who helped carve out the genre of glamour films in Malayalam cinema from the 1970s through the 1990s. These films were not necessarily explicit; rather, "glamour" was an industrial code that indicated a range of elements, including erotic dance sequences, illicit relationships, crime, and awakenings of sexuality. In my analysis of these directors' film practices, I argue that low-budget glamour filmmakers employed specific tactics to reduce wait-time and manage precarity. They provided aspiring actors with opportunities and hands-on experience to build connections in an industry that had traditionally been a multi-tier structure; without these connections, it remained hard for outsiders to enter it. I suggest that Kodambakkam as a tinsel town has been shaped by such temporally motivated practices, which emerge at the confluence of precarious labor and risk management.

In her work on Bombay cinema, Ranjani Mazumdar views the cinematic city as an "archive that is deeply saturated with urban dreams, desires and fears."[10] Mazumdar complicates ideological readings by emphasizing how cinematic practices and urban experience inform the cinematic portrayal of city life. For Mazumdar, experiences of loss, nostalgia, pain, community, and anger can be perceived in spaces such as the "footpath"—a mix of "part village community, part cosmopolitan city street."[11] The tinsel-town economy that I foreground in this chapter taps into the space of the footpath as it intersects with labor and wait-time. In the case of Bombay or Chennai, urban space cannot be divorced from large-scale migration from the rural hinterlands. Footpaths are not only traces of homelessness, but also spaces of negotiation where laborers—both native and migrant—wait to find work. For example, in Kodambakkam, junior artists wait for agents to pick them up outside the junior artists' union office, and aspiring actors often wait near shooting locations to be introduced to the film directors. Films such as *Annakutty Kodambakkam Vilikunnu* (Annakutty, Kodambakkam is beckoning you; dir. Jagathy Sreekumar, 1989) and *Halo Madras Girl* (dir. J. Williams, 1983) that depict Kodambakkam as a cinematic city regularly show these waiting crowds. This kind of spatial, waiting practice is predicated on a deliberate deployment of hope—what Hirokazu Miyazaki describes as a way of capturing the prospective, future-oriented momentum inherent in the anticipation of "what has not-yet become."[12] In a tinsel town, the anticipation of prospects renders waiting a mode of buying time to work out career options. Simultaneously, such practices also produce a community of "waiters" who learn from each other's experiences and collectively negotiate wait-time in the industry.

Many of my interviewees used the word "waiting" in English, as opposed to its Malayalam or Tamil equivalent (*kathiruppu*, in both languages). In response to my questions about what exactly they were waiting *for*, many referred to an "apt time," "conducive factors," "right support," or "god's graces" that would turn their aspirations into reality. "Waiting for a break is like waiting for the visa to arrive. We all know that it will come but don't know when. Like the different routes used to get [the] visa, we are all at the mercy of other people," said Shenoy, who had come to Kodambakkam to be an actor in the 1980s and at the time of the interview worked in an eatery in Vadapalani.[13] Many who came to Kodambakkam in search of a film career and ended up doing odd jobs in the industry expressed a belief that wait-time might guarantee them a break. At the same time, waiting can also point toward reserve labor, which is sought only when there is a deficit in the labor pool, or unutilized labor that is either wasting away or not allowed to realize its potential. This reserve labor is constitutive of the spatial construction of the tinsel town, as waiting through and with hope becomes a mode of connecting with the world of filmmaking.

Tinsel town differs from terms such as "cinematic city" (the city as represented in film) or "film city" (the city where the film is shot). Although cinematic city, film city, and tinsel town all refer to spatial organizations of filmmaking, they are distinct in their relationship to waiting. If the cinematic city encapsulates urban experience, a film city refers to a simulated one. It is an ensemble of infrastructures that are mobilized in one place to enable the film's production, as, for example, the Ramoji Film City (RFC) in Hyderabad, which Shanti Kumar describes as a coalescence of fantasy space and profit, where the existence of the entire place is meant to reduce the expenditure of time by speeding up processes and linking different segments into one unified space.[14]

Tinsel towns, though, are more closely related to cinema cities—urban spaces that are associated with film production, often drawing in crowds who witness the shooting as part of the experience of film production in the urban space. Unlike the cinematic city and the film city, which exist partly as representation and partly as simulation, cinema cities and tinsel towns are tangible urban spaces that intersect with cinematic practice. In relation to the cinema city, Madhusree Dutta, Kaushik Bhaumik, and Rohan Shivkumar, the authors of the multimedia *Project Cinema City*, map the space of Bombay and its intersection with varied cinematic practices. They write that the relationship between cinema and the city is "imaginary yet tactile, complementary and also ambivalent, momentary and still recyclable—in short it speaks of a form and its apparition as well."[15] In the context of Indian cinema, Bombay is the cinema-city par excellence—"Bombay" is the city where the Hindi film industry is located, but its modalities of life are dispersed across its different urban locations. The cinema city points to an urban imagination in which the *entire* city is seen as a part of the cinematic industry. This is where tinsel towns differ from cinema cities: the difference between the two is primarily one of scale and relational locality. A tinsel town such as Kodambakkam preexists as a neighborhood or an urban zone within a larger city—Chennai/Madras in this case. It is "Kodambakkam" and not "Chennai" that defines the physical area and the reach of cinematic practice (Fig. 10). Although the term "Bollywood" is regularly used in the case of Bombay, there is no actual place with that name. Unlike Bollywood, Kodambakkam refers to an actual zone marked out within Chennai. This difference between Bombay as a cinematic city and Kodambakkam as a tinsel town also points toward practices of informal urban zoning that mark out specific trades within certain localities.

Kodambakkam intersects with space and wait-time in three significant ways: the representation of Kodambakkam as a cinematic city in filmic references; Kodambakkam as a tinsel town in its everyday workings; and Kodambakkam's intersections with filmic regionality. To use David Harvey's terms, we can approach Kodambakkam as both a represented space (appearing in memorial accounts) and a space of representation (working through signs and signifiers).[16] This latter aspect allows new spatial practices, spaces of representation, and cinematic practices to emerge across Kodambakkam's cartography. Tracing the historical

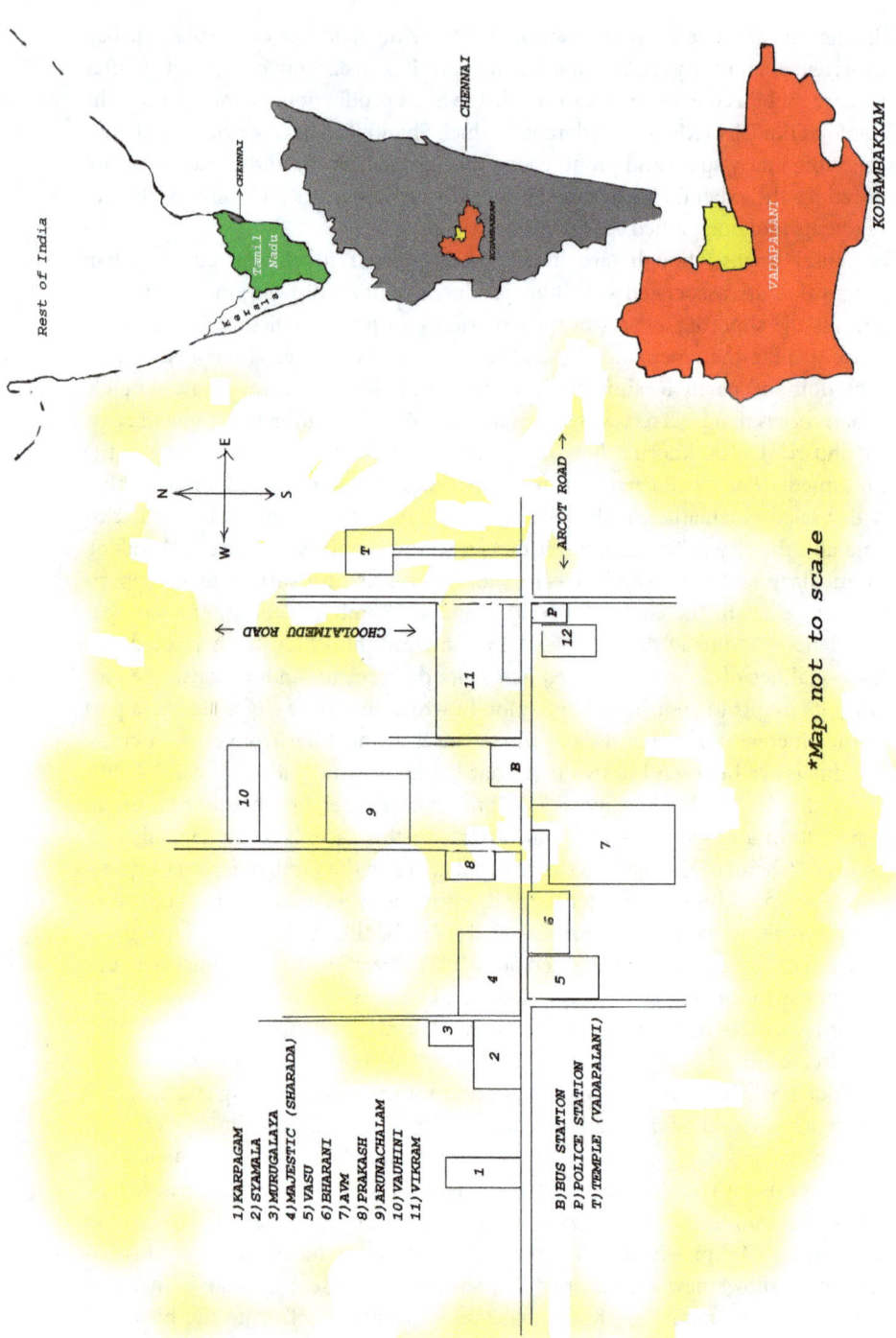

FIGURE 10. Artist's rendition of the map of Kodambakkam showing the location of various film facilities, including studios and labs. Image concept and model by S. Padhakrishnan; composite by Anirban Baishya.

emergence of Kodambakkam as a tinsel town allows us to unpack these two layers of representation.

ORIGINS AND DEVELOPMENT OF KODAMBAKKAM AS TINSEL TOWN

There are many contesting narratives about the origin of Kodambakkam. In some oral accounts, it forms part of the Shrotrium Village in Puliyur Kottam, one of the twenty-four subdivisions of Thondainadu.[17] According to the *Sthalapuranam*, the name Kodambakkam comes from one of the two Siva temples in the area. Between the seventeenth and nineteenth centuries, the stretch of land that now comprises Kodambakkam and its adjacent localities, Vadapalani and Saligramam, was the fiefdom of the Nawab of Arcot. Until 1964, one footpath extending only as far as Vadapalani was seen as the city limit. The place-name Kodambakkam derives from the Hindi term *Ghoda Bagh*, the name given to the Horse Gardens by the Nawab of Arcot.[18] The gradual development of Kodambakkam as the nerve center for film production in South India began with its incubation of an early film culture in the late nineteenth and early twentieth centuries, with the establishment of several studios and theaters in the city of Madras. During the colonial regime, the four states—Kerala, Tamil Nadu, Andhra Pradesh, and Karnataka—were collectively called the Madras Presidency. In the 1950s, Madras was at the center of a dispute between Tamils and Telugus, who both wanted Madras to be included in their state as part of the linguistic reorganization of independent India. Despite this contestation, Madras functioned as a base for the production for South Indian films in Tamil, Kannada, Telugu, and Malayalam until the 1980s.[19] These films were colloquially called "Madras" films by distributors and exhibitors based in Hindi-speaking regions of India.

The first studio in Madras, Tower House, was set up in 1917 by Nataraja Mudaliar,[20] and several other studios, such as Star of India Glass-Studio and Sreenivasa Cinetone, were soon built in the same vicinity. Initially, the locality of Purasawalkam was the locus of film production in Madras; this shifted to Kodambakkam in the mid-1940s due to demands for electricity. Kodambakkam was an ideal location because it had a powerhouse built by the Madras Electricity Supply Corporation (MESC) during World War II.[21] Kodambakkam was a sparsely populated area according to the 1939 census, but by the 1950s it had become the main site of film production for most of the South Indian states. The Kodambakkam Bridge, which connects the rest of the city with the prime area of film production, is a landmark that cannot be missed by anyone traveling to the city's west side. The bridge was built in 1965 by the Highways Authority of India and the Indian Railways, under the initiative of Minjur Bhaktavatsalam, the last Congress chief minister of Tamil Nadu (1963–67), and during a time when anti-Hindi protests were flaring there.[22] Before the bridge was built, a railway crossing gate known as "Periye Gate" (also called Rajagopuram Gate) connected the city with the studios in Vadapalani.[23] The term *Periye*, which is derived from the root word *peruma* common to both Tamil and Malayalam, means "famous," and thus hints at the landmark's proximity to the star-studded film business. Onlookers were fascinated by the view of actors waiting in their cars for the railway gates to be opened, and there was no scarcity of crowds at the gate.[24] Thus, the spatial imaginary of Kodambakkam mediated its star culture, with each part of the town associated with some aspect of the film industry.

Areas such as Kodambakkam Bridge, Periye Gate, Saligramam, and Vadapalani are anchor points that are crucial for understanding the film production and labor procurement practices that formed its tinsel-town economy. The varied trades and production-related tasks are spread across different localities that are demarcated informally as specialized zones. For instance, home-based business establishments flourished in and around the residential areas of Nungambakkam and Valluvarkottam in the 1960s, demonstrating how people living in Kodambakkam incorporated filmmaking into their lives, making it into jobs that sustained their families. Huge stretches of the town's thoroughfares were dotted with shops and businesses related to film, such as accessories suppliers, wig makers, carpenters, costumers, and hairdressers. Women also managed catering units from their homes.[25] Many took up businesses related to film as an extension of the traditional vocations of preceding generations, who mainly catered to the theaters and the mythological cinema of the 1930s and 1940s. The remnants of this film-based culture persist in signboards in Kodambakkam, like that of Hotel Hollywood, which was established in Trustpuram in the 1950s, and Bombay Hollywood, a tailoring and costume firm on Karunanidhi Road established in the 1960s (Fig. 11).

Lodging facilities were arranged in Rohini (T-Nagar), Raj Home (Numgambakkam), Palm Grove (Kodambakkam High Road), Amarawati, and Mosabi, depending on the "grade" of the technicians, production staff, and actors. Raipetta is another site famous for housing prominent actors. Production crews preferred the mess units based in Pondy Bazar, like Shanta Bhawan, Gita Café, and Narayanan Mess, due to their reasonable prices. Initially, most junior artists lived in one-room lodgings around Subarayan Street that charged daily rent, but beginning in the 1970s, they moved to Mosque Street. In a practice that is still followed today, agents frequented these localities to select extras for background and crowd scenes. The residential localities of Saligramam, Dasaradapuram, VOC Street, and Florist Street offered low-cost housing for newcomers. Whereas the area of Sowcarpet was demarcated as the hub for financiers, distributors were mostly based on Meeran Sahib Street near Mount Road. In the 1970s, film labs also began to open shop in Kodambakkam. These included R. K. Labs, Kamal Black and White Lab, Vijaya Black and White Lab, Prasad Labs, Gemini Labs, AVM Lab, Sarada Lab, and Vasu Lab.

Although it is not surprising that businesses providing housing and food thrived in this urban space, perhaps what is unique about Kodambakkam is that

FIGURE 11. Bombay Hollywood Tailors in Kalaingar Karunanidhi Road, Saligramam. Photo by author.

film permeated all aspects of its social life. Consider, for instance, that the Murugan Temple at Vadapalani became another central landmark of film production in Kodambakkam. During the 1970s and 1980s, the performance of prayers outside the temple was an everyday sight for people staying in the locality of S. Perumal Kovil Street. Before sending film reels out for circulation, distributors would mark the cans with sandalwood paste from the temple premises and, regardless of religious beliefs, most distributors and exhibitors would offer the first print to the deity for blessings, in a kind of urban cinematic ritual. Sometimes, reluctant producers who had reservations about the ritual's Hindu nature were made to compromise by shrewd distributors and production managers. As Mathews, a production manager—an agnostic who was raised as a Christian—said during one of our meetings: "Film production is a gamble at the end of the day. So, even though I am an agnostic, I would not mind doing a *puja* (prayer) at the Murugan Temple before sending the cans to the theaters."[26] In fact, Murugan Temple's growth from a thatched shed built by the devotee Annaswami Nayakar to a full-fledged temple in 1920 owes a lot to Kodambakkam's bustling film production units.

The history of Malayalam cinema was closely associated with Kodambakkam until the 1990s, even though the first Malayalam films were not based in Kodambakkam—the first, *Vigatakumaran* (dir. J. C. Daniel, 1928), was made in a studio based in Trivandrum, while the second film, *Balan* (dir. S. Nottani, 1938), was made by Modern Theatres, Salem. Studios based in Coimbatore, such as the Pakshiraja and Ratna studios, also contributed to the making of Malayalam films in the initial phase. The establishment of studios like Udaya and Merryland in Kerala in the late 1940s stirred popular interest in cinema, and many migrated to Madras in search of opportunities to work in film.[27] Madras was always thought of as a city that welcomed newcomers to its fold, as the phrase "Vantharai Vazhavaikkum Tamilagam" (The Tamil land that welcomes everyone with open arms) indicates. With an increase in the number of Malayalam films produced in the 1950s, the influx of migrants to Kodambakkam began to increase substantially. The success of the 1954 Malayalam film *Neelakuyil* (dir. P. Bhaskaran) led to a rush of talent to Madras.[28] Migration was boosted by the informal bonds that supported aspiring film workers during trying times in Kodambakkam, and the shared vocabulary of the Dravidian languages spoken by migrants opened channels of communication.

Cultural and linguistic affinities were boosted through infrastructural support systems such as housing facilities, as well as restaurants that allowed Malayalis to convene and emerge as a substantial presence in Madras. Community spaces such as Poona Home and a cafeteria run by a proprietor known only by the surname Varghese supported employment opportunities for those who migrated to Madras in search of film jobs. P. A. Becker opened Poona Home in 1960 to support aspiring Malayali film workers who had returned to Madras after completing their studies at the Film and Television Institute in Pune (previously known as Poona) in Maharashtra in western India. It gradually developed into a hub for discussions and scripting workshops. Patrons of Poona Home included the likes of John Abraham, K. G. George, M. Asad, Ramachandra Babu, Balu Mahendra, and Vipin Das, who later became iconic figures in Malayalam cinema. Varghese's establishment was a small, one-hall kitchen set up near the Kodambakkam Powerhouse that was frequented by many aspiring film workers. Film critic P. K. Sreenivasan reminiscences of Varghese: "Varghese's ledger had names of many star figures who would later rule South Indian film industry."[29] Other popular Malayali establishments included Quality Hotel, run by a Malayali owner; Swamy's Lodge in Mount Road, which offered cheap accommodations; and Kilpauk's Malabar Hill, named after a Bombay locality, a popular lodging option for those with a slightly higher budget.

In the 1980s, as part of a larger process of strengthening the regional industries, Malayalam cinema moved its official base back to the state of Kerala, and the Kannada and Telugu industries moved back to their respective states. After this official relocation, however, Kodambakkam began to function as a shadow economy and simultaneously emerged as a significant strand in the imagination of Malayalam cinema. During the 1990s, Kodambakkam was seen as a space for low-budget films and one that held the key to Malayalam cinema's underbelly. During my initial inquiries about soft-porn films, many prominent Malayalam filmmakers told me to find contacts from Kodambakkam. In the layered imaginary of Kodambakkam, the town was both a place-signifier for Malayalam cinema and a space where cinema's informal and infrastructural practices could be mapped.

KODAMBAKKAM AS REMEMBERED SPACE

Autobiographical accounts and memoirs of erstwhile technicians, actors, and production personnel reminiscing on their experiences working in Madras in the 1960s and 1970s paint varied pictures of Kodambakkam. Often partial and fragmentary, these accounts purport to offer a glimpse of people whose voices are lost in official histories. In *Beyond Frames: The Autobiography of a Cinema Still Photographer*, P. David, who worked in the film industry from 1961 to 1978, inflects his account of his struggling phase with the time he shared with film personnel. A preface by P. Zakir Hussain, titled "The Invisible Film Historian," locates David and his book within the rise and fall of many aspiring film workers who had to negotiate the industry's labyrinthine networks. The figure of the invisible historian evoked in this preface is invested with the task of unearthing lost voices. Although the book was promoted as an autobiography, it was in fact a compilation of articles by Hussain, who was a journalist and biographer. Hussain's name appears under the heading "thayarakkiyathu," meaning "prepared by," and the preface refers to the previous publication of some of the material as vignettes in *Mathrubhumi* magazine.[30] Arranged chronologically, the accounts begin with David's entry into Kodambakkam and subsequent chapters center on a specific figure or film. David evocatively narrates how he confronted the experience of waiting in an industry that is keen on time-bound work. In his constant run from pillar to post, he realized that "wait-time" had become a frequent phrase used to refer to the time that hardens one up to face the world. For many film hopefuls, waiting signified a testing time that could make or break their prospects in the industry.

David also writes about Kodambakkam's need-based housing arrangements, which offered low-budget lodging for job seekers who could not afford monthly rent and advance payment. These lodging arrangements were colloquially called "waiting rooms" and allowed job seekers to occupy a space without having to rent it. They were, in a sense, veritable "waiting technologies [that regulate] the compartmentalization of space and the provision of a space dedicated to waiting."[31] The temporary arrangements provided lodgers with a bed to sleep on, and they could leave their belongings at the hotel reception desk when going out.[32] This interim status meant that the lodger's space was marked by the bed they occupied, while the space adjacent to the hotel reception was used as a cloakroom. Sleep time was regulated so that the same bed could be occupied by multiple people at different points in the same day; ownership of the space thus varied over the course of the day. This wait-time arrangement hinted at a practice that distinguished between spatial occupation and spatial belonging as integral parts of negotiating wait-time. Spatial belonging could be earned after traversing wait-time.

FIGURE 12. Artist's impression of a continuity album for a 1996 film shared with me by a director. Image courtesy S. Radhakrishnan.

The spatiotemporal technology of the waiting room is replicated in a different filmic artifact—the continuity album. These albums perform a functional role in documenting the continuity of shots and collating a serialized view of time and space. Whereas publicity photographs are "rehearsed tableaus from the film [that] showcased key dramatic moments and other promised pleasures,"[33] continuity albums are devoid of aesthetic ornamentation. In his memoir, David refers to continuity albums as spatializing time within the "arena managed by a still photographer."[34] These artifacts not only arrange the sequence of the images in the order of shooting, but they also act as a trace that connects an otherwise dispersed shooting process. Just as the waiting room houses film aspirants who may never meet, the continuity album documents disparate, fragmented segments of the shoot. At the same time, continuity albums also document extras or struggling actors who may have appeared in a scene in the shoot but may not have made it into the final cut of the film. They are not merely nostalgic documents of a film's making but also a roster of those who waited through its production. They house not just the stars of the film but also the people who may have waited outside production facilities or studio offices to appear in one of the scenes. Continuity albums thus also become a resource for research—one that has helped me spark many a conversation with filmmakers about their experiences in Kodambakkam (Fig. 12).

A contrary picture of Kodambakkam emerges in the 2010 memoir *Chitratheruvukal* (Film streets) by the National Award-winning author M. T. Vasudevan Nair, in which he looks back at Kodambakkam in the 1960s and 1970s. Unlike that of David, who left the film scene in the 1980s and moved to wedding photography, Nair's presence in Kerala's literary and cinematic publics sustained his privileged status. The book is structured in the form of remembrance columns by Nair focused on people he befriended in his time in Madras. Nair's memoir is woven around the theme of loss—the loss of people whose deaths remain central to his memory of the place and the loss of memory itself, which made him pen the memoir in the first place. Illustrations by the artist Nampoothiri serve as reminders of the spaces that have changed or been reorganized but are reawakened through Nair's narration. Nair returns to the trope of "time-bound writing" and the importance of spatial memory in recollecting moments from the past. Nair recounts that there were days when ideas would flow freely, while on others the process was slower and required time to allow latent ideas to manifest through images.[35] The places he stayed during these writing sessions played a crucial role in germinating his ideas. An idea of space as containing suppressed time emerges in these recollections. Realizing the importance of the spaces of hotel rooms to his "art of waiting" for ideas to emerge, Nair would frequent the same hotels to recreate the mood for literary outpourings, sometimes to find that hotel management had changed and the layout of the rooms had been altered.

Nair's account includes an interesting reference to the perception of Kodambakkam films in the national imagination. He narrates his experience of attending the NFDC's board meeting in Bombay in the 1980s, which discussed proposals for loans submitted by filmmakers. In the meeting, a bureaucrat lamented that the proposals were all "Kodambakkam style," gesturing to the fact that the offbeat art cinema style that the NFDC was responsible for promoting had been put on the back burner in favor of "low-budget films" from Madras.[36] The presence of stalwarts like the film director L. V. Prasad did not stop the bureaucrat's tirade against seemingly low-quality films from the south. The chair of the NFDC, B. A. Karanjia, decided to resolve this quandary by conducting the next board meeting in Madras and including a tour of a couple of studios to offer a firsthand experience of Kodambakkam film production. As a former editor of film magazines such as *Filmfare, Screen, Cine Voice,* and *Movie Times,* Karanjia wanted the facts to be supported by evidence and felt that nothing could fall short of field experience for the officials who were in charge of selections for funding programs to support filmmakers. Nair does not mention if visiting the studios changed the bureaucrat's perception of Kodambakkam films, but the chair's insistence on changing the venue of the board meeting from Bombay to Madras indicates the need to actively advocate for a nonjudgmental attitude toward regional film industries. The connotation of "Madrasi films" as sex films was not uncommon in the 1980s and 1990s, as is evident in news reports on raids in theaters and anti-obscenity marches organized by

South Indian groups based in cities such as Bombay and Delhi.[37] *Madrasi* became a widely (and derogatorily) used term to refer to those hailing from South India, regardless of where they originated in South India. Despite protest from South Indian communities in Bombay and New Delhi who contested the use of this regional marker as a stand-in for taste, class, and linguistic subnationalism, soft-porn films exhibited in B- and C-circuit theaters in Bombay are to this day referred to as Madrasi films.

In contrast to the glossy and glamorous image associated with mainstream cinema production in Madras, K. S. Gopalakrishnan's 1980 film *Goodbye to Kodambakkam* captures Kodambakkam as a space of dirty dealings and compromises. The film begins with the disclaimer that the characters and events portrayed are fictional, but it draws on many real-life stories that the director witnessed over the course of his career.[38] The narrative centers on the trials and tribulations of Nandini, a female scriptwriter from Kerala who moves to Kodambakkam in search of opportunities in film.[39] *Goodbye to Kodambakkam* provides a meta-commentary on the role of informal networking in procuring jobs in the film industry. This includes casting arrangements mediated by brokers or film journalists such as Selvaraj, who offers to introduce Nandini to the top directors. Throughout these meetings with key people, she is addressed as "the girl from Kerala," and the film intersperses Tamil, Malayalam, and English in the dialogue, perhaps as a way of gesturing toward the cosmopolitan nature of Kodambakkam as a space of film production. The film also portrays Nandini's relationship with a much older director and his betrayal when he uses her as a pawn in an industry power play. After multiple rejections and sexual exploitation, Nandini finally gets to pen her own experiences in Kodambakkam in the form of a film script. The film muses philosophically about the futility of sincere labor in a competitive industry in which sexual favors, monetary benefits, or future returns determine support and mentorship. The film concludes with Nandini being conferred the State Award for her script. In her acceptance speech, she talks openly about how her bitter experiences in Kodambakkam strengthened her and her script. She ultimately decides to leave Kodambakkam because it made her compromise her personal beliefs. Her farewell to Kodambakkam is accompanied by a montage of the town's identifying geographical markers. For Nandini, her time in Kodambakkam provides the experience she needs to attain the strength to navigate an industry that promotes a patriarchal value system and would never accommodate a female scriptwriter. *Goodbye to Kodambakkam* is not alone in portraying the figure of a Kerala girl who is led astray in the city of Madras. As the tagline for *Avalude Ravukal* (Her nights) goes: "The story of a girl from a village in Kerala who is waylaid and gets morally corrupted in Madras city."[40]

Like all places, Madras and Kodambakkam simultaneously meant different things to different people. Collectively, accounts such as *Beyond Frames,*

Chitratheruvukal, and *Goodbye to Kodambakkam* do not give us a monolithic or "true" view of the space of Kodambakkam; rather, they produce a *sense* of space—a polyvocal understanding that emerges from subjective experience. Such variegated spatialities give birth to an uncanny space that is outside of all spaces, similar to what Foucault calls "heterotopias"—places that are counter-sites, where real sites are simultaneously represented, contested, and inverted.[41] These accounts invoke a sense of time that is individualized and subjective, and that requires understanding space by working through experiential memories that transcend the boundedness of absolute, abstract space. Spatial practices attain their efficacy only if they are placed within the social relations that condition their existence. P. David's reference to "wait time" and Nair's to "time-bound" writing can only be imagined within film production culture and the power relations that structure the interaction between different social actors.

In the context of film production, wait-time assumes the same resonance as the phrases "in the meantime" or "meanwhile," which denote a kind of waiting that is allied to other happenings. The emphasis is on temporary arrangements that can help individuals upgrade their skills or procure a better job. In my case, it meant waiting *long enough* to gather resources, strengthen my job profile, and look for fresh pastures that could help me with research. The position of helper that I was offered had a very nebulous job description. Its requirement that I work across many departments may have made for tenuous working arrangements had my entire livelihood depended on it, but it was a boon for research as it allowed me to make contacts across a wide field. Shadowing the production manager, then, became an integral part of my method, and shaped the conversations I had during my research.

WAIT-TIME ECONOMY AND THE PRODUCTION MANAGER

In the summer of 2013, equipped with limited Tamil, I started living in Trustpuram, a locality adjacent to the Kodambakkam Bridge. While trying to find personnel who worked in soft-porn cinema, I was faced with a conundrum: everyone knew glamour films were produced in Kodambakkam, but no one knew exactly where. I also had to negotiate the significant, related problem of accessing material and people. In laying preliminary groundwork for my project, I had collated a list of possible contacts who might help me explore Kodambakkam's past—specifically, the era when it flourished as the production site of glamour films, which preceded soft-porn films. Little did I know that I was entering a vortex of fake names and identities. Despite my relentless efforts, my attempt to track down key street names in Kodambakkam came to naught—they simply did not exist on maps of Chennai. The story was the same with people's names. I received blank looks from acquaintances in response to my queries about "Joseph Breeze," a one-time producer who made a handful of sex education films, or about a particular editor who was so adept at splicing the sexually explicit cut-pieces that he was known among his peers as "cut-piece Nanu."

To decode such fictional identities, I took up temporary jobs that could sustain me and my research in Chennai. My initial industry experience involved figuring out if I had any prospects as a dubbing artist. But in a month's time I had to give up, after the Dubbing Artistes Union warned me about the membership requirements needed to pursue opportunities. Breaking into its small circle was not easy, and membership conditions were certainly not encouraging for a newcomer. Per the union rules, a one-time deposit of one lakh rupees (approx. $2,000) was necessary before determining whether I had a future in dubbing. Since that was a luxury I could not afford at the time, I bid adieu to my dubbing career after a series of auditions.

The unionization of twenty-three trade guilds under the Film Employees Federation of South India (FEFSI) meant that membership norms were quite stringent. The minimum guarantee of the wage rate and *bata* (daily wage) was favorable to employees, who would be eligible for payment even if the production stopped midway or for any other contingency that would affect their individual roles in the production. But union membership was also expensive; to join, newcomers had to work in at least three projects and furnish letters from the directors authorizing their status as employees. Such requirements meant that newcomers took whatever jobs they could find, regardless of whether or not they were paid. Most agreed to be part of this unpaid workforce with the consolation that once they gained membership, they could ask for the wage rate stipulated by the union. Membership fees were perceived as a fixed deposit with "returns," or as insurance in times of emergency. Even during bouts of severe job insecurity, unionization gave workers the power to bargain with producers. This was such a strong lure that nobody wanted to challenge the exorbitant membership fee. The time lag between starting off with unpaid jobs and becoming able to pay for union membership was seen as a compulsory initiation ritual, with a few exceptions. "If you are well-connected or from a family with connections to films, you can bypass the wait-time. If that's not an option, one would certainly require a strong network of powerful friends who can smooth your risks," said Raveendran, a production manager, in response to my questions about whether waiting was integral to the tinsel-town economy.[42]

Since insider knowledge and immersive fieldwork were crucial to understanding the production practices of glamour films, I decided to try my luck in the production unit. In the framework of the FEFSI, women are not considered for the job of production assistant, even though for a newcomer like me it would have allowed for an entry without barriers. The regulations were strict and it was a male-only workforce, so without proper accreditation I could only accompany a production manager as an observer who sometimes helped out with odd jobs. The field experiences of anthropologists such as Tejaswini Ganti and Anand Pandian in film production in Bombay and Chennai were certainly an inspiration;[43] however, lack of previous experience in film production coupled with a rush of aspirants who had been working in the industry scouting for opportunities meant that gaining access to a production unit was not easy for me. For a new hire (a woman, no less!) with no bankable production experience, I was told quite sternly by most of the production managers I approached that it would be nearly impossible for me to get an opening.

In order to negotiate the boredom and anxiety that accompanied waiting for a job, I frequented shooting locations and postproduction facilities like Prasad Lab at Saligramam to get acquainted with prospective contacts who might give me a chance. Prasad Lab soon became a common place where I met with interviewees. As I became a regular face there, no one paid much heed to the purposes of my visits. From the security guard outside who waved when I entered, with his unchanging tone of *vanakkam* ("Good morning"), to the people at the canteen with whom I chatted while I gulped mouthfuls of *sadam* (rice mixed with curry), I was welcomed into the circle of film hopefuls who lingered around the premises. A mixed crowd frequented the lab: some had completed diploma courses from one of the many acting schools that mushroomed in the vicinity of Chennai, while others were assistant directors making strategic moves by socializing in the right circles. My circle of acquaintances increased day by day, but it was still insufficient for digging up the history of glamour films. My acquaintances at the lab provided me with often contradictory descriptions of the "contacts" for whom I should be on the lookout. For example, Partipan, a production executive, described the main production agent for glamour films as "a sturdy man who wears gold rings on all his fingers (with a green stone on his thumb finger!), dressed in white shirt and white pants," while Raghavan *chettan* (colloquial term for brother), the owner of the tea shop, described the same person as a man in his late forties "carrying a diary under his arms, wearing *mundu* [single-cloth lower garment worn by men in Southern India], chewing betel leaves."[44] These clues were distressing because so many people could fit these generic descriptions. On one of these days, I was introduced to "Auto" Jayarajan, a film journalist turned "mediator" whose main duty was to obtain distributors on behalf of producers. His frequent weeks-long trips to Chennai on a rented autorickshaw had earned him the name "Auto" Jayarajan, and his presence at a location was announced by the vehicle parked outside. This meeting gave me insight into the world of glamour cinema and led to an introduction to Narasimhan (name changed), a production manager who had been working in low-budgets films for more than forty-five years.

The next day, I got a call at about seven in the morning from Narasimhan, who told me that he had thought over my request for a job and had convinced the producer to allow me to accompany him as an observer and a helper, on the condition that I take my work seriously. Narasimhan and the production unit thus

FIGURE 13. Interior of the workshop of a catering unit that serves film crews in Kodambakkam. Photo by author.

became part of my daily routine for the next four months. I accompanied Narasimhan in his routine business of arranging shooting houses and procuring letters from various places to start production. Accompanying him to the dingy hotel rooms of fly-by-night producers, wig makers' and caterers' workshops (Fig. 13), and even the stable of an animal supplier, I became his "apprentice," as he preferred to introduce me. If there were more questions, he would add *Keralapennu* (the girl from Kerala) to halt them. Narasimhan stressed my secretarial, accounting, and administrative skills as my strengths in his introduction to the producer. All the while, he did not hesitate to point out the major obstacle—my safety—or to express that others suspected that my entry into the unit would upset the normal order of things. I could see his enthusiasm in telling the unit that I was engaged, marking my "unavailability" with the retort "getting married next year."

My attempt to balance being an observer and a researcher (my real job) was not easy, as the on-the-clock hours were as strict as any other job, and perhaps even more demanding because they threw additional challenges at me to see if I was capable of handling a "man's job." In the first few days, my inquisitive nature and constant habit of jotting down details in a notebook became a bit of a joke in the unit, but it also encouraged many of the crew members to open up about their experiences of Kodambakkam. Warnings from "Narasimhan Sir" would immediately arrive in the form of text messages instructing me to behave modestly "like a girl" (which included wearing a *dupatta*, a long scarf used to cover the neck and chest) and not invite unwanted attention by attempting to "act smart."

As time passed, I noticed myself taking extra care in handling receipts for stationery, food, or daily wages; renting utensils in a narrow alley adjacent to the Vadapalani bus; or negotiating with lodges to confirm the dates for bulk booking, almost as if it were my real job. This immersion was not without its perks, though, for it allowed me to effortlessly code-switch in my roles as researcher and helper. By the time I spoke to Narasimhan about my research interests, he had become a confidant. In spite of his initial reservations about my project's emphasis on "porn," he agreed to help me to meet the director Gopalakrishnan, who was seen as the improviser of "budget films." Having worked with "KS" (as Gopalakrishnan was known in film circles), Narasimhan knew people who were part of his productions. With Narasimhan, I would revisit the production histories of some of the films in which he had doubled as production manager and production controller and visit the various shooting locations with him.

Yet even when Narasimhan shared stories with me, he was cautious not to entertain their "sex" aspects. This was a pattern among many of my respondents, who struggled to reconcile conflicting values when I asked them about the production-related aspects of glamour films. Some refused to acknowledge their association with these films outright, but they were willing to share information that they had learned from other sources. Some dictated that there were to be no follow-up questions, while others wanted the interview itself to be kept secret. Some respondents believed that stories about glamour cinema production were hyped, so the anecdotal accounts took on the value of the real only through their repeated circulation and in some cases, a kind of selective amnesia was at play. This became clear when I asked more than three people who were part of a production the whereabouts of the actress who had played the lead role. Although I had seen photographs of these people with her and knew from other sources that my respondents were known to the actress, all of them pretended they did not know her at all. After repeated meetings, some of my respondents did open up with a few details, but only after receiving assurance from the actress that she was comfortable with information about her being shared. This pattern of revealing information that came by after spending substantial time with the respondents helped me get insights into the production of glamour films in the 1980s and 1990s.

UNCOVERING "GLAMOUR" CINEMA: ALTERNATIVE PRODUCTION CIRCUITS

Wait-time became natural to the aspirational economies of Kodambakkam's cinema-ecology, and my own experience of trying to uncover this history were framed within practices of waiting (for respondents, for events, for clues). Yet there is another way in which wait-time becomes important to our understanding of Kodambakkam. Wait-time was not unique to aspiring actors and those in the lower rungs of the production hierarchy; negotiating wait-time or rather reducing wait-time was also a core concern of the directors I interviewed, although the forms of negotiation were different. Many directors and technicians who ended up working in glamour films and soft-porn worked as assistant directors for a relatively long period of time, with seemingly no prospects of making a film of their own through the regular circuits. Wait-time was an important element, and its negation came to structure the parallel studio systems that these glamour filmmakers began to build.

My foray into film production in Kodambakkam was mediated by my interactions with two directors, K. S. Gopalakrishnan and P. Chandrakumar. Both gained currency in the 1980s on account of the "glamour" sequences that were a staple of their film repertoires. Interactions with them allowed me to uncover some pseudonyms and fictitious identities, which were a common practice in Kodambakkam's low-budget productions. In some cases, cast and crew were credited by name even when they were not a part of the production, while in others, their names were deliberately left out of the credits of films in which they had visibly worked. For instance, the 1989 film *Ayiram Chirakulla Moham* (Hundred-winged desire; dir. Vinayan), which explores the extramarital sexual adventures of a professor-couple in a jungle, later came to be known under the credits of a director by the name of Ashokan, and even IMDb identifies him as such. However, it is unclear whether this is by the same director, as there was another director named Ashokan whose association with glamour films like *Ardharathri* (Midnight, 1986) was quite widely known in the late 1980s.[45]

Unless one has access to insiders who have leads about the production, the journey to find directors remains an arduous task since fictitious names were widely used in soft-porn production. *Ayiram Chirakulla Moham* came back into circulation with the boom of soft-porn in the early 2000s. By then Vinayan had entered the league of mainstream directors, and his directorial debut had been forgotten for some time. But the story of *Ayiram Chirakulla Moham* came back to haunt him in the aftermath of his election as the general secretary of the Malayalam Cine Technicians Association (MACTA), a body comprising nineteen organizations that represents the collective interests of everyone associated with filmmaking, from directors to drivers to script writers, with the exception of producers and actors. In a closely fought election in 2008, Vinayan, who supported laborers' demands for wage increases, was alleged to have used the support of "low-profile" technicians to rig votes.[46] In the context of this development, Vinayan's credentials as the producer of "good" films came into question. His debut film, which had largely been forgotten in popular memory, was recalled thanks to entries under Vinayan's name in websites like *Malayalanchalachithram*—a Malayalam movie and music database.[47] His rivals strategically used his association with low-budget films to mark his inferior status as the maker of glamour films and to "declass" Vinayan as someone who shared affinities with technicians of lower grade.

It was often alleged that directors and producers of glamour and low-budget movies resorted to shady dealings, like using "open shots" (sexually explicit, reusable shots) to sell their films. Open shots are performed by credited actors and actresses, not dupes. The term also refers to sex scenes shot with a limited crew. These films were colloquially called *orazchapadangal* (one-week films) because they had a very short shelf life of seven days, during which they reaped maximum profits—sometimes twice and thrice the initial investment. These films included *kananacinemakal* (jungle films), set in the wild with the hero and heroine clad in fig leaves, and "revenge films" exploring female sexuality and action sequences, featuring the female lead as a *madakarani*.[48] Many of these films were about women's quest for companionship—some were cautionary tales, while others used revelatory or confessional modes drawn from *kambipustakam* (erotic fiction) to explore youthful sexuality. However, even though these films mobilized sex as one of their central structuring principles, it would be shortsighted to see them as merely sexually explicit pornography with full frontal nudity and acts of penetration. The sexual roles of the *madakarani* were indeed the unique selling point of these films, but that does not necessarily qualify them as aesthetically and technically "poor." To some degree, this generalization was retroactive—a result of the notoriety generated by the production and reception of certain films in the late 1990s, which employed low-budget techniques and were marketed as "soft-porn." In hindsight, it is possible to trace the genealogy of the soft-porn films of the late 1990s and early 2000s to these glamour films. But to call glamour films "soft-porn" would be anachronistic, as the term only came to be used in the late 1990s.

The term "glamour film" has its own historical specificity in the 1980s, when filmmakers themselves used it to refer to their work. When I asked a few of these films' distributors why the label became widely popular, one said, "It was thought to be milder in tone and less 'revealing.'"[49] Made with limited budgets of ten to fifteen lakh rupees (approx. $14,000–$20,000), these films were reminiscent of American exploitation cinema of the 1960s. It was a common sentiment that their low budgets and promise of financial gain with minimal investment were the only motive for producing these films. But if these films used *exploitation* (in the sense of widening the marketing possibilities) as a mode in any way, it was by emphasizing the same sensational overtures featured in the *painkili* stories that were serialized in the magazines of the time. Verging on sentimental excess and exploring mundane lives, *painkili* novels either featured lovelorn couples struggling to consummate their desires or were crime thrillers based on the theme of revenge. They are frequently set in high mountain ranges and feature rubber-tapping laborers and their frustrated attempts to escape the confines of the rural landscape. But literary culture at the time derided these weeklies as smacking of "low brow taste" and their readers as indulging in affective excess.[50] In contrast to *kambikathakal*, the popular perception of *painkili* as consumed mostly by women led to the feminization of the genre. When asked about the audience for *painkili* literature, one of my respondents, a journalist, recounted: "There were times when the *Manorama* weekly editor Padmanabhan Nair was asked to take the submitted manuscripts of the novels to the chief editor's house. It was the taste of the women servants who were working there that decided what was popular and hence publishable."[51] The magazines that featured *painkili* literature were called "Ma" magazines, a label popularized by E. V. Sreedharan, a film reporter for the *Kala Kaumudi* weekly, who pointed out that they appeared in publications like *Manorama, Malayala Nadu, Malayala Rajyam, Madiram*, and *Mangalam*, whose titles all coincidentally began with the syllable "Ma."[52] Stories in these magazines were accompanied by illustrations that used transparent watercolors to render naturalistic color and depth. The full-bodied, buxom female figures in the illustrations were a favorite collectible item. In the Facebook page of the illustrator Mohan Manimala, many fans nostalgically shared their experience of growing up reading the fantasy scenarios portrayed through Manimala's illustrations.[53] An article in *India Today* on the production of *painkili* literature alleged that "episodes woven into the stories . . . were similar to the sex-tinged moments incorporated in K. S. Gopalakrishnan's films."[54] Thus, the similarities between *painkili* literature and glamour films came to be discussed in the context of the moral anxieties around the incursion of transgressive desires into familial spaces.

My conversations with Narasimhan about low-budget film production often ended with him reminiscing about his shooting schedules with Gopalakrishnan, the director with whom he worked for the longest period. A soft-spoken man in his sixties, Gopalakrishnan was surprisingly responsive to my questions and agreed to a series of meetings over the next two months. Our discussions sometimes focused on the whereabouts of people who had worked with him or on the backstories on the making of certain films. Even today, Gopalakrishnan remains the primary reference point for ailing cine-workers in Madras who were part of the industry in the 1980s; he writes letters of introduction to recommend beneficiaries for the pension and medical assistance scheme supported by the Kerala State Chalachitra Academy, the government body in charge of film and cultural management in Kerala.

Gopalakrishnan gave many hopefuls their breaks, and some, such as Bollywood stars Sridevi and Kamal Hassan, became famous in later years. His crew hired many newcomers who came to Madras looking for jobs, and they often ended up working consistently with him. For instance, Chunakara Ramankutty or Bharanikavu Sreekumar often wrote the lyrics for his films, K. J. Joy composed the music, and Thyagarajan Master or Bheeman Raghu—who also acted in Gopalakrishnan's films—choreographed the fight sequences. Gopalakrishnan's heyday was between 1989 and 1991, when he produced more than four films a year. In the late 1980s and 1990s, studios began to lose their charm and outdoor locations were increasingly preferred; the guarantee of permanent work made many turn to Gopalakrishnan for work. This arrangement created a sort of an "alternative studio" system and, in the uncertainties of the time, his budget films were financially profitable. But in the late 1990s, Gopalakrishnan had to contend with a changing film industry, as soft-porn started to eclipse glamour films. Although he attempted a comeback, he had to compete with new contenders in the field. This included his erstwhile still photographer A. T. Joy, who became a sought-after soft-porn director after making several films with Shakeela, the most iconic soft-porn star. Trying to distinguish glamour films from "Shakeela films," Narasimhan told me, "Low-budget films were never 'sex' films. The crew and the production team who associated with the project were quite serious about the work they were engaged in."[55] This response emerged from a distinction he wanted to maintain between low-budget films and soft-porn, as he felt that Gopalakrishnan was often incorrectly remembered as a soft-porn filmmaker.

P. Chandrakumar was a prominent director of glamour films and a contemporary of Gopalakrishnan. In addition to directing, Chandrakumar managed Kiku Films, a distribution agency for English films founded in 1984. It bought films from agents based in Bombay and Bangalore and sold them to smaller agents in the towns of Kerala. On one of his trips to Bangalore, Chandrakumar conceived the idea for a film based on the biblical story of Adam and Eve. The story was made into the film *Aadyapaapam* (The first sin) in 1988 (Fig. 14).[56] Produced with an investment of approximately twelve lakh rupees (approx. $14,452) under the banner of R. B. Choudary's Super Good Films, *Aadyapaapam* was the first Malayalam movie to feature frontal nudity.[57] Chandrakumar told me that his interest in experimenting with a shoe-string budget motivated him to make *Aadyapaapam*. Chandrakumar's brother, P. Sukumar (who would later appear through his films with the screen name Kiran), was in charge of the camera, while another brother, Vijayakumar, took up the role of production assistant.[58] The film was shot with minimal camera equipment and no track, trolley, or crane shots. Despite its low budget, it became a trendsetter, becoming one of the few films to commercially succeed without a recognizable star cast. Abhilasha, a Telugu starlet who had come to Kodambakkam in search of opportunity, got her break in *Aadyapaapam*. Reminiscing about the film's production, Chandrakumar recounted that he hired Abhilasha when, after a chance encounter

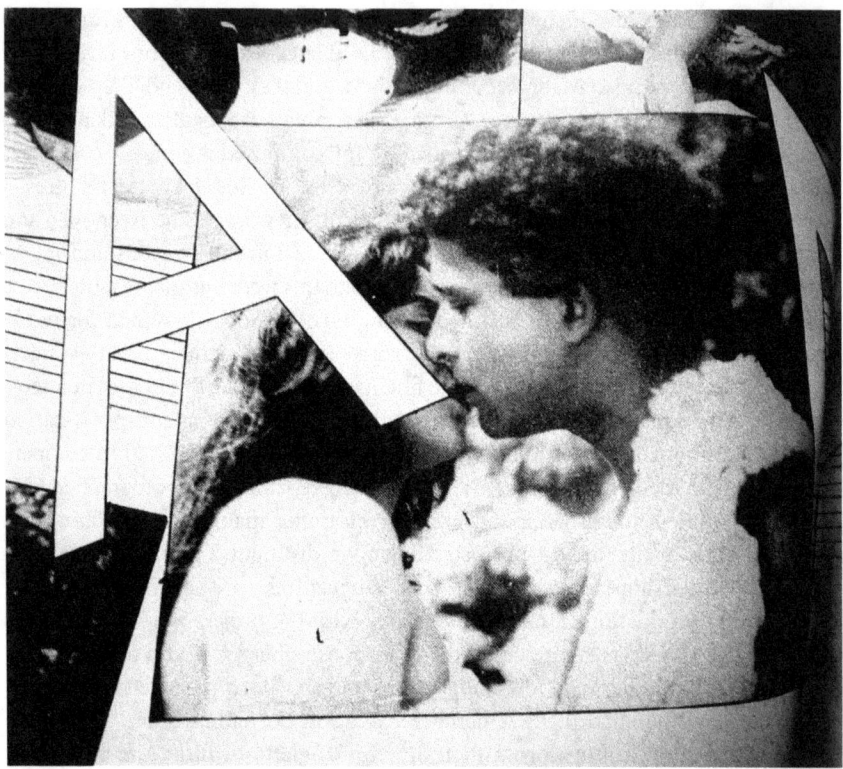

FIGURE 14. Publicity image for *Aadyapaapam*, in 1988, prominently featuring the "A" for adult sign. Author's personal collection.

in Madras, she expressed an interest in acting in the film despite knowing the theme and the risks.⁵⁹

The production of *Aadyapaapam* mobilized an untapped pool of hopefuls, collectively referred to as "talent-in-waiting," who hopped from one studio to the other in search of acting opportunities. Advertisements for auditions regularly appeared in film magazines and vernacular newspapers, with details about the studio and specifications for the roles. Chandrakumar's "package films" (a colloquial term for low-budget films) attracted this crowd. *Aadyapaapam* was released simultaneously in four languages (Kannada, Tamil, Malayalam, and Hindi) and was a huge box-office hit. It had only three scenes with dialogue. Shot in the forests of Karnataka, it also availed itself of a subsidy of one and a half lakh rupees (approx. $1,200) offered by the Karnataka State Government to encourage film production in the state. Yet Karnataka was selected as the shooting location for another reason: a member of the censor board who had agreed to help the filmmakers with certification had been transferred there. When the film was released, many alleged it was pornographic, with the biblical story being the pretext by which the filmmakers sidestepped censorship regulations. The censor certification committee included priests who were invited to give their opinion of the film's incorporation of the biblical story. Surprisingly, they deemed the film to be "educational" and found nothing offensive in its depiction of nudity. However, for distribution purposes, the educational label stood in the way of marketing the film. The film consequently had to be sent for re-censoring, and it was finally given an "A" (Adult) certificate.

Gopalakrishnan and Chandrakumar did not invent an alternative film-industrial structure, but they were prominent examples of early experiments in low-budget filmmaking in Malayalam cinema. These experiments were a kind of "wayfinding," or what Jason Pine calls "making do"—a way of coping with the precarity of business and livelihood through multiple acts of innovating, preparing, speculating, and applying instrumental reason.[60] The budgetary improvisations and limited shooting schedules of glamour filmmakers allowed for a system of tactical moves to reduce or bypass wait-time. The arrangement was premised on collective benefits that were not dependent on workers' roles in the film's production or on the magnitude of box-office returns.

The guarantee that the director/producer would support the cast, crew, and technicians, even if the film failed at the box office, allowed for a different kind of patronage, which I refer to as "pastoral filmmaking"—directors such as Gopalakrishnan and Chandrakumar were almost like shepherds who guided and protected their stable of film hopefuls and regular collaborators. In the context of low-budget Malayalam glamour cinema of the 1970s and 1980s, pastoral film-production units such as theirs were based on the principles of reducing risk, ensuring a minimum return, and offering consistent employment to a set of labor-agents. Unlike the unconditional obedience and surrendering of personal will that underlined mainstream studio practices, pastoral forms of low-budget filmmaking based their risk-mitigating practices on a trust-based economy. While the mainstream film industry's practices were deeply hierarchical and internally divided to mark different tiers, including separate dining and accommodation privileges to the main cast, low-budget filmmakers forged a quasi-familial bond. These arrangements were not completely free from hierarchies, but they entailed an ethical code of relationality that connected all labor-agents in the unit as equally integral constituents.

CONCLUSION

Waiting in and for Kodambakkam entails recognizing the relationality built into the subjectivity of labor-agents whose individuality is subsumed within the waiting crowd. In the face of this erasure, this crowd was united in its shared expectation of getting a break—that luck would favor them at some point in the future. This optimism reflects a unique relationship to time *and* space. In a slightly different context from northern India, the anthropologist Craig Jeffrey refers to two different kinds of waiting: "timepass" and the "waiting game." Whereas unemployed youth use the term "timepass" to rationalize their whiling away of time as the process of acquiring skill sets, wealthy farmers used the term "waiting game" to describe their readiness to invest in their children's future mobility with the expectation that they will support them in their old age.[61] In Kodambakkam's film economy, wait-time lies somewhere between these two. My respondents thought of their wait period as a process of acquiring skills, but they also equated it with the waiting game.

Throughout this chapter, I have argued that Kodambakkam's spatiotemporal arrangement exerted a strong imprint on its labor practices. The quasi-formal and informal nature of these arrangements and the assemblages of making do that glamour filmmakers were forced to build filtered down to the production of soft-porn films in the 1990s and 2000s. Yet whereas the glamour cinema of the 1970s and 1980s is still traceable to some extent, the circuits of soft-porn were assumed to be far more invisible to me as a researcher—for instance, anonymous practices were more rampant in soft-porn production, as were modes of bypassing censorship. More importantly, like glamour films, soft-porn cinema was marked—perhaps even more so—by conditions of precarity. The next chapter follows this thread by exploring precarious labor practices in the era of soft-porn cinema, thus recasting the popular memory of soft-porn cinema, its actors, and its exhibition and consumption practices by attending to their agency. Soft-porn personnel—especially actresses—are remembered through pin-up posters and "known" through channels of gossip, and a feminist history of soft-porn that is attuned to precarious labor reinstates them as equal producers of discourse.

3

Embodied Vulnerabilities

Precarity and Body Work

Questions of vulnerability and precarity in the film industry are not merely institutional and economic but are enmeshed within matrices of caste, gender, and class. The management of wait-time is one way in which cine-workers who are entangled in film's infrastructural pathways navigate the rhythms of precarious employment cultures. In this chapter, I extend the theorization of wait-time by examining its effect as a particular kind of precarity that I call "embodied vulnerability," which emerges out of uneven power relations in which some subjects are more precarious than others.[1] Embodied vulnerability inscribes the vagaries of cinema's infrastructural modalities into the bodies and social presence of cine-workers. The survival logic that sustains embodied vulnerability is imbued with what Kathleen Kuehn and Thomas Corrigan call "hope labor": "un- or undercompensated work carried out in the present, often for experience or exposure in the hope that future employment may follow."[2] Hope labor is a temporal relationship between present and future work that shifts the costs and risks onto the individual.[3] Although embodied vulnerability shares hope labor's future-oriented optimism,[4] it is distinct in its attention to the subject's awareness of the risk and uncertainties that accompany nonstandard and contingent work portfolios in the film industry. Soft-porn cine-workers are doubly disadvantaged by their association with soft-porn films, as the form itself comes with risks related to respectability, reputation, and future work. Workers are aware that they must take calculated risks to succeed in the informal economy.[5] Informality can open up job opportunities but also reinforces expectations of loyalty and noncombative collegiality as the norm. These stringent yet informal or quasi-formal protocols discipline cine-workers into docile, conforming subjects.[6]

Embodied vulnerability is thus both a shared problem and a condition with potential to forge solidarities between cine-workers as they negotiate "relations of production and quality of social life" in the informal economy.[7] Although the role of capitalist structures in this is crucial, precarity is not exclusively economic or wage-related; it also impacts affect, emotions, and social mobility. Embodied vulnerability thus resonates with Lauren Berlant's notion of cruel optimism: "a relation of attachment to compromised conditions of possibility whose realization is discovered either to be impossible, sheer fantasy, or too possible, and toxic."[8]

I focus on these affective, emotional, and mobility-related conditions to understand the survival strategies employed by soft-porn's labor force, which includes, but is not limited to, distributors, producers, actresses, and body doubles. Using a hybrid methodology that incorporates media industry studies, textual analysis, and an ethnographic study conducted intermittently between 2012 and 2022, I weave together a cultural history of soft-porn drawn from interviews with technicians, artists, production units, distributors, and exhibitors. In so doing, I explicate how filmmakers use the cultural marginality of soft-porn films as a creative avenue to contest rigid structures of censorship. I also examine how actresses wield stardom in soft-porn as a temporary opportunity. Identifiable as emblems of soft-porn films, these actresses are also rendered ignominious by their hypervisibility. Through the case study of Shakeela, one of the most famous soft-porn actresses in the 2000s, I interrogate general and more specific aspects of precarious film labor, especially as it relates to its female workforce. Finally, I examine "body work"—working as a body double—an example of uncredited, precarious labor and contextualize it within debates about body doubles in the soft-porn industry. In sum, I argue that precarity impacts not just the financial stability of these subjects but also their very subjectivity as cine-workers.

The Film Employees Federation of Kerala (FEFKA), a consolidated body that represents more than seventeen trade guilds, has taken up the mantle of arbitrating on behalf of cine-workers. FEFKA was formed after the dissolution of MACTA in 2008. Despite Kerala's long history of left-wing political culture and trade union mobilization, film labor has not been a core vector for unionizing and a lack of sustained policy-level interventions constricts long-term goals that can support it. Even though FEFKA speaks the language of trade unionism, it and other unions implicitly and explicitly address an abstract cine-worker who implicitly remains a male worker unmarked by class, religion, gender, and caste inequalities. Further, while FEFKA's actions and policies are ostensibly aimed at improving the quality of its members' lives, cine-workers' agency is simultaneously co-opted by the neoliberal system, which puts the onus squarely on the worker's ability to make themselves employable.[9] At the level of policy interventions, trade guild formations have limited scope in pursuing proactive measures for supporting inclusivity, gender justice, and worker safety. Because union membership is a precondition for employment (as well as contingency money, pension benefits, and compensation for work-related death and injury), it also pressures workers to subscribe to their union's stance at all times.

The efforts of soft-porn filmmakers to collectively mobilize resources and make low-budget films during a lull in industrial production becomes important in this context. Most filmmakers who made soft-porn films in the 1990s came from different film-related trades, including still photography, costume, cinematography, production, sound, and editing. With experience in mainstream cinema, many were aware of the barriers that prevented below-the-line workers from becoming directors and producers. Whereas popular discourses associate low production values and sexual exploitation with soft-porn films, these filmmakers approached it as a legitimate form—many of my interviewees noted that these films featured songs penned by prominent lyricists and sung by mainstream artists, thereby framing them as being made with the same commercial impetus as the mainstream industry. In response to questions about labor and the vagaries of luck, they foregrounded the inside workings of an industry where only a very few would end up being successful. While the fictitious names used in soft-porn films underplayed the labor that went into the making, distribution, and exhibition of these films, for many of my respondents the bracketing of these films as *thattikoottu padangal* (trashy films) was tantamount to erasing their association with them. Their willingness to talk openly about these films also stemmed from the need to recuperate their labor in accounts about Indian cinema.[10] With films being produced about B-grade and soft-porn cinema (most recent case in point, Netflix's docuseries *Cinema Marte Dum Tak* [dir. Vasan Bala, 2023]), things have begun to change. Over the past few years, many of my respondents expressed interest in speaking about their films as media material that experimented with sex narratives and transgressive sexual relationships.

THE FORMAL AND INSTITUTIONAL CIRCUITS OF SOFT-PORN

In the 1990s, soft-porn emerged as an industrial form that paralleled mainstream Malayalam cinema after strikes organized by exhibitors and distributors over profit shares brought the film industry to a standstill. The box-office failure of many big mainstream productions starring A-list actors forced exhibitors to forge alternative business arrangements with distributors and producers to stay afloat. Colloquially referred to as *neela chitrangal* (blue films), they bore material traces of their mode of production in things like lack of continuity editing, reliance on stock footage, tight shooting schedules, and repeated use of ensemble casts and crews. Such referential resonances can be seen in some soft-porn film titles as well: *Neela Thadakatile Nizhal Pakshikal* (The shadow birds in the blue lagoon; dir. Venu B Pillai, 2000), for example. Amid the financial slowdown, soft-porn films offered work to lower-rung artists, technicians, below-the-line workers, distributors, and exhibitors who, facing impending unemployment and debt, worked out distribution deals and profit-sharing arrangements. Most of these films starred newcomers and were often produced with budgets not exceeding twenty-five lakh rupees (approx. $35,000).[11] The year 2001 marked the high point of soft-porn production: of the eighty-nine releases in the Malayalam film industry that year, fifty-seven were soft-porn films.[12] The popular press and the mainstream film industry expressed anxieties that the immense popularity of these low-budget films would spread low-brow taste. An article in *India Today* declared:

> Kerala is steaming, and the reasons have nothing to do with the onset of summer. Bare breasts, hairy chests and various other parts of the human anatomy are erupting like a rash across the state's cinema screens and the audience is literally lapping it all up in lascivious delight, unmindful of censors and other sundry guardians of public morality.[13]

Because of such reactions, crew members and distributors who wanted to maintain their status as part of the more "respectable" mainstream film industry had to carefully distance themselves from it. Because these films were produced in Kodambakkam, close to yet at a relative distance from Kerala, clandestine production practices became possible, and anonymity was almost a norm. Although most film crew assumed fictitious names on their credit lines, the actresses remained identifiable by their faces and names and prominent place in publicity posters.[14] The actresses' hypervisibility in these so-called heroine-oriented narratives also compensated for the limited inclusion of male actors. The prominence of these actresses also led to the popular perception that these films pandered to the commercial market through salacious story templates and skin show.

Although using pseudonyms was not itself an expression of worker dissent, it meant moving away from the mainstream film industry and its alienation of lower rungs of production units. Soft-porn filmmakers were invested in promoting change that would open filmmaking opportunities to those outside what I call "proximate networks" of film production. Proximate networks are powerful, guarded, and close-knit networks that facilitate opportunities through contacts and connections with those in decision-making capacities. Bollywood producers have long been accused of nepotism and allowing only entrants with social capital and familial lineage in the film industry to survive. Such proximate networks are often gendered, caste-ridden, and classed spaces premised on unearned privileges and selective gatekeeping. Membership in proximate networks is highly prized: both cinematic wait-time and precarious labor rely on subjects' aspirations to gain membership in such exclusive groups, and the risk of failure is higher outside of such proximate connections. Those who entered soft-porn production were largely deemed failures, because without the support of proximate networks, they were not able to translate their talents into jobs in the mainstream film industry. Soft-porn filmmakers consequently formed alternative survival networks to counter the negativity that surrounded them. By privileging female sexual desire as the fulcrum of their narratives, these films provided a critical look at the power hierarchies and exclusionary practices that structure the film industry as a whole. One recurrent trope that appeared in these films is the open expression of female sexual pleasure: they showed women enjoying sex, as opposed to providing pleasure for their male partners. But despite the recollection of filmmakers, some actresses have stated they were sometimes unhappy with the end result. For instance, Shakeela said in response to her films, "I'd go to the theater and suddenly see myself emerging from nowhere and going into the bedroom with a guy. . . . I could've pursued such matters further, but I needed the money."[15] Thus, even while these filmmakers worked outside mainstream proximate networks, their own use of sexualized images raised questions about compromised ethics.

In addition to the improvisational, flexible, and entrepreneurial qualities associated with soft-porn's economy, the soft-porn wave also brought to the fore questions of risk, insecurity, and unstable work arrangements that are taken for granted as part of the toil of filmmaking. Soft-porn's anonymous circuits permitted slippage between the underground and the mainstream, allowing technicians to move between the two industries. Even though soft-porn filmmakers and crew had links with the larger formal institutions of filmmaking, transactions between personnel within the industry were often based on trust and bypassed the formal routes of trade and censorship institutions. Alongside borrowed capital from private financial institutions with high interest rates, money was pooled from Gulf-based Malayali migrants who took up the role of producers, either individually or collectively.[16] These trust-based systems relied on deferred payment, which ultimately casualized labor. Employees were assured that they would be paid a lump sum after the film recouped costs and was profitable at the box office. Notwithstanding the precarious modes of production through which these films were put together, they proffered a certain degree of bargaining power to the technicians and actors.

Film production was based on credit rather than instant payment for work. Even when producers did not have cash on hand for immediate payment, actors and technicians were promised remuneration as soon as the film was sold by the distributor. In the meantime, they would work in other films by the same director or production manager. When I asked soft-porn filmmaker Thrikkunnappuzha Vijayakumar what motivated personnel to work without contracts or immediate payments, he said:

> For this informal monetary arrangement to work, we need complete transparency of the financial situation. We can't give them false promises on when exactly we would repay them. It is seen more as a repayment than a payment because if it were a mainstream production, they wouldn't work with mere assurances. Here, they know us personally and we know that they can trust us, and our reputation matters in these monetary arrangements.[17]

Even distributors and exhibitors used soft-porn films to reshape profit-sharing arrangements and informal labor practices. In my conversations with many exhibitors and distributors of soft-porn films, many recalled the sway that soft-porn films had on viewers and their ability to negotiate a crisis that had left the film industry with dwindling audiences. For instance, the film distributor Sreekumar told me, "Many thought these films were nothing but an excuse for showing sex. But it saved us when mainstream Malayalam films of the time flopped in the box office, leaving us in debt. It was the soft-porn boom that helped us to recover the loss."[18]

As a mainstream distributor, Sreekumar's business was steady until multiple films flopped at the box office during the financial crisis of the 1990s. He then decided to try his luck distributing soft-porn films, and he worked out a suitable profit-sharing model with exhibitors that did not involve much risk. For instance, he used a clause that allocated 65 percent for the distributor and 35 percent for the exhibitor until the film's run hit the fourth week, when it became a 50–50 flat share for both parties. Sreekumar was able to recoup his losses and, in a short time, he returned to distributing mainstream films. Another strategy was to execute sales immediately after the completion of the project and divide the distribution rights into three territories within Kerala—Travancore, Kochi, and Malabar—for twenty lakh rupees (approx. $28,436); this was distinct from outside-state rights, which were sold separately. At the peak of the soft-porn success in 2000, each territory could fetch a profit of forty lakh rupees ($91,872) for the distributor.[19]

Beyond such industrial aspects, the conditions of precarious life manifested differently for actors, starlets, and directors, who were each impacted by financial instability, risk-taking, and lack of success. The fact that soft-porn thrived in an economy of fictitious names, rumors, and gossip also posed a methodological challenge for me, especially in separating fact from fiction. Despite the availability of many of these films on DVD format and as digital files on media-sharing sites, YouTube channels, and porn sites, the details of productions, including the technicians and even the shooting locations, were hard to come by. The names in opening credits were mostly fictitious, and the production and distribution companies existed only until business transactions were completed. As soon as outside-state rights, satellite rights, and DVD rights for the films were sold, these companies were dissolved. The picture was further muddied by the fact that production crew members removed identifiable details about themselves from the films, as did technicians who had moved from mainstream film hoping to profit from the windfall and financiers who funneled in money using third-party deals. The only person in the production unit who could link the preproduction, production, and postproduction phases of these films was the production manager, whose job included procuring capital and delivering the prints from the lab to the distributors. Although the function of such negotiated anonymity was to keep the production process going, it also reframes the terms by which we understand film authorship. The substitution of real names with pseudonyms was not aimed at erasing individual contributions or labor but was a recognition of the precarious production practices at play. The pseudonym-mediated circuit was not a one-off arrangement; many filmmakers and technicians went on to produce, direct, and edit films consistently with the same pseudonym.[20]

Some respondents in the Gulf (particularly in Abu Dhabi and Dubai) spoke to me about collectively viewing soft-porn films through video cassettes that were brought from India, some with Arabic subtitles. Many of them recounted trying to figure out whether the names in the end credits were real or fake. One of my respondents, Nanda Kumar, a carpenter in his fifties who came to Abu Dhabi in the 1970s, said: "I don't think anyone exists by these names. Seeing names of popular mainstream directors in the credits like Bharatan or Padmarajan is different from Purushan Alappuzha or RDX . . . most of us were quite entertained by the credit sequences."[21] Unlike prominent directors like Bharatan and Padmarajan, whose larger repertoire of films were marked by their authorial imprint, pseudonyms such as Purushan Alappuzha (literally "the man from Alappuzha") assert the implausibility of attaching genuine personhood to cine-labor. The name Purushan Alappuzha cropped up a few times during my fieldwork in Kodambakkam as well, but it took me another two years to verify that such a person actually existed and that he had produced a handful of soft-porn films. An article in *The Indian Express* in 1978 had a news item on the film *Ponnil Kulicha Rathri* (Gold-bathed night) that mentions his name as the script writer. Similarly, some of the censor scripts that I accessed at the National Film Archive of India (NFAI) in Pune also mention him as the director of a few films.[22] This indicates that the ecology of soft-porn film production was so steeped in anonymity or pseudonymous practices that even real names were sometimes mistaken as fake ones. And in a context where the crew sought anonymity, the hypervisibility of the female star replaced the filmic author.

Such anonymity, combined with low budgets, the exploitation of "glamour," tailor-made shooting schedules, and hurriedly written dialogue, added to the dismissal of these films in dominant accounts of Malayalam cinema history as *thattikoottu padangal*.[23] In contrast, one of the recurrent ideas that cropped up in conversations with my respondents was an unwritten code of ethics that governed the production of soft-porn. Director A. T. Joy told me, "I am not saying that women were not exploited in soft-porn. But there was a verbal agreement on what actresses were comfortable with and they can work without any external pressure."[24] The director Thrikkunnappuzha Vijayakumar similarly recounted: "Even though we had access to many intimate shots of the actresses that could have fetched us a good price in the market, there was a collective consensus on the risk involved in circulating or trading in sexually explicit bits (*thundu*)."[25]

Although it may be true that some films included extraneously shot and edited erotic sequences that entered different circuits, these films and the one-sided reviews they received were caught in a larger discourse about their notoriety as sexual exploitation. Voicing his criticism of mainstream Indian cinema's portrayal of soft-porn as nothing short of prostitution, a producer who had made a string of soft-porn films under a fictitious identity said:

> It was not like the mainstream cinema where the actresses after being cast are told to agree to "compromise" to retain their roles. Whoever comes to soft-porn enters with the full knowledge of what is involved. . . . In spite of the sex and desire, there was a certain ethics that governed our inter-personal relations. It was not that everything was out there free for all.[26]

Vijayakumar and others regularly worked with a pool of actresses (a remnant of what I described as K. S. Gopalakrishnan's "pastoral" style of film production), and nobody wanted to endanger their business by breaching this trust. The soft-porn industry has always been concerned with distinguishing itself from hardcore pornography. The soft-porn filmmakers and production personnel who I interviewed were keen to describe how they used the term "soft-porn" as an oppositional phrase that distinguished their work from "hardcore pornography." Some even rejected the designation of their work as involving pornography.

The soft-porn film industry's promotion of relatively unknown female starlets also contributed to anxieties about female stars. The film magazines that showcased these starlets were keen to foreground their willingness to act in roles that required "modern" and "bold" looks—phrases that signify sexually tinged roles—and they thus began to associate this group of ambitious aspiring actresses with the *madakarani* and her sexual autonomy. This sexual politics is not unique to Malayalam soft-porn; as Linda Ruth Williams demonstrates, even film noir incorporates sexual intrigue into its storylines to motivate on-screen softcore sex.[27] The foregrounding of female characters in soft-porn cinema's narrative organization by default implied demasculinizing the figure of the male hero. Journalistic accounts investigated Malayalam soft-porn industry from the vantage point of male actors who were barely visible on the margins. These articles reveal an impulse to *remasculinize* the cinematic screen, which has seemingly been threatened by the upsurge of soft-porn actresses. An *India Today* article writes of male actors who were featured in soft-porn films:

> They are heroes, but only in name. For male porn actors of Malayalam and Tamil cinema, life is removed from the affluence and glory associated with reel life. Not only are they overshadowed by porn heroines and paid measly salaries but they also have to contend with the prospect of never making it to mainstream cinema. . . . Even after twenty movies, the assistant director tells them how to grin sheepishly when the heroine reveals her cleavage. Will they ever get to perform? Unlikely as long as the bottom line requires the heroines to be visibly bare and the heroes, well barely visible.[28]

Conversely, as transient figures, the actresses cast as *madakarani* in soft-porn films were simultaneously seen as a threat and a source of exoticized desire. Most of these actresses came from states such as Tamil Nadu, Andhra Pradesh, Karnataka, Maharashtra, and Punjab—that is, from outside the state of Kerala.

Casting actresses like Reshma, Sindhu, Sajini, and Roshni from other linguistic and regional spaces was a deliberate strategy to not have to rely on local, ethnically Malayalam talent for sexualized labor.

These actresses' "stardom" was not the same as that of big-budget, mainstream stars. Instead of appearing on advertising billboards and in television ads, these actresses became the new pin-up girls who fed the fantasies of men in places as varied as B-circuit cinema halls and public toilets, as well as film magazine centerfolds. Their on-screen personas became manifestations of forbidden sexual fantasies, and they were counterpoised to the idea of a morally pure and culturally virtuous Malayali woman. Their personal lives and private interactions were perceived as a continuation of their filmic roles. In fact, a proliferating genre of pulp fiction focused entirely on their sex lives.

The conflation of their on-screen roles and private lives, coupled with the many moral edicts and compunctions around soft-porn film production, meant that these actresses' stardom was figured as a precarious form caught between hypervisibility and invisibility. Foremost among these new and emerging actresses was Shakeela (Fig. 15), whose impact on the industry was so strong that soft-porn films soon came to be known as "Shakeela films." Shakeela's rise as the beacon of Malayalam soft-porn across the nation and her formidable bodily presence exposed the sexual contradictions of Malayali society. Soft-porn's language of sexual excess allowed figures such as Shakeela to speak to diverse constituencies of desire, yet it also fixed their off-screen lives into the image of the sex siren. Most of them disappeared from the industry after short stints and, for many, working in soft-porn blocked them from ever entering the mainstream film industry. Thus, even as the genre of soft-porn proved ephemeral, fizzling out in the early 2000s, its effects on the careers and lives of certain actresses were longer lasting.

Figures such as Shakeela force us to rethink precarity beyond conditions of economic instability and focus instead on a "set of concerns about relations of production and the quality of social life."[29] Although financial insecurity remains part of soft-porn's networks of production, the precarious stardom of Shakeela and other starlets of the Malayalam soft-porn circuit brings us into the arena of gender roles. This kind of precarity comes closer to Richard Dyer's description of the star commodity as something produced "out of their own bodies and psychologies." If soft-porn actresses such as Shakeela were "part of the way films [were] sold," the precarity of their stardom was as much a function of the friction between norms of sexuality and the licentiousness of the films.[30] Although the figure of Shakeela is localized in the specific context of one of India's many regional-language film industries, the lessons of this investigation reach further and foreground the need to discuss precarious female labor in the context of disparaged genres such as soft-porn. Following Judith Butler, we can think of this kind of precarity as a "fundamental dependency on anonymous others."[31] Soft-porn actresses such as Shakeela were caught between the image of sexual autonomy and the realities of social

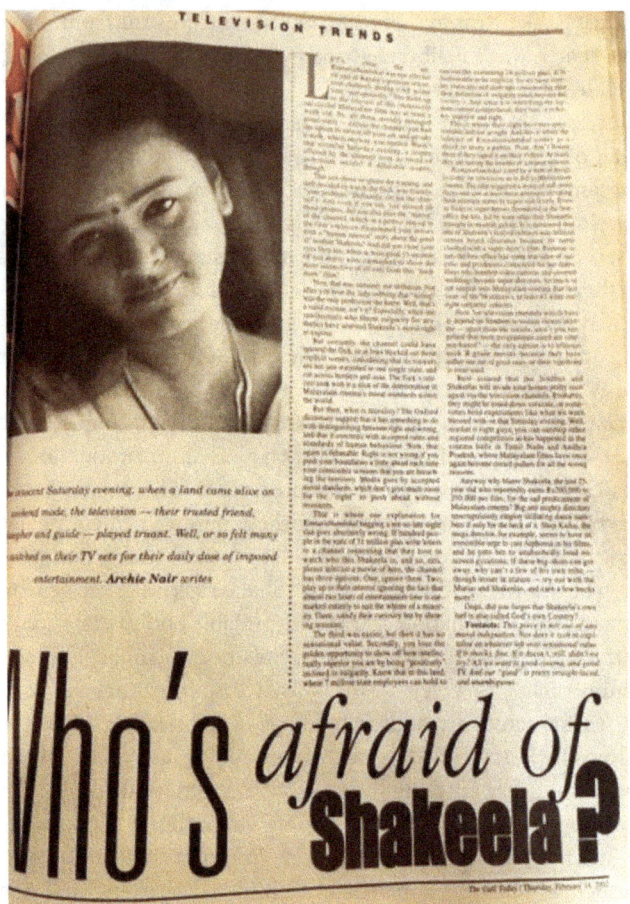

FIGURE 15. "Who's Afraid of Shakeela?" *Gulf Today*, February 14, 2002, 4. Image courtesy Rajeev.

dependency. This precarious stardom is produced at the confluence of infrastructural routes, censorial regimes, and norms of social acceptance and permissiveness.

SHAKEELA'S PRECARIOUS STARDOM: SAVIOR, SEDUCTRESS, "AUNTY"

In her autobiography, Shakeela writes that her films catered to an audience who found expression for their fantasies in certain parts of her body.[32] Shakeela's status as an outsider enabled the public imagination of her as a series of desired body parts that could be zoomed in on and magnified. The mainstream Malayalam industry would never have allowed an "indigenous" actress, so to speak, to be foregrounded as a sex siren.[33] In fact, the history of Malayalam cinema has been peppered with a slew of "outsider" actresses who emblematized an exotic, desirable, and yet objectified body, for instance Vijayashree in the 1970s and Silk Smitha in the 1980s and early 1990s. Like the prejudices around "Madras films" prevalent in North India, in the public imagination promiscuous actresses from other states were preferred to native Malayali women. Moreover, there were also concerns that identifiable Malayali actors might be sought for sexual services, as opposed to the relative distance that the "outside" actress would wield in public imagination. Thus, the porn-star aura that Shakeela embodied in the late nineties and 2000s was a particular variant of the sex siren enabled by overlapping social and industrial configurations of the time.

Born as Chand Shakeela Begum to a Muslim family of mixed Tamil-Telegu descent, Shakeela hailed from the tinsel town of Kodambakkam in Tamil Nadu. She debuted at the age of seventeen in a supporting role in *Play Girls* (dir. R. D. Sekhar, Tamil, 1994), a "sex education film" where she co-starred with Silk Smitha. Her entry into the film industry was quite accidental, as Shekar, a makeup artist (and Shakeela's neighbor), offered her a role. As an indication of the low-budget format that soft-porn films would later adopt, Shekar handled the responsibility of story, screenplay, editing, production, and direction. Shakeela went on to act in *Shobhanam* (dir. K. S. Sivachandran, Malayalam, 1997) after *Play Girls*. The media celebrated Shakeela's success by calling her *sexpuyal*, the "sex tempest," whose sheer screen presence allowed low-budget films to outpace even mainstream films at the box office.

The B- and C-circuit theaters increased Shakeela's marketability as a star, especially as they expanded soft-porn films' reach and scale into the hinterlands and rural spaces, which were removed from the entertainment offered by A-circuit theaters. Shakeela acted in a string of films between 2000 and 2002, including *Thankathoni* (dir. A. T. Joy, 2000), *Rakkilikal* (dir. A. T. Joy, 2000), *Manjukalapakshi* (dir. R. J. Prasad, 2000), *Rasaleela* (dir. K. R. Joshi, 2001), and *Yaamini* (dir. U. C. Roshan, 2002), which allowed her to create a brand value. Some of her older films, like *Swargam* (dir. S. Chandran, 1995) and *Kalluvathukkal Kathreena* (dir. A. T. Joy, 1999), were rereleased as "Shakeela films" during this period. The prefix "Shakeela" was added to identify soft-porn films in general, and theaters that screened Shakeela films were called the "Shakeela Camp."[34] A field representative who had been sent to the Shakeela Camp remembered that theater owners would demand that he confirm whether the film print had the real or the fake Shakeela—"real" and "fake" being operative terms used to identify films in which she acted throughout and those that featured her for a few minutes as a token presence. Films such as *Miss Shakeela* (dir. K. Alexander, 1999) were released to cash in on her presence, and her makeup man, Ravi, even came to be known in the film circles as "Shakeela Ravi."

The film that cemented Shakeela's position as an "adult film" actress in Malayalam cinema was *Kinnarathumbikal* (Lovelorn dragonflies; 2000), a debut venture

FIGURE 16. Newspaper advertisement for *Kinnarathumbikal*, prominently displaying the "A" certification. The success and popularity of the film is denoted by the word "housefull," and the number "2" refers to the second week after the film's release. Image courtesy Sarat Chandran.

by the hitherto unknown associate cinematographer R. Jay Prasad, who used the pseudonym "R. J. Prasad" in his directorial credit (Fig. 16). As a serious film aficionado who was part of the regular film screenings at the Chitralekha film society, Prasad had long desired to do an independent project, and *Kinnarathumbikal* was it.[35] Although the mainstream film he had planned had to be shelved for lack of funds, a low-budget film was planned to funnel in money needed for the main project. The title *Kinnarathumbikal* was derived from *Ammanamkunnile Kinnarathumbikal* (The dragonflies of the Ammanam Hills), the original title that he had planned for the mainstream film. The initial money for the project was procured through a loan scheme offered by the Kerala State Financial Enterprises, a state government body that had introduced plans to provide a rotating savings and credit to customers. Reminiscing about those days, Prasad said:

> The sweat and hard work that went into the making of the film went down the drain and instead *Kinnarathumbikal* got reduced to a sex-film. My debut film was a nail in my coffin. There were *thundu* that were inserted into the film, and these were interpolations made without my consent.[36]

Kinnarathumbikal was made with a meager budget of 13.97 lakh rupees ($29,000) and was shot with an Arri IIC camera that was converted to

Cinemascope by changing the gate and lens.[37] In our conversation, Prasad shared the response of T. E. Vasudevan, the producer who headed Kerala Film Chamber of Commerce, where the mandatory title registration of the film was done. "This looks more like a hotel bill of a mainstream film," Prasad recounted Vasudevan saying to him, a sentiment that clearly reflected the mainstream film industry's attitude toward soft-porn films as low cost.[38] The package scheme offered by the Kerala State Film Development Corporation (KSFDC) through the Trivandrum-based Chitranjali Studio was a boon, as it allowed the filmmaker to acquire film stock, camera, a production unit, and postproduction for a payment of one lakh rupees (approx. $2,100). *Kinnarathumbikal* went on to gross four crore rupees (approx. $856,900), capitalizing on what one reviewer described as Shakeela's "dreamy eyes, puffed-up flesh squeezed within a low-cut blouse and her deep, deep cleavage."[39]

Set in a tea plantation, the film explores the conflicts caused by the blossoming of complex desires amid the exploitative labor arrangements underlying the everyday lives of its laborers. Shakeela plays Dakshayini, a tea-plucker who is in a live-in relationship with the plantation supervisor, Sivan, but also has sexual escapades with the teenager Gopu. Gopu desires to be with his elder cousin Revathy, who is the daughter of a tea-plucker, while Sivan also desires Revathy's hand in marriage. A similar storyline involving intergenerational desire was explored in *Rathinirvedham* (Sexual ecstasy; 1978), starring Jayabharti, and *Layanam* (Dissolution; dir. Thulasidas, 1989), starring Silk Smitha. But in those films, narrative closure demanded that the female protagonist be punished for her transgressive desire, which resulted in their deaths. In contrast, *Kinnarathumbikal* empowers Dakshayani, who feels betrayed by Sivan's desire for Revathy. Rejecting Sivan's advances, she incites Gopu to murder Sivan, thereby helping the cousins to elope.

Shakeela's oft-quoted line "Is there anyone among us who hasn't committed sin?" resonates with viewers of the film and is known to many who have heard about the film but not actually seen it. The statement is directed at a heteropatriarchal structure that berates women who are alleged to have multiple sexual partners as warranting social sanctions while giving men a freehand to engage in extramarital relationships. As a strong statement against the double standards and hypocrisy of middle-class moral values, the film's dialogue now surfaces as memes and quotes shared on fan sites and Twitter, long after the film's original release and run.[40] There are even fan-created trailers for the film, with fictitious details of the production addressing Shakeela as "universal star."[41] The film banner in one of these trailers was inventively phrased as "Kanyaka Films" (Virgin Films), a turn of phrase that was later adopted by the 2013 film *Kanyaka Talkie*, which presents a ficto-critical history of soft-porn films, which I explore in chapter 5. Similarly, The Lost Entertainment, a YouTube channel that creatively edits trailers of older films, curated one for *Kinnarathumbikal* compiling the highlights to evoke the original experience of watching it on-screen.[42] In the specific context of

FIGURE 17. Screen grabs from the fan-created teaser for *Kinnarathumbikal* (left) and trailer by The Lost Entertainment (right).

Kinnarathumbikal, this curation reimagines the publicity material and contexts of reception to conjoin different generations of viewers (Fig. 17).

Although soft-porn films were perceived as addressing mostly male viewers, one cannot completely ignore female viewership. Between 2001 and 2002, these films were telecast on cable channels as part of "Midnight Masala"—the late-night segment, which according to David Andrews is "soft-core's most distinctive habitat."[43] The reference to *masala* (spice) refers to scenes that could not be broadcast during prime time. *Kinnarathumbikal* was also telecast in 2002 on Asianet, a Malayalam-language satellite television channel. The appearance of a soft-porn film during prime time created a huge controversy, unleashing debates about televisuality and obscenity in domestic interiors, and the channel publicly apologized.[44] This has become common lore in the Malayali televisual public and found reflection in contemporary renderings. For instance, *Perilloor Premier League* (2023), a Malayalam web series streamed on Hulu, begins with the protagonist Sreekuttan looking at a copy of *Nana* film magazine with Shakeela on the cover page showing her cleavage in a classic massage scene. Hiding the magazine within his notebook, he discusses with his schoolmates the impending telecast of *Kinnarathumbikal* on the local cable television channel at 10 p.m. that night. He plans to view the film when his family is asleep, but an unsuccessful robbery attempt wakes his parents, who catch him watching the film. Sreekuttan receives a beating for watching porn, and it becomes public knowledge as the villagers who gather outside the house to catch the thief also learn of his nocturnal adventures. From then on, Sreekuttan is teased by his friends as *thumbi* (dragonfly), in reference to the film *Kinnarathumbikal*. This rendering in *Perilloor Premier League* is fictional but has a real-life basis in the experiences of many young men and women.

Similarly, in a 2017 Facebook post, the literary commentator Deepa Nisanth recollects the surreptitious pleasures the film provided many female viewers. Nishant explains that she watched *Kinnarathumbikal* secretly when it was telecast on Surya TV (another satellite channel that regularly showed late night soft-porn films),

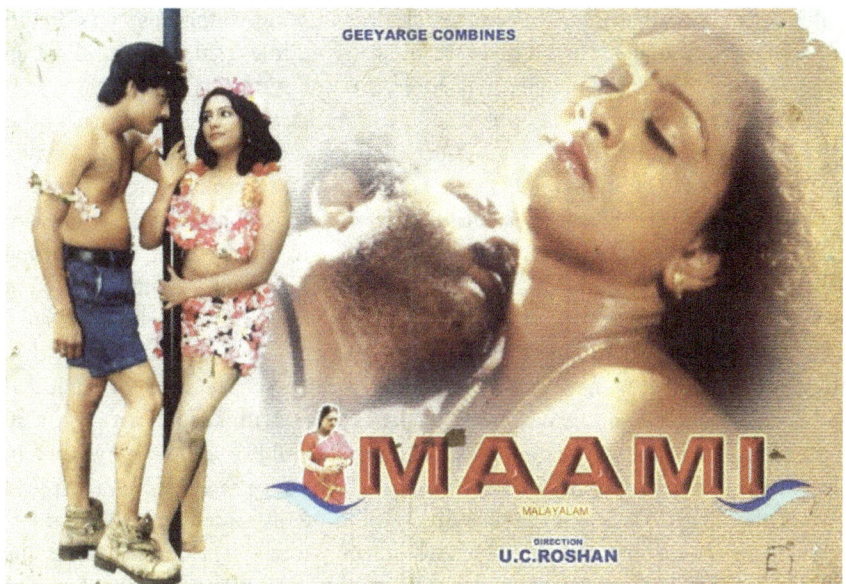

FIGURE 18. Promotional poster of *Maami* (Aunty) directed by U. C. Roshan. The poster features Shakeela and an unknown actor. Shakeela's prominence as a symbol of soft-porn films is indicated by the icon of her next to the title. Image courtesy National Film Archive of India.

knowing all too well that her mother wouldn't approve.[45] Her curiosity as a teenager was stirred by conversations in her college and the teasing repartee directed at heavy-set girls whom boys teased as "Shakeela." In her deeply personal note, Nishant writes about how Shakeela's autobiography became crucial to understanding the "real" Shakeela and the trials and tribulations that made her into a force to be reckoned with. Nishant's post was widely shared and commented upon by many Facebook users, who also added their own reminiscences of watching the film.

Shakeela's heavy-set body allowed her to fit into the archetype of the amorous "aunty," a recurring figure in both visual and written forms of pornography throughout the country and a stereotype that gave imaginative access to the middle-aged woman next door. Shakeela confirms this in her autobiography: "My large breasts and heavy body was what excited the audience.... If I didn't have this body I had, I may not have been able to make my career."[46] These films often paired Shakeela with young actors, and this stamped her public image as that of a sexually depraved middle-aged woman. Frequent use of the word *chechi*, not only in *Kinnarathumbikal* but in other films and erotic pulp fiction, suggested her "cougar-like" figure. In Malayalam, *chechi* literally means "elder sister," but colloquially it also connotes an older woman with whom one intends to engage in sex (see Fig. 18).[47] In relation to this, sex-advice columns published in literary magazines often speculated that the excessive sexual drive among young boys was due to unwarranted sexual exposure given to them by middle-aged women who trap impressionable boys for sexual satisfaction. In a column titled "What is the Reason for Excessive Sex-Drive?" published in *Chitrakarthika* in 1977, a writer who goes by P. A. G. Nair writes, "it is because they are forced by middle-aged women to have sex with them; moreover, they are being told to prolong the duration of holding off the semen before ejaculation to satisfy the woman, and the deferral of orgasm leads to increase in sex drive." According to this rhetoric, upon growing up, such men prefer young girls over middle-aged women, and are uninterested in sex workers because any monetary transaction makes them lose interest in sex.[48] This frames the sexually active middle-aged woman as the causal factor for dysfunctional families—young girls who end up with these men later are subjected to violence, and the young men are also portrayed as victims of this arrangement. Imagined as a sexually deviant but also sexually desirable middle-aged woman in line with such descriptions, Shakeela's body became a locus of excess that spilled out of the diegetic space of the narratives, spinning off-screen fantasies that circulated in sensational yellow magazines like *Fire* and *Crime*. After the decline of soft-porn films in the early 2000s, this template of intergenerational erotica would become popular in erotic cartoons, especially in popular comic series such as *Savita Bhabhi* and *Velamma*, which regularly featured the sexual extramarital adventures of the eponymous characters.[49]

With the decline of soft-porn by 2005, Shakeela's success also dwindled and she made only cameo appearances in comic roles. She did have cameos with mainstream actors such as Mohan Lal (*Chotta Mumbai* [Small Mumbai], 2007), Vikram (*Dhool* [Dust], 2003), and Vijay (*Sukran*, 2005) capitalizing on her past glory. But in contrast to her prior heroine-centric roles in soft-porn films, these roles would have been forgotten, were it not for the fact that she shared screen space with mainstream actors from a system that had always disparaged her films. As she was marginalized after 2005, Shakeela's career began to mirror that of many other starlets who had come from outside and enjoyed a short stint in the industry (Fig. 19). A handful of legal cases were registered against Shakeela for obscenity in different parts of South India, including Nagercoil, Salem, and Tirunelveli (all in Tamil Nadu). In one of her court appearances, Shakeela, a Muslim by birth, arrived clad in a burqa, earning the ire of an Islamic women's group that went on record as saying: "She doesn't wear any clothes in films, how dare she choose symbols of Islam?"[50] Another controversy arose over the Malayalam film *Kadambari* (Wine; dir. Jayadevan, 2002), around which the Dalit activist group Ayyankali Pada (Fighters of Ayyankali) organized a cleansing campaign against the soft-porn wave in Kerala. A group of activists attacked Lata Theatre in Muvattupuzha with locally made bombs and burned a reel of the film in front of the audience.[51] Although the attack was aimed at exposing the culpability of the film industry in the sexualization of women, the action was also driven by respectability

FIGURE 19. A newspaper article in the *New Indian Express* (2004) headlining the decline of soft-porn films, with the image of Shakeela (spelled "Shakila") standing in for the "dark" state of the industry. Image courtesy A. T. Joy.

politics, as many of the actresses in the film came from caste-oppressed backgrounds. In such narratives, soft-porn films were accused of having extended the violence and sexualization imposed on Dalit women.

Even after the decline of her soft-porn stardom, Shakeela continues to be remembered as a soft-porn actress—in fact, this becomes a selling point in sex education programs in Tamil television such as *Antharangam* (Personal intimacy; 2016, telecast on 1TV) and *Samayal Mathiram* (Cooking tricks; 2016, telecast on Captain TV). Following a phone-in, talk-show format, both programs elevated Shakeela to the role of an information expert who mediated sex-related queries for the sexologist. Interestingly, while the sexologist in the program is presented as a peddler of sexual myths who focuses on masculine performance from a strictly heterosexual perspective, Shakeela's presence as the caller's initial point of contact allows for a collective sharing of her on-screen roles and their relevance to sex education.[52] Shakeela's presence as a visual icon of soft-porn is evoked time and again, as most of the callers are elated to speak with her and show off their knowledge of her films. Thus, Shakeela's career in soft-porn also enabled her to stand in as a facilitator for the callers to seek out information about sex, as well as share their queries about sex-related concerns. Another sex education program titled *Thitthikkum Iravukal* (Sweet nights, 2016) made Shakeela's on-screen significance a prominent part of its strategy, devoting substantial airtime to sequences from Shakeela's films in between the sexologist's responses to caller queries. Most recently, Shakeela has also been roped in as a sex education expert in a Malayalam promotional sketch (2023) for the Netflix show *Sex Education*.[53] In the sketch, "Shakeela's Driving School" stands in as a metaphor for sex education itself, her tips about driving being innuendos about sexual intercourse as she tells a couple that she is going to talk to them about an important chapter that may have been skipped by their teachers in school. Shakeela's words of wisdom range from pointers on intercourse and foreplay, to ethical dictums about consent and slut-shaming, the importance of self-pleasure and protection, and, quite ironically, the importance of finding out each other's likes and dislikes instead of copying what is shown in porn. Significantly, in one sequence Shakeela tells off the male partner for slut-shaming, and as the man apologizes, Shakeela responds with the lines, "thettu cheyyathavarayi arumilla." This translates as "there is no one who has not made a mistake" (subtitled by Netflix as "Everyone makes mistakes"), a direct reference to an iconic Shakeela dialogue from *Kinnarathumbikal*. Thus, in a strange way, these sex education programs tapped into Shakeela and her precarious labor for their own instrumental use.

Shakeela's influence on the industry was phenomenal, but she did not direct any films during the peak of her career. In 2013, a flurry of publicity announced her return to Malayalam films, this time as a director of *Neelakurinji Poothu* (Neelakurinhi is in bloom). As part of the film's promotion, both Shakeela and the producer, Jaffar Kanjirapalli, appeared in many interviews and television shows. Shakeela emphasized that her directorial debut was a new beginning, and this film was in no way connected to the sex films she had previously been part of.[54] Kanjirapalli, who was also the vice president of FEFKA, was also an erstwhile producer of soft-porn films. Crucially, like Shakeela, Kanjirapalli was not ashamed of his soft-porn phase despite his decision to switch gears to catering for film units in the mid-2000s. However, the project ran into trouble when Shakeela expressed her discomfort with Kanjirapalli's insistence that she take the lead role as well as direct the film. This disquiet was also partially an effect of print and visual media's speculations about the film's plot, even before shooting started. For instance, a *The Times of India* report quoted Kanjirapalli as stating: "The movie will be a complete entertainer with spicy scenes of Shakeela underwater and in the attire of a fish seller. The shots will be taken in such a way that the censor board can never deny us certificate."[55] *Neelakurinji Poothu* was shelved halfway into preproduction. Shakeela finally made her directorial debut two years later, in 2015, with the Telugu film *Romantic Target*. In response to an interviewer's question about its genre, Shakeela described it as dealing with a "lady-oriented subject."[56] The film centers on a female vigilante who murders sexual predators who pose a threat to women's safety and dignity. Despite Shakeela's cameo role as a police officer, it failed to win over audiences.

Depictions of Shakeela in mainstream films also align with the popular tendency to frame the soft-porn industry as the arena of an exploitative mafia. This occurs in *The Dirty Picture*, which focuses on Silk Smitha but briefly references Shakeela. "Shakeela" appears as Silk's young, zesty rival who displaces her as the next sex bomb, but there is some anachronism in this narrative. A song sequence portrays Silk and Shakeela in a competitive relationship and posits a causal relationship between Smitha's decline and Shakeela's rise, even though the industrial configurations they inhabited were different. By situating Silk's character in a narrative of moral and professional decline and associating it with a particular industrial form, *The Dirty Picture* not only vilifies the soft-porn industry but also collapses two temporal moments. This temporal slippage allows all *madakarani* figures to be perceived as soft-porn actresses, no matter that Malayalam soft-porn emerged, strictly speaking, as a genre during Shakeela's reign; Smitha had died by the time Shakeela became a major presence.

Shakeela's autobiographical account and her biopic, *Shakeela*, released in five languages—Hindi, Tamil, Telegu, Kannada, and Malayalam—are part of a recuperative effort to reinstate her voice and performance as important interventions in rethinking sexual politics. Whereas *The Dirty Picture* sparked allegations that it watered down Silk Smitha's life experiences and led to defamation suits from her family, *Shakeela* was endorsed by Shakeela herself. The production house released photographs and news stories showcasing Shakeela as a consultant for the film who helped Richa Chadha prepare for the role. Director Indrajit Lankesh claimed that *Shakeela* would be a "rags-to-riches-to-rags story" that mapped "the hardships and rough phases when she was not getting films and was trying for character roles."[57] The film's first-look poster presents a complicated picture of Shakeela that both embraces and distances her from the peculiar kind of stardom she inhabited. Under the film's tagline, "Not a Porn Star," the Bollywood actress Richa Chadha, who plays Shakeela, looks defiantly at the camera, the upper half of her body covered in gold jewelry. She stands in front of a wall scribbled with negative comments in Hindi about her skin color, weight, and religion. The Malayalam word *veshya* (prostitute) and a Tamil word that loosely translates to "fuck" appear amid the Hindi words, localizing Shakeela as a South Indian figure, even though her films had a pan-Indian appeal, thanks to the dubbing industry that flourished alongside soft-porn films. The filmmakers drew inspiration for the image from Silk Smitha's film *Miss Pamela* (dir. Kottayam Chellappan, 1989) and this image indeed pays homage to Smitha (Fig. 20).[58] Chadha shared a photograph of the poster on Twitter with the caption "Bold is Gold," with the filmmakers claiming, "It was Smitha's . . . untimely tragic demise which led to the rise of Shakeela's popularity and had it not been for Silk to pave the way with her unapologetic choices, Shakeela wouldn't have been so popular."[59]

The film's fragmented storyline with episodic narration capitalizes on preexisting narratives about Shakeela's life—being forced into acting in adult films by her mother, being disowned by her family after they benefited from her money, and being left with no financial security and forced to take refuge in the one-bedroom house where she started her life as a junior artist. It opens with a song sequence that gives a glimpse of her career trajectory—photo shoots, dance sequences, protests by activist groups, press conferences by directors' and producers' associations

FIGURE 20. Artist's impressions of the posters for *Miss Pamela* (left) and *Shakeela* (right), inspired by the *Hindustan Times* comparison of the two posters. Image courtesy S. Radhakrishnan.

calling for her films to be banned, and, finally, shots of her film posters defiled by eggs and charcoal. The narrative proper begins with Shakeela visiting the house of a scriptwriter who, despite his initial reluctance, agrees to pen her biopic, provided she agrees to take a narco-test to reveal the truth about her life—a character like Shakeela can only be seen a reliable narrator/witness with recourse to such pseudo-scientific routes. Flashback sequences provide her backstory as the film moves from the ban on her films to her attempts to restore her image through a comeback film. Her plan to work in a "clean film" backfires when the director, in collusion with her "dupe" (body double), Suhana (Ester Noronha), splices explicit bits into the final cut without her knowledge. Egged on by the superstar Salim (Pankaj Tripathi), who feels threatened by Shakeela, a Muslim group attacks Suhana. The film ends with Shakeela facing journalists who have gathered outside the hospital where Suhana has been admitted. In response to their allegation that her films are responsible for an increase in rape and other sexual crimes, Shakeela redirects these allegations to the male audience, producers, and the journalists, who are united in the efforts to isolate her as the cause for all malice.

The era of the 1990s serves as the backdrop for the film's exploration of Shakeela's career, and a sequence involving Silk Smitha and Shakeela repeats some of the problems that the film set out to avoid. The film falls back on a cliched narrative about Smitha becoming jealous of the younger actress, who, according to industry rumors, might replace her. A dance sequence pitting the two against each other, with Shakeela emerging as the victor, replicates *The Dirty Picture*'s problems. Even though the actress Shakeela was never a dancer (unlike Smitha), the film shows her effortlessly stepping into Smitha's shoes. Although the filmmakers used "Not a Porn Star" as a rhetorical strategy to outwardly avoid sensationalism, the film rests on Shakeela's aura as a soft-porn star and sensational stories and rumors about her. Shakeela's unique selling point was her porn-star status—and its corollary, precarious stardom. Thus, despite Lankesh's efforts to foreground the "humanitarian" angle of making the film "as truthful as possible," its sensationalism backfires and weakens its ability to carry the story forward. The fictional Shakeela becomes the poster woman for issues of wage equality, sexual harassment, and unethical practices in the film industry. Although the inclusion of the "actual" Shakeela in the production process was meant to index biographical fact, the film renders the public imagination of Shakeela as incapable of escaping the trappings of popular journalism, rumors, and pulp-fiction sensationalism.

The vicissitudes that followed in the real Shakeela's life after soft-porn fizzled out as an industrial genre are best understood when contrasted with the trajectory of Bollywood actress Sunny Leone (Karenjit Kaur Vohra). This comparison is not random: both Shakeela and Leone appeared in the trilingual film *Luv U Alia* (dir. Indrajith Lankesh, 2016), leading some in the media to speculate that Leone might be playing the role of Shakeela in her biopic. But there is a marked discrepancy between how Leone is now addressed as part of India's mainstream film culture and how soft-porn stars such as Shakeela are still made to publicly defend their life choices. Leone, of Canadian, Indian, and American origin, is a former adult film actress who moved to Bollywood and entered the mainstream Indian film industry in 2011. She has since been able to successfully use her porn-star image to carve out a new fanbase. Although Leone has not acted in any porn features since her Bollywood debut, she has strategically used her past association with the adult film industry to self-fashion her identity in Hindi cinema. On the other hand, while Shakeela temporarily enjoyed the limelight as the emblem of soft-porn films, this identity did not give her much momentum on the film production front. Despite her attempts to start afresh in comic roles, the excess associated with her on-screen and off-screen images stalled her opportunities to partake in mainstream films on equal terms. Under the careful supervision of a public relations management team, Leone was able to smooth her entry into Bollywood and successfully negotiate her porn-star image after some initial hurdles. This created a humanizing narrative that emphasized her heterosexual coupledom through marriage and her adoption of a child, making it easy for the film fraternity to welcome her into their fold. Shakeela's familial connections are different; she has spoken at length about the need to have an adopted family instead of a family in the strict sense of blood relations. She has adopted transgender community members as part of her family and was adopted in turn by trans groups as their ally. In an interview in 2015, Shakeela mentions her relationship with the *thirunangai* (trans women) community in Chennai and the need for support structures that can help them get their due rights and respect in society.[60] Identifying herself as an ally, Shakeela speaks about the multiple roles in which she doubles as sister, confidante, and friend for community members and the alternative family she has been able to build. Shakeela says, "The society has considered *thirunangai* and actresses as just bodies. We also have dreams and lives more than just what's seen on the surface level."[61] Shakeela's alliance with the trans community extends the bonds of caring and sharing instantiated in the queering of family. By building an adopted family, Shakeela is also thinking about alternative kinship networks that can sustain her through tough times—a potentiality that challenges the heteronormative ideals that characterize her films.

Shakeela's and Leone's experiences are united, however, by the enforced exposure of their pasts on public platforms. Both Leone and Shakeela have also been subjected to hostile treatment in television interviews, with hosts constantly reminding them of their pasts and their need to make amends for the damage their films have done. Leone had to endure offensive remarks from a leading English news anchor, CNN-IBN's Bhupendra Chaubey.[62] Shakeela's talk show, *Janakeeya Kodathi* (People's court), telecast by the Malayalam channel 24 in 2019, was publicized as *thurannu parachil* (exposure/confession). The show re-created the courtroom format, in which a judge hears the charges from both sides and passes a verdict. However, the anchor, Ranjini Menon, asked prying questions that pushed Shakeela to narrate her experiences of child sexual abuse and sex work, which she had written about in her autobiography. The questions were designed to cross-check details she had already revealed, as well as to elicit her comments on the exposure triggered by the #MeToo movement. Menon subjected Shakeela to a hostile interrogation, questioning her autonomy by holding her culpable for destroying her own career.[63] In what seemed like an attack meant to force Shakeela to take responsibility for her association with soft-porn films, she bombarded the actress with allegations that cast her as a cause of moral disarray, including personal questions about her stint with sex work. Shakeela took the questions in stride and responded that no one can judge her for her decisions, as they emerged from a certain set of experiences and her need for survival. The media's incessant demand that these subjects own up to the repercussions of their choices is nothing less than an invasion into their private lives.

In Kerala though, Leone's experience is markedly different from the tepid response that Shakeela received from the Malayalam film industry after her stint with soft-porn films. Leone entered Malayalam cinema in 2019, in an item number with the prominent actor Mammootty for the film *Madura Raja* (dir. Vysakh). If in the past, item numbers as a dance form were performed by actors who appeared on-screen solely for spectacular and sensual appeal and exited playing this "marginal role in the narrative without ceremony," contemporary item dances are often performed by A-list actors.[64] Leone's appearance in the same film as Mammootty was ironic, as the actor is often alleged to have spearheaded the campaign to put an end to Malayalam soft-porn films in the early 2000s. With the changed times and crossover of Bollywood stars into regional cinema, it seems only logical that an item dance starring Leone could gather a sizable audience.

FIGURE 21. Screenshot of Sunny Leone's tweet about her Kochi visit.

Even before entering Malayalam films, Leone was stupendously popular among Malayali men. In 2017, when Leone visited Kochi for the inauguration of a retail showroom for phones called Phone 4 Digital Hub, thousands of people gathered on adjacent roads and around nearby buildings to catch a glimpse of her. Chanting "We love Sunny," they blocked the roads, forcing the police to disperse the crowd with batons. An aerial shot from the inauguration showing hordes of peoples climbing the roofs of moving buses and nearby buildings circulated on social media (Fig. 21), leading the Twitterati to comment that Kerala cannot shed its soft-porn past, or rather cannot reconcile the moral contradictions in the expression of sexuality. The photograph also gave way to popular memes comparing the crowds gathered in Kerala to those for rallies for former US presidents Barack Obama and Donald Trump.⁶⁵ The presence of the All Kerala Sunny Leone Fans Club as a prime player in organizing the event and galvanizing the crowd (especially in a state where male stars and their fan clubs wield enormous power), as well as her contribution of five crore rupees (approx. $732,475) during the 2017 Kerala floods furnished support for her from women—quite unlike Shakeela, who had to defend herself on television.

While Sunny Leone's Kerala visit was one side of the story, a virally circulating image in 2018 gives us a few more clues. This image includes portraits of current and former porn stars including Mia Khalifa, Keiran Lee, Ava Addams, Johnny Sins, Jordi, and, crucially, Sunny Leone, all painted on a private bus in Kerala. The owner of the bus used this novel strategy to attract young patrons and considered it a statement about the influence of porn stars in Kerala's popular culture. Although decorating buses with painted posters is not new in India, including porn stars is.⁶⁶ This public visibility of porn stars differs from moral qualms associated with the exhibition of soft-porn posters or the broadcast of soft-porn films on television. While Leone's popularity or the bus's painted posters may very well be within the ambit of the permissible, debates about obscenity posit soft-porn as a disruptive, dangerous object. Consider, for example, the telecast of *Kinnarathumbikal* in 2000, which caused such an uproar that the channel Asianet had to tender its apology in their program in response to readers' letters.⁶⁷ Unlike Leone, figures like Shakeela belong to this register of unsettling objects. Her association with the trans community, her vocal articulation about questions of labor in the industry, and her constant refusal to toe the heteronormative line contribute to the construction of this image. Thus, while Leone becomes acceptable as a glossy, convertible image, the perceived "dirty" nature of Malayalam soft-porn sticks to Shakeela's body. Thus, although soft-porn itself has petered out as an industrial form, its residual effects still mark Shakeela's life and career in the present. Although no longer a porn star in the strictest sense of the term, Shakeela embodies precarious stardom and remains an index of the way the industry works to legitimize or delegitimize gendered (bodily) labor in response to cultural and economic demands.

SO MANY SHAKEELAS

Reading Shakeela's career trajectory as a form of precarious stardom gives insights into the historical formations of gender and sexuality within the film industry and Malayali society at large. In these films, Shakeela's presence as a sexually liberated woman who can give free rein to her desires and ignore hegemonic moral edicts destabilized Kerala's hero-centric, mainstream film industry, leading to what was popularly called "Shakeela *tharangam*"—the wave of Shakeela.⁶⁸ The camera lingered on her buxom, heavy-set figure—an anomaly in the Malayalam film industry at the time—and this concentrated focus on her face, breasts, and thighs equated the realm of desire with her anatomy. The emphasis on "women-centered" narratives in soft-porn films led to acrimonious debates among feminists and women's groups, which were quick to furnish the relevant obscenity clauses of censorship regulations.[69] Even as protests and theater blockades were organized to prevent the screenings of these films, their popularity increased instantaneously. Nevertheless, when obscenity cases were filed against Shakeela, none of the men's or women's groups advocating gender equality or sexual liberation lent support, leaving her to wage her own battle. Her location outside the space of conjugal sex also inaugurated Shakeela's fame as a "porn heroine," an almost impossibly paradoxical category in a cultural context that associated stardom exclusively with male actors and scripted female roles to foreground the normative codes of conduct expected of the women in a patriarchal society. Her gaze as it was directed at pleasure-seeking male viewers subverted earlier tropes of heterosexual intimacy, in which the male partner and his sexual drives structured scene composition.

If success, popularity, and influence over production decisions are the criteria for stardom, Shakeela was way ahead of many mainstream actresses whose memory faded the moment they left the industry. Many still feel that Shakeela's image as the veritable signifier of soft-porn films hijacked the successes of other actresses who starred in films but were forgotten in the accounts of the era. An actor who had starred opposite Shakeela recounted how many films that were distributed as "Shakeela films" were recycled from footage from her earlier films, yet they easily managed to break even and even reap profits. This process of recycling included duplicating and editing together small segments that featured Shakeela, and often resulted in films that were a hodgepodge of exploitation films in Hindi and English. Shakeela's image was the connective tissue binding together fragments that otherwise would have amounted to a random mix of sexploitation shots. Familiarity with Shakeela's image as a soft-porn icon was fundamental to this fragment economy, the visual dynamics of which both foregrounded the artifice behind the image and invited audiences to break down visual and aural sequences into smaller units. The precariousness of Shakeela's stardom and the limits of performative labor coalesce here. Speaking about Shakeela's star value, my respondent added:

> Shakeela's remuneration was on a day-to-day basis, which was beneficial for her in some ways, but proved fatal to her career. There were many producers who were willing to pay her more than Rs. 1 lakh for a day. But what she did not know was that these shots formed part of three to four films which were in the pipeline. There were even agents who helped mediate the selling of "unused" shots to prospective buyers.[70]

If Shakeela's stardom gave her some visibility, however precarious it may have been, the same cannot be said about other actresses who were part of soft-porn films. Actresses such as Roshni, Maria, Sajini, and Alphonsa disappeared from the film industry after finding little success and were never heard from again. In 2007, after soft-porn films had lost their initial allure, Reshma, an actress who starred prominently in soft-porn films like *Lovely* (dir. A. T. Joy, 1995) and *Sundari Kutty* (dir. Vinayan, 2003), among others, was arrested by police in Kerala as part of series of raids following a tip-off that "prostitution rackets" were operating in residential areas in the town of Kochi.[71] In keeping with the tendency of institutional and legal systems to view all kinds of sex work as forced human trafficking, a moral panic arose about male visitors frequenting a flat rented out by a few non-Malayali women. Yet the news item that ran the next day focused on Reshma's public exposure, not the busting of the racket of sex workers and middlemen from states like Karnataka and Andhra Pradesh. In contrast with that of Shakeela, Reshma's film career was mostly limited to soft-porn films, and she remained identifiable to viewers only through her screen roles.

The police inspector manning the station to which Reshma was brought used his mobile phone to illegally shoot and leak video of her interrogation.[72] The footage circulated widely on MMS (Multimedia Messaging Service) and social media sites. The uploaded video received mixed responses, with many viewers pointing to its unwarranted humiliation of the actress. Some even pointed out that the officer's zooming in and out had a stripping effect. The video was marked by a confessional drive that conjoined Reshma's personal history with her involvement in soft-porn films. Although the police inspector who was interrogating Reshma is absent from the screen, his presence is apparent in his handling of the mobile phone camera, directing Reshma's gaze to the center of the frame. Beginning with his use of Malayalam-peppered Hindi to his passing reference to his colleagues about soft-porn films, his looming presence determines Reshma's humiliation. At the same time, the officer asserts his knowledge of soft-porn films by mentioning his experience of having seen these films and noting that he recently conducted a raid at a CD shop where Reshma's films were widely distributed. Other media reports on Reshma's arrest make note of the fact that the other two women arrested with Reshma were also soft-porn actresses—an allegation that one of them refutes in the interrogation video.[73] The officer questions Reshma about the details of the soft-porn films she acted in and the whereabouts of other soft-porn actresses, such as Shakeela and Sindhu. By addressing her in broken Hindi and asking how much Malayalam she had learned by acting in soft-porn films, he invokes her outsider status.

The interrogating officer's framing of Reshma is reflective of the larger discourse on sexuality and the public sphere. The frequent zooming in and out on Reshma's face, the demand for immediate responses, and the instructions to look straight at the camera all reflect a shift of control. Although Reshma's presence on-screen in her films was marked by her control over her image, the interrogation video reduces her to a failed actress who turned to prostitution because of her straitened circumstances.[74] An *India Times* article titled "Tragic Life of Indian Porn Star Reshma" goes so far as to blame the soft-porn industry for her plight: "Reshma never made it big in mainstream cinema, in fact pimps got the better of her, and she got involved in the dirty business of adult films."[75] This exposure video not only constitutes a violation of privacy but also sets up soft-porn as the catalyst in this story of alleged moral decline. Framed as both a perpetrator and a victim of the "flesh trade," Reshma's stint as a soft-porn actress is used against her to circulate her interrogation video as a public image.[76] Here the idea of outing or publicly displaying unauthorized images contributes to a disciplining process that is meant to counter nonnormative modes of conduct. The act of "slut-shaming"—that is, publicly humiliating women perceived to be promiscuous—has become a widely used disciplining strategy, especially on social media, to inscribe codes of morality.[77] Starlets such as Reshma are refused the right to appeal violations of their privacy because they are already presumed to be morally questionable subjects. This denial of personhood and agency reduces them to the machinations of the camera-wielding institutional apparatus.

SOFT-PORN AND THE PRECARITY OF BODY-DOUBLING

If the lives and travails of soft-porn starlets expose one form of encoded and embodied precarity, the arena of body-doubling presents a form of labor relations that has been made even more invisible. Whereas dubbing artists have been unionized, people who work as body doubles have yet to enter trade guild discussions. Many soft-porn films, in fact, were dubbed by prominent dubbing artists, who, despite providing the recognizable moans that accompanied sex scenes, had successful careers in the mainstream industry. The same is not true of body doubles. Surayya Bhanu's autobiographical account *Dupe*, published in 2010, offers an alternative narrative of soft-porn from the vantage point of such invisible labor. As a body double who performed for actresses such as Shakeela, Bhanu incorporates invisibility and failure as the organizing principles of her narration. The book is dedicated to "actresses who were unknown," like her—a statement she reiterates in the preface and when she writes:

> No one who has failed has revealed what happened to them. I think that the readers ought to know the stories of those who have failed as well ... stories of those who have left their dreams to take up a career in cinema after having gone through unspeakable traumas.[78]

Bhanu's account corroborates many insider stories that I encountered during my fieldwork in Kodambakkam. In the parlance of the film industry, *body double* signifies an actor or junior artist who performs sequences that are attributable to stars. It is a process of investing labor and time into a role for which one's name can never be credited. Contractual terms sometimes forbid these actors from identifying themselves as body doubles or giving out any information about the production process. The disconnect between the body and the face means that body-doubling rests on an attrition of value. Erased of all identifiable features, the double's body is provided for a reduced wage. The double's labor is distinct in its invisibility insofar as it disappears the moment it is associated with someone else's face and credited to their name. The body double thus exists in an economy in which she is doubly disposable: she takes up the scenes left behind by stars and, at the same time, is pushed to the brink of job insecurity given the highly replaceable nature of her task. Bhanu's narrative teases out these complicated meanings of being a body double and provides insight into the actual work of soft-porn production.

The double's work involves consciously giving up ownership over one's on-screen body by allowing it to be edited onto the star's head. This leaves the body double in the precarious position of inhabiting a screen image that they cannot reclaim. The fragmentation of the body into different parts leaves the body double with no agency to make their identity public or to openly assert that the body seen on-screen is theirs. The body double's identity is perched on the precipice of obscurity—neither faciality nor labor can allow her individuation. Body-doubling pays abysmally, and many doubles are primarily motivated by the hope that by being part of the industry they will catch a break. If apprenticeship is the norm in the tinsel-town economy, for the body double it is the willful erasure of one's identity. And whereas apprentices may lay claim to the credits that are rightfully theirs, for body doubles, laying claim is tantamount to exposing the inner workings of the industry.

Bhanu also refers to the disposability and devaluation of labor that is central to doubling. Because bodies ultimately do not bear individual signifiers as strikingly as do faces, many newcomers to Kodambakkam were attracted to the job of doubling (always replaceable by another acceptable body). The job's popularity made it harder for Bhanu to land other roles and effectively cost her bargaining power to negotiate terms. The unacknowledged nature of body-double work means that the immediate impact of her labor and performance are constrained by the need to remain discreet. All throughout her stint in the industry, Bhanu's status was that of someone else's "dupe"—a generic English label that also stands in for cheating, hoodwinking, or deceiving. Shakeela's reluctance to perform topless scenes was known to production personnel who arranged for a body double to perform the sequences she refused to take on. Shakeela also recounts that when she entered into contracts for films, she was very clear that she would not perform any topless shots and these would be filmed separately by a body double or dupe.[79] This body double performed not only the topless sequences but also any intimate scenes that were shot separately as cut-pieces. These cut-pieces were purportedly circulated as images of Shakeela, blurring the otherwise sharp lines of distinction that separate the star from the double.

Shakeela's use of a body double might seem counterintuitive given her status and iconicity as a soft-porn star. The work of Shakeela and Bhanu demonstrate that body-doubling operates by foregrounding the primacy of the star and the embodied value of her stardom. Shakeela's face and status remained the primary motivation for doubling. Shakeela's use of what I call "visibility capital" could be leveraged by Bhanu, but Bhanu's body could assume value only when conjoined with Shakeela's face at the editing table. Visibility capital is premised on the recognition of star value. Shakeela's image was used as currency for generic recognition at her peak and in her association with sex education programs after the soft-porn boom. At the same time, Bhanu's bargaining power was curtailed because visibility capital does not entail equal benefits for all parties.[80] Bhanu writes that she had to be satisfied with what the producer paid her and that she had to discover short- and long-term strategies to manage her resources. Body doubles are the film precariat par excellence, not just in the soft-porn industry but in film at large.[81]

CONCLUSION

In attempting to unravel the constitutive roles that precarity plays in soft-porn production cultures, I have examined how Kodambakkam's tinsel-town economy shaped the social life of subjects and impacted tasks such as body-doubling that are often marginalized or made invisible. The soft-porn industry's casualization of labor and transformation of work arrangements had ramifications for how actors, technicians, and body doubles engaged with freelancing. The idea of discontinuous labor that I have elaborated in the case of soft-porn cinema is distinct from the idea of the "new precariat," which conjoins precariousness and the proletariat to signify the emergence of a new political subjectivity that involves forms of collective organizing and modes of expression.[82] Scholars such as Louise Waite have argued that precarity can offer hope and possibilities for disparate groups that have been marginalized and fragmented to unite.[83] At the same time, precarity is an experience without uniform ramifications that can nevertheless contribute to conversations about structural inequalities. Although sparks of organizing took off in soft-porn filmmaking, they were sidelined by backlash from the mainstream film industry and the social stigma that marked the soft-porn industry as a morally reprehensible and socially infectious machine.

My respondents expressed an awareness of the industry's exploitative arrangements, and their accounts suggested they sought to make the best of the given opportunities. Cine-workers in soft-porn film production attempted to reinvent the rules of the game in order to manage contingencies. Be it Shakeela's precarious stardom or the body double's performance, this labor remained hinged on performers' awareness of their own identity as risk takers. Even though many failed to sustain their careers after the soft-porn industry fizzled out in the mid-2000s, they offered resistance to the dominant, exclusionary industrial patterns and networks that were crucial to subsequent discussions in trade guild forums. As one of my respondents put it, "we might have failed miserably, but still we tried to work against the odds and speak about expropriation of our labor."[84]

4

The Alternative Transnational

Migration, Media, and Soft-Porn

Malayalam soft-porn emerged through various native and foreign influences, mobilizing transnational circuits and traversing national and regional boundaries. Whereas its native influences included erotic pulp fiction and sex literature that circulated through the formats of *kambikathakal* and *rathikathakal*, among its foreign influences, American exploitation cinema imported into India in the 1970s and 1980s was the most immediate. Similar mechanisms of flow can be seen in Nitin Govil's analysis of American film prints that entered South Asia after successfully transiting other international markets.[1] Transit, then, is central to understanding cinema as a circulating cultural object that has meanings beyond the text and the frame. Further, many Malayalam soft-porn films were financed by expatriate Indians living in the Middle Eastern Gulf, and they, in turn, began to circulate in the Gulf through pirate networks. Thus, Malayalam soft-porn is not an isolated cultural and industrial form, as the specificity of the descriptor "Malayalam" may suggest, but "transcends the national as autonomous cultural particularity while respecting it as a powerful symbolic force."[2] In this formulation, Malayalam soft-porn reflects the potential for "local, regional and diasporic film cultures to affect, subvert and transform national and transnational cinemas."[3] Such regional and local film cultures, as Govil shows, can "provincialize" dominant film cultures (in his analysis, Hollywood). This requires an epistemic reorientation that "defies the grammar of mobility through which the narrative of global domination is most often communicated."[4] A similar provincialization becomes necessary when discussing Malayalam soft-porn, which, as a filmmaking practice, aligns with all three of these formulations: it transcends the local, it interfaces with other locals in a field of porous exchanges, and it transits through various kinds of markets.

But while it is almost natural to talk about "transnational" cinema in terms of its opposition to national cinemas (i.e., in terms of treaty productions, international distribution, and labor outsourcing),[5] the uncritical adoption of the idea of transnationalism, as Mette Hjort warns, can often result in treating the concept as a general qualifier that can be made to stick to almost anything in a largely globalized world.[6] In an era where porous borders and outsourced labor form the general environment for film production, the nation's boundaries are not the only portals to the transnational. Although such official infrastructures of transnationalism remain important for cinema, I explore the more informal underground circuits of Malayalam soft-porn, their meanings for diasporic populations, and their work in negotiating cultural imaginaries between home and abroad. Caren Kaplan and Inderpal Grewal's postulation that transnationalism is constituted by migration flows, the emergence of alternative identities that are not primarily national, and diasporic formations, is also key.[7] Accordingly, I approach Malayalam soft-porn through the lens of what I term the "alternative transnational"—a paradigm for understanding media flows that centers regional formations to map transient connections among stakeholders who are situated outside the boundaries of the nation-state.

The process of vernacularizing cinema's forms and possibilities, as well as tracking its global flows, allows us to reread the region and the ways its diasporic communities use it to consolidate their identities and navigate structures of belonging and ownership under uncertain conditions of citizenship. The dominant perception of the Non-Resident Indian (NRI) community, at both a state level and in popular discourse, is that its members connect the home country and its diasporic satellites; further, they are seen as a core constituency for replenishing the home country through remittances.[8] The unilateral celebration of successful western-bound NRIs in dominant narratives excludes Indian diasporic communities in the Gulf from those in the skilled and semiskilled sectors who are considered beneficiaries of welfare. Kerala's relationship to the Gulf is marked by this multifaceted and uneven connectivity: as Kerala's unofficial "satellite" colony, the Gulf is a place of prosperity and vocational mobility, but it is also a location of anxiety in terms of its strained relationship with Kerala's lower-income group of expatriates.

Tracking these dispersed histories requires a blend of archival research, discourse analysis, and ethnographic observation in sites such as Mumbai, Chennai, and the UAE. Conducting fieldwork among both diasporic Indians and Indian officials on issues such as pornography presented a very particular set of problems. Citing confidentiality clauses, officials at the NFDC in Mumbai were unwilling to entertain questions on the failed NRI scheme that facilitated the import of American exploitation cinema and pushed me to approach retired officials and agents who had imported films to India. On the other hand, questions about pornography often alienated my respondents in the Gulf, who were motivated to portray themselves as ideal immigrants unsullied by negative stereotypes. This necessitated developing an array of alternative approaches to data collection that included interviewing returned emigrants and circulating a separate questionnaire that emphasized diasporic media consumption practices more broadly. Such methodological conundrums point out that the "object" (soft-porn), as well as its traces and coding, transform as it travels and merges with the varied cultural and social positions of my subjects. Negotiations between regional identities (as "Malayalis"), national identities (as "Indians"), and diasporic identities (as migrant workers in the Gulf) become central both to the status of Malayalam soft-porn as an object and to the subject positions it inaugurates in its audiences.

THE MANY (REGIONAL) LIVES OF MALAYALAM SOFT-PORN

In relation to Indian cinema, the term "regional" is usually affixed to cinemas in languages other than Hindi. The popular Bollywood cinema of India that often stands in as "Indian cinema" outside the country is a significant (and dominant) constituent of India's cinemascape, but hardly represents the complexities of the country's diverse linguistic and regional groups, which have their own cinematic traditions. India's many regional cinemas often have to compete with Bollywood's overwhelming popularity and financial resources.[9] Correspondingly, regional cinemas that have distinct and flourishing production and exhibition practices are relatively understudied or discussed as part of the "national cinema" paradigm (although things seem to be changing slightly in the era of streaming networks and the national and global success of south Indian films such as *Pushpa: The Rise* [dir. Sukumar, 2021] and *RRR* [dir. S. S. Rajamouli, 2022]).

Andrew Higson argues that the paradigm of national cinema is "prescriptive rather than descriptive, citing what *ought* to be the national cinema, rather than describing the actual cinematic experience of popular audiences."[10] As a phrase, "Indian cinema" drums up an image of a nation that is territorially bound and unified. But cinema has been at the center of conflict between mainstream India and regions that are marked as ridden with insurgents, as, for instance, in some northeastern states where separatist groups have unofficially banned Bollywood films.[11] Such measures react to the government's hypersecuritized management of civilian populations in these states under the pretext of curbing militancy—a reflection of Ravi Vasudevan's postulation that the state "puts together diverse cultural and linguistic formations within a somewhat forced political and administrative integrity."[12] With this in mind, I turn to what Gayatri Gopinath posits as a "South-South relationality between seemingly discrete regional spaces that in fact bypasses the nation."[13] Following her cue, I approach Malayalam soft-porn through the conceptual lens of the alternative transnational, which allows subsumed regional identities to be articulated as simultaneously local and global without being constrained by the national. Joining "soft-porn" with "Malayalam" affixes a regional qualifier to the cinematic object and mobilizes diverse imaginations of the regional, national, and transnational that are mediated by class and cultural norms.

That said, my use of the phrase "Malayalam soft-porn" elicited discomfort from some respondents, forcing me to rephrase my area of research depending on the interview subject and the institutional frameworks in which they were embedded. Although "soft-porn film" emerged as a generic label in the Malayalam industry only in the 1990s, the history of the term can be traced back to its journalistic use in the 1970s and 1980s to refer to Malayalam films with sexually charged narratives that were distributed outside the state of Kerala. A 1983 article in the *Maharashtra Herald* reported that the screening of the "Malayalam soft-porn" film *Crazy Lady* had to be canceled after demonstrations outside central Delhi's Odeon cinema hall by women activists from Janawadi Mahila Samiti (People's Women Group) and Young Women's Christian Association.[14] The author lists erotic titles such as *Sexy Boy, Sexy Night, Only One Night, Sex and Play, Sex and Rape, Sex Hungry,* and *Midnight Affairs.* As a result of the protests by women's groups, South Indian films with English titles were scrutinized to monitor the spread of soft-porn. Section 30 (3) of The Cinematograph (certification) Rules, 1983, requires that the duplicate of the censor certificates (both parts 1 and 11) be exhibited in the cinema halls on the days the film is shown. This was hardly followed by the cinema hall owners, as many of these "films were not always exhibited in the form they were certified."[15] The use of "erotic titles" in English and not in Malayalam or Hindi parallels the distribution of American exploitation films in India in the 1980s. The demonstrators' primary demand was for restrictions to be placed on the screening of "dubbed films," which allegedly flouted censorship regulations by inserting pornographic sequences. The categorization of these films as "dubbed films" positioned them as coming from outside the jurisdiction of the dominant Hindi-language belt and thus hinted at the geographical otherness that was imposed on them. Journalistic reports highlighted this as an example of Malayalam filmmakers' use of exploitation tactics—an allegation that often contrasted these films with the realist art cinema that was also associated with Kerala's film culture.

Although New Delhi is a cosmopolitan city with a mix of linguistic communities and migrants from all over the country who have moved there for work, the Malayalam soft-porn controversy put the Kerala-based community on tenterhooks. The Malayalam films that were retitled and circulated with English titles included *Night Duty, Evils of Rape, Sexy Body, Sexy Nights, Crazy Nights, Sex Life of Heroine, Sex Love, and Charm.* The debate and protests over obscenity and censorship assigned the Malayali community with the moral responsibility of taking a strong stance to guard their regional cinema from association with sex films. The Delhi Malayalee Association of Mayur Vihar addressed a letter to the Information and Broadcasting minister H. K. L. Bhagat asking for the stoppage of films "that are full of perverted sex scenes added illegally by the distributors and exhibitors" and noting how they have negatively affected the image and prestige of Keralites.[16] In the aftermath of the protests, a Delhi-based Malayali association organized a film discussion forum to showcase Kerala films in the right perspective and a seminar titled "Sex and Violence in Indian Cinema" that was attended by art cinema proponents like Adoor Gopalakrishnan.[17] In Ambala, in Haryana, the posters for *Private Life*, a Malayalam film, were removed under order of the deputy commissioner to weed out obscene material.[18] The South Indian Chamber of Commerce alleged that these concerns about South Indian films emerged from Bombay cinema's "step-motherly" treatment of regional cinemas, which did not get the visibility and loan provisions available for "purposeful films" funded by Film Finance Corporation (FFC). It was not just Malayalam films that bore the brunt of allegations that they were pornographic; the South Indian film industry in general received such rebuke. Thus, the circulation of Malayalam soft-porn in other parts of India was always preceded by notoriety—a trend that started with the distribution of *Avalude Ravukal* (Her nights) as a "sex" film because of the way it was marketed outside Kerala.

The term "Malayalam soft-porn" thus raises questions about what constitutes regional cinema in India's multilingual context. Malayalam cinema's association with unbridled sex unsettled regional filmmakers, who saw it as licensing both a dismissive attitude toward regional cinemas from South India and a forceful homogenization of all the South Indian film industries as the "other" of mainstream Indian cinema—something encapsulated by the catch-all label "Madrasi films." Journalistic reportage of the time gestures to the sexualized imagination of South Indian cinema—Malayalam films, in particular—that peddled the notion that an infectious South was threatening the chaste character of the country. This devalued status partly explains why pseudonyms were so widely used in soft-porn production to guard the identities of the film crew.

This tension was palpable when I interviewed Ravi Kottarakara, chair of the South Indian Chamber of Commerce, during the Indian Cinema Centenary Celebrations in Chennai in 2013. He perceived my work as "delegitimizing" regional cinemas' rich traditions by appending "Malayalam" to "soft-porn."[19] For Kottarakara, the combination of "soft-porn" with the regional marker "Malayalam" contributed to the stereotyped depiction of "Madras films" as the harbinger of sex and violence. The perceived "devaluation" of the regional in these responses points to two versions of the area—some of my respondents were specifically speaking about Malayalam films when they uttered the phrase "regional cinema," whereas others spoke of a larger category of "South Indian cinema" that had to constantly mark its difference from Bollywood.

The region, as it is invoked in these reactions, exposes a built-in boundedness that can elicit protectionist measures to safeguard their interests. Regional cinemas have always tried to protect their distribution-exhibition interests from the influx of content from Hollywood and Hindi cinema. For instance, the South Indian state of Karnataka had an informal ban on dubbing films from other languages until the Competition Commission of India intervened and passed an order allowing it in 2018.[20] The ban, instituted by private, trade-related bodies associated with Kannada film and television in the 1980s, also draws from the pro-Kannada cultural movement.[21] Intended to support local creativity, the ban paved the way for an alternative culture of remaking films in Karnataka. The remaking protocols meant that films in other languages could not be dubbed into Kannada, but Kannada films could be dubbed into other languages to be distributed outside Karnataka and overseas. This is significant because soft-porn filmmakers took advantage of this arrangement very early on by making original content in Kannada and then dubbing it into other languages. *Aadyapaapam* (The first sin, 1988), a film that is often seen as a direct precursor to the soft-porn wave of the 1990s, was produced in Karnataka. The director of the film, P. Chandrakumar, used a subsidy instituted by the Karnataka Film Chamber of Commerce that was originally meant to promote Kannada filmmakers. Curiously, while *Aadyapaapam* went on to become hugely popular as a Malayalam soft-porn film, today it essentially means a version that is dubbed from Kannada. Thus, even when linguistic and regional specificity are invoked, they can unsettle the logic of protectionism that undergird them.

The regional status of soft-porn surfaced in my fieldwork when a handful of my respondents based in the Middle East narrated their experiences of watching soft-porn on video tape—a format that allows for relative safety as it can be watched in the privacy of the home. In different cultural contexts in the 1980s, video was perceived as a "bad" cultural object that was seen as "creatively impoverished" because of its association with porn.[22] In the Indian context, video was also the harbinger of piracy; in the 1980s, video was reported to be the format with "the latest releases from Hindi and regional cinema, as well as a reasonable selection of pornography."[23] Video porn coexisted with celluloid pornography and encouraged the production of direct-to-video films sold through video libraries. Affordable and easy-to-use, magnetic tape allowed pornography to circulate widely and be easily reproduced, which made it a lucrative investment that turned quick profits. U-Matic and Betamax tapes featuring adult content were sold in video libraries in India and Dubai, along with clandestinely sold copies of *Screw* that were passed around among patrons on the lookout for "foreign" magazines. Many of my respondents recounted how they came across Malayalam soft-porn films among the pirated CDs that were sold by door-to-door salesmen in Dubai and Sharjah, and in Dubai's Karama Market, which was famous for counterfeit goods.[24] In Bahrain, Malayalam soft-porn was available for rent in places like Gold Souq, a neighborhood in Manama, where shops that sold phone cards also sold videos.[25]

Describing his encounter with Malayalam soft-porn in Bahrain, one of my respondents, Narayanan, recounted that erotic magazines such as *Muttuchippi* were available in stationery shops that sold Malayalam newspapers and magazines.[26] Sometimes the magazines were published with a Gulf Malayali audience specifically in mind. *The Sex Education Encyclopedia*, published by Moral Books in 1978, included a separate announcement for Gulf Malayalis that listed the details of book marketers based in the UAE, Kuwait, Doha, Bahrain, Oman, and Saudi Arabia.[27] Many adult magazines, such as *Honeymoon Guide*, also advertised soft-porn films and featured catchy quotes and images from the films to directly reach out to prospective viewers in the Gulf. The adult magazine *Crossfire* featured storylines exploring the double lives of Malayali women who were recruited to work as maids in Dubai but ended up performing sex work. Like the narrative tradition of first person used in *Rathikathakal*, many of these stories feature women directly addressing the readers as they write about their experiences in the Gulf.

In the censorial atmosphere of the Middle East, it was common practice to label porn films as "mythological films" or "home videos" to minimize risk if a purchaser were caught by the Mutawa, the special police unit that enforces religious observations and public morality. Recounting an early encounter with soft-porn in Dubai, another respondent, Thampy, stated that when he was approached by a vendor who tried to sell him soft-porn films, he was too scared to even look at the CDs: "It was as if being in Dubai made it seem like soft-porn films were illegal. . . . I have watched these films in theaters in India, but never felt like they were illegal there."[28] Soft-porn DVDs were bought and sold with a sense of trepidation, arranged alongside mainstream films with genre labels such as "melodrama" and "thriller" to hide erotic content from the authorities, while leaving it open for those who possessed the cultural and contextual knowledge to decode them. In contrast to the "backroom" section of American video stores that Dan Herbert describes as cordoning off adult video from the rest of the inventory, Gulf Malayali video rentals hid adult films in plain sight.[29] Isaac, a former video library owner who sold soft-porn along with his regular fare of Hindi, Tamil, and Malayalam films in Dubai, stated that soft-porn CDs sold in video parlors might look to an outsider like "any other Malayalam film," except for the text in Malayalam promising juicy elements. Often, cover images would be sanitized, transforming, as Isaac described it, even Shakeela into "a schoolteacher or a middle-aged family woman."[30] Some of my Pakistani informants also spoke of soft-porn films that were available in Karachi's Rainbow Center in Saddar, one of the hubs of video piracy in Pakistan. For instance, Wahab, a cleaning worker, said:

> In the laborer camp that I worked in the industrial area of Mussafeh, I stayed with a group of Indians. I knew of these films from them, but never thought I would find them in a kiosk in Saddar. My immediate response when I found these films stacked with Bollywood was to tell my friend, this is from Kerala, not Bollywood.[31]

Responses like Wahab's starkly contrast the uneasiness demonstrated by officials such as Kottarakara. For this other set of diasporic respondents, the experience of recognizing "Malayalam soft-porn" was marked by nostalgia for the homeland. Such starkly different responses in conceiving how illicit media objects evoke different senses of relationality in transnational contexts resonate with Kathryn C. Hardy's argument that the region "is constantly on the move."[32] The circulation of soft-porn in the Gulf illustrates how the consolidation of regional identities and diffusion of generic markers create alternative transnational imaginations that are speckled with regional traces. Alternative transnationalism then, is mediated by two contrasting poles of formal and informal networks: first, the formal circuits that national film institutions envisaged as they promoted trade relations by inviting the Indian diaspora to trade in "foreign" made films in India; and second, the specific infrastructures of diasporic media that targeted the Malayali audience in the Gulf.

TRANSNATIONALISM, THE NRI SCHEME, AND THE SEXUAL IMAGINARY

As Sudha Rajagopalan demonstrates in her work on Indian films in the Soviet Union, transnational flows that are initiated and mediated by national institutions often involve adjustments that betray the planned logic of diplomatic treaties and trade exchanges, as more informal networks come into play.[33] The transnational history of Malayalam soft-porn likewise involves the failure of a state-initiated scheme that exceeded its intended purpose and caused a major setback to government policies on importing films. In October 1984, the Indian government initiated the NRI scheme, which allowed emigrant Indians to import foreign films to India with a payment of $15,000. The emergence of NRIs as an important constituency that could contribute to the home country's overall financial welfare was an important development in the mid-1980s. The NRI scheme was envisioned to increase the flow of foreign exchange into India. The NFDC, the centralized body tasked with promoting Indian cinema, was authorized to manage it, and the administrative officer of the CBFC oversaw it. The profits accrued through the scheme were not repatriable and had to be invested in India. The scheme was a culmination of a tense atmosphere that arose from institutional constraints on bodies such as Indian Motion Pictures Export Corporation (IMPEC) and the CBFC, and was part of the government's attempt to concretize NRIs as a crucial node in India's development.

In the late 1970s, "black money" in the Indian economy became a cause for concern as hoarding and speculation reached an all-time high. In response, the Indian Government introduced the Manufacturing and Other Companies (Auditor's Report) Order, 1975 (MAOCARO), which obligated management to maintain records and auditors to carry out physical verification of same. Interestingly, amid calls to identify hoarders, news reports portrayed the Indian film industry as one of the primary sites bypassing regulations by using black money for transactions ranging from remuneration for stars to advance payments for exhibitors.[34] The speculative nature of filmmaking, high rates of interest, and uncertain returns meant that the calculation of box-office receipts and tax collection did not always lead to a neat figure. Strategies to put black money into circulation included using false vouchers to inflate production costs, forging arrangements with distributors to pilfer the prints directly from labs as a part of the 8 percent permissible waste, and even misusing subsidy schemes such as the one instituted by the Maharashtra government for color films in 1975.[35]

Issues with the foreign exchange reserves, for which such black money was partially blamed, had loomed large since the 1960s. As Nitin Govil notes, India's reserves were depleted in the 1960s, and this pushed the country to expand the reach of its cinema into the UK and the US in a bid to reach globalized markets.[36] This resulted in India issuing a blockade on repatriations of profits accrued from distributing and exhibiting Indian films in the US. In 1964, officers of the Enforcement Directorate of the Reserve Bank of India raided the residences of nine leading film personalities in Bombay and recovered four hundred foreign gold coins, currency worth thirty lakh rupees ($630,000), and unmanufactured gold.[37] The Public Accounts Committee of parliament even suggested opening a databank that could keep tabs on expenditures in film production. In 1957, a proposal was put forth by the Indian government to the Motion Picture Export Association of America (MPEA) to reduce film imports to 10 percent of the figures from 1947. The quota was later raised to 75 percent under the condition that remittance would be restricted to 12.5 percent and the remaining funds were to be placed in a blocked account in India.[38] Called "blocked funds," this arrangement meant that if distributors earned one hundred rupees in India, they could only take back twenty five, and the remaining seventy-five rupees, called the "interest fee," had to be used in India. Consequently, studios blocked funds to finance co-productions and to lease theaters in India. Indian film producers were allowed quotas to spend the foreign exchange abroad to encourage export.

Until the 1980s, the only agencies that could import films to India were the MPEA, NFDC, and Soveksportfil'm. The responsibility of film export fell on the Film Import Contract Registration Committee, but in 1979, IMPEC, formed in 1963, took on the sole responsibility of exporting feature films from India.[39] Because IMPEC sold Indian films to other countries and charged a commission on all export deals, the Indian Film Exporters Association (IFEA) and the All India Film Producer's Council (AIFPC) perceived IMPEC as a monopoly and placed a hold on supplying films to it.[40] In 1980, IMPEC and FFC merged to form the NFDC. In the 1980s, the Indian economy began to face further fiscal imbalances due to problems in the balance of payments.[41] The quasi-welfare system of Nehruvian socialism coupled with the red tape involved in procuring licenses (referred to as "license-raj") constrained entrepreneurial prospects. Despite increase in exports, interest payments and imports rose faster, leading to an external payment crisis.[42] The NRI scheme emerged because of the convergence of this history of larger economic forces and film-institutional histories. The move to incorporate

NRIs as stakeholders reflected the Indian government's need to articulate its commitment to acknowledging the economic potential of the emigrant community.

The 1980s also saw the emergence of a consumer economy routed through the diasporic community and their import of foreign goods to India. The popularity of video cassette recorders (VCRs), video cassette players (VCPs), and video cassettes in India allowed for a distinctly transnational imagination to develop. For instance, the Japanese-made Aksai VS-23 was sold in India with a warranty that could be used for service and replacement of parts in Egypt, India, Jordan, Pakistan, the Philippines, Syria, and Thailand. It was advertised with the slogan: "Why settle for the national favorite when you can get the international leader?"[43] Locally made video cassettes and cassette players soon followed. In 1984, Pakistan removed the import tax duty for VHS video recorders, which also boosted their importation from the Gulf.[44]

The consumer economy of the 1980s was joined by a shadow economy of smuggling and piracy, as human carriers brought video equipment and computer parts into India from regions such as Southeast Asia (including Hong Kong) and the Gulf.[45] Along with the usual tactics of using carbonized paper to circumvent X-ray scans and strategically placing contacts at customs offices and checks, carriers brought in dutiable items like VCRs and stereos. Paying the required duties on these items was meant to distract officers from noticing contraband items carried in separate bags, the rationale being that customs personnel would not suspect a person who paid a substantial amount of duty of being a smuggler.[46] In addition to concerns about smuggling, anxieties about film piracy also became a core concern of the 1980s. In a 1986 statement, the Film Federation of India (FFI) noted that video piracy affected the export of Indian films to the Gulf countries.[47] The immediate causes of concern included the unlicensed nature of video libraries; the ease of under-the-table transactions, such as renting sex videos; the availability of bootleg copies of newly released films; and the projection of illegally made copies of 35mm films.[48] The massive spread of video came to be seen as a phenomenon that the law could not keep up with. The state governments, in the meantime, established regulatory mechanisms to check the proliferation of video parlors. By 1986, the number of video libraries had increased to 3,000, while the number of theaters had decreased to 2,400, creating a panic that signaled the invasion of video.[49] In March 1984, the Cinematograph Act of 1952 was amended to include the provision that all video cassettes must carry a new censor certificate.[50] Because state governments collected entertainment tax, it was considered their responsibility to ensure that regulatory mechanisms were devised to contain video piracy.[51]

In this period of the 1980s, such developments gave rise to new anxieties about culture and industry. The import of American exploitation films into India under the NRI scheme, which directly impacted Malayalam soft-porn films, is one important ramification. The increase in the import of American films was seen as a cause for concern because they were oversaturating the market and depriving

Indian feature films of a fair run in the exhibition circuit. Contrary to the figure of the NRI as the booster of foreign exchange and the upwardly mobile social class envisaged in the film-import scheme, many interested parties based in India used their connections abroad to import foreign films without consideration of aesthetic value or film form. In Madras, the dealers of NRI films included G. B. S. Mani of Kartik Enterprises, Dr. Sreenivasan of Subasri Pictures, Y. M. Elias of Indo-Overseas Films, and J. Jaya Kumar of Metro Film Corporation. At times, their deals were mediated by agents based in Southeast Asian countries such as Singapore and Malaysia who would connect the NRIs with procurers based in India.[52] Many clients who imported these films were based in the UK, Chile, and the Middle East.[53] The details of foreign films were handed over to diasporic Indian agents who imported and exported films in Southeast Asia at large. *The Times of India* reports that "Local film distributors with blood brothers, cousins, miscellaneous relatives and friends settled abroad saw this as a whopping business prospect. Films were brought in by the NRI but in many cases sold or co-opted to Indian distributors."[54] In contrast to foreign films, which were labeled based on the country from which they were being imported, the imported films were publicized as hybrid packages that included a mix of Swedish, Danish, and English films. Despite efforts to prevent unauthorized circulation, many of the films were distributed illegally to theaters and were featured as "English" films. Because import duties were associated with these films, the NFDC issued permits for import in the form of a letter addressed to customs. To facilitate the selection of films, the Indian government recommended the constitution of a Film Imports Committee. The films cleared by the committee were sent to the CBFC. It was during this stage that officials at the CBFC realized the discrepancy between the written scripts and their audiovisual execution. When the CBFC denied certificates to films that were screened by the committee, they were in effect questioning the rationale behind the selection of these films. From 1985 to 1987, 558 films were submitted for clearance, of which only 296 were cleared and imported. Another report puts the number of films submitted for clearance during the same time at 198, of which 45 were refused certificates by the CBFC.[55] The discarded prints entered distribution networks, and the execution of the import policy was blamed for giving leeway to NRIs to import questionable content without much oversight by the Film Imports Committee.

Questions were raised by institutional bodies like the FFI about the rampant presence of sexually explicit sequences in the films that were cleared by the import committee without any note of disapproval. In raids conducted in the aftermath of the controversy, officials discovered that sex sequences unrelated to the storyline had been interpolated into some of the films. Even editing labs like Vijaya Vauhini were raided to check if the negatives were in order. As Reddi, who managed the lab, said: "If there was any interpolation, the lab wasn't involved. If anyone comes to us with a censor certificate, that's enough. Whether a film is aesthetic or rubbishy is not our look out. It's humanly impossible to keep a quality check."[56] Similar sentiments were expressed by the Prasad Lab personnel when asked if they had come across *thundu* in their editing of the films.[57] Moreover, it was common practice to organize secret previews for imported NRI films or screen them from an unexpurgated video print to assure the distributor that the "bits" were included in the package.[58] In an attempt to clarify the procedures in the certification of NRI films, then CBFC chair Vikram Singh stated: "Our functions end with the recommendation of an "A" or "UA" certificate. We also make physical cuts—the objectionable portions from a film are deleted from the positive and negative prints. There's nothing more we can do by way of censorship."[59]

Voicing the need to set up a "cinema cell" to monitor film screenings and keep interpolation at bay, Singh emphasized that enforcement was the responsibility of state governments—the central government had decided that the state governments should be the ones to step in and seize the illegal prints. While the Ministry of Human Resource Development blamed the exhibitors' and distributors' "distorted publicity" for influencing the public perception of these films as low quality, cinema hall owners turned on the press, alleging that they had exploited the crisis by running magazine stories about the same film posters they had condemned and profiting from the sales.[60] By 1986, the tug of war between the CBFC and the AIFPC regarding explicit scenes resulted in a temporary pause in sending films for certification. In their memorandum to the Human Resource development minister, the council urged that Singh be replaced by someone "from the film industry itself."[61] At the end of the day, the tussle over censorship boiled down to who oversaw it. Singh was seen as representing the film critics, and he was associated with the institutions he had been part of—namely, *The Times of India* and *Filmfare* magazine. Amid these controversies, the Ministry of Information and Broadcasting decided to review the NRI scheme in 1988, and a panel was constituted to vet the films before they went to the censor board. An eleven-member Import Selection Committee (ISC), headed by film producer Kantilal Rathore, was appointed in January 1988, following the new import policy for films. The ISC decided that in order to be imported, films should have run in international film festival circuits or have received "rave reviews" in "prominent film journals."[62] They should also provide "clean healthy entertainment" and not violate governmental regulations. Reports soon began to circulate that the subcommittee rejected 50 percent of NRI films, emphasizing that the guidelines were in place and arbitrary imports would no longer be entertained.[63]

Realizing that the NRI scheme had become a quagmire, the Ministry of Information and Broadcasting intervened and issued a notification to the censor board that their purview was limited to certification and they need not worry about the quality of imported films. In the absence of any guidelines, the first fifty-seven applications for import passed through the committee without screenings of the films; the only condition was that they were accompanied by a check. In hindsight, even NFDC officials agreed that quality had never been a priority and that the complaints that these films included sex and violence were valid.[64] The imported films, some of which the CBFC had objected to, were left at a government warehouse to be destroyed. But these prints reached distributors through scrap dealers and agents and eventually hit the exhibition circuit. The prints were salvaged because the agents had managed to get lab negatives before they sent the films for certification. Many of these films were screened in theaters across Calcutta, Bombay, Madras, and Delhi. The NFDC could not curb their circulation without acknowledging that the prints that were in the warehouse had been smuggled in by their own people. Statements by NFDC officials expressed their sense of helplessness in streamlining the rejection process. Even during my correspondence with officials, many refused outright to talk about the scheme. Others who were part of the handling of the scheme wanted assurance that they would not be quoted.[65] The failed scheme exposed the limitations of censorship's regulatory framework. When faced with the allegation that the imported films celebrated sex and violence, some NRI importers met with the joint secretary of the Ministry of Information and Broadcasting to appeal the scrapping of the scheme. "A miniscule 10 percent of the importers maligned the NRIs as 'nonreliable Indians,'" said Jaya Kumar, an importer based in Madras.[66]

Some of my respondents who imported these films were forthcoming about the varied methods they used to bypass the system: some reduplicated negative prints at the time of import, while others smuggled reels in their hand luggage or paid carriers to smuggle them from abroad. While a film was stuck at the censor board awaiting certification, duplicated copies would be processed and dispatched to distributors.[67] One importer cleared a film by using Section 126 of the Customs Act, which allows the importer to pay a penalty to customs to clear the objectionable material. Another frequently used technique was changing the title of the film during import. For instance, Puran Chawla of Lord Films imported a film titled *Hot Heir*, but the real film was *My Tutor*, a teen exploitation film.[68] Similarly, the Greek exploitation film *Revanche* (dir. Nicos Vergitsis, 1983) was retitled *Pyar Phir Ek Baar* (Love once again).[69] Additionally, many exploitation films were illegally transported to India from the Middle East under the guise that they were waste celluloid headed for bangle factories.[70] This method of smuggling film prints was not unique to India: in the 1970s in the US, Cosmos Films made 16mm films featuring full nudity of "beaver films" (featuring female frontal nudity but not much sexual activity) and distributed the prints in mailing containers disguised as other kinds of freight.[71]

Distributors of soft-porn films were not the only ones who tricked Indian's censorship system by reworking the plot outlines that had been submitted to the NFDC or using the category of "sex education films" to justify their import.[72] Films from a wide variety of genres were illicitly brought in. One genre that stood out were nature documentaries such as *Sex and Animals* (dir. Harold Hoffman, 1969), which explored the mating rituals and sexual habits of different animals.[73] Exploitation films such as *Adam and Eve* (dir. Enzo Doria and Luigi Russo, Italy, 1983), *Carry on Emmanuelle* (dir. Gerald Thomas, UK, 1978), *Lonely Lady* (dir. Peter Sasdy, US, 1983), and *Daughter of the Jungle* (dir. Umberto Lenzi, Italy, 1982) formed a major category of imported films. Foreign sex education films were also cleared for general viewing in India and met packed audiences. Some of these films also came as a package deal in the form of an anthology, without credits or details of the director or production; this included titles such as *Tomboy* and *Life and Birth*.[74]

Although most of the films imported were unavailable to source for this book, I was fortunate to access a copy of *Main Aur Tum* (You and me; dir. Harihar, 1987), a 16mm film provided to me by its producer. As an indigenized version of sex education films, *Main Aur Tum* sourced footage from *It Could Happen to You* (dir. Stanley A. Long, Australia, 1976), which addressed sexually transmitted diseases (STDs); reels from the British Health Education Society; as well as a blow-up of 16mm film illustrating childbirth from other imported films.[75] Thus, like the insertion of *thundu* in soft-porn, NRI films allowed for an assemblage of practices whereby fragments of reels could easily transmute from one context to the other, carrying material traces from different source texts. Made in the tradition of educational material aimed at facilitating discussions around sexuality and intimacy, *Main Aur Tum* offers a critique of the conservative upbringing in India that deprives youth of having healthy interactions with the opposite sex. Framed through the figure of the sexologist (Om Shivpuri) and his handling of patients who consult him for treatment and advice, the documentary covers misconceptions around what couples should do on the "first night"—popular parlance for the wedding night, when a couple has sex—the film draws on popular cinematic imaginations, showcasing a series of still photographs from various Hindi films where stars like Randhir Kapoor, Rajesh Khanna, Amol Palekar, Jitendra, and Sanjeev Kumar are shown enacting the first night scene. *Main Aur Tum* received a fair amount of press; one newspaper article referred to it as the "sexyclopedia of the country" and noted the performance of actress Sonika Gill.[76] Through the figure of the expert, the film attempts to demystify stigmas about premature ejaculation and masculine performance during sex and makes a case for allowing couples to understand each other's sexual preferences by spending time together and to plan children when they are ready for it. Information about contraceptives, including foreign-brand condoms such as "Bugger," "Fourex," and "Sultan," and Indian-made Nirdodh, were interwoven into the film. Further, the film also offered information on different birthing methods and the need to preserve lactating mothers' milk so that working mothers can better negotiate their job responsibilities and child-care needs. In its pedagogic drive, the film also highlights the differences between male and female orgasm to show how partners could support each other in pleasurable sexual experiences. In fact, there is a direct takeaway for the audience that is inserted into the text of the film after discussing each phase of the relationship.

FIGURE 22. A news article on sex education films. Image courtesy National Film Archive of India.

This pedagogic legitimization was also supported by references to sexological tracts, including *Human Sexual Response* (Masters and Johnson), *Women's Experience of Sex* (Sheila Kitzenger), *The Hite Report* (Shere Hite), *Breast Feeding in Practice* (Elizabeth Helsing), and *Love and Sexuality* (Romie Goodchild), right at the beginning of the film. The film interpolates the viewer through direct address, asking them to partake in the case studies that the sexologist reveals through the discussion of the couples. The film's educational status enabled it to procure tax exemption from the Tamil Nadu Government. Interestingly, even though the film distanced itself from sexual titillation or erotic undertones in the use of nudity or female bodies, there were allegations that it used documentary format to showcase female nudity. News reports were quick to add that the film was produced in Madras, even though it featured a mix of actors from Bombay and Chennai, and then CBFC chief Vikram Singh alleged that the film was censored at Trivandrum (Kerala) and the Bombay office had asked the censor board in Kerala to provide all the requisite files, thus, placing the responsibility of illicit eruptions on the errant region.[77] Another article lamented that the film was directed by Hariharan (who used the pseudonym Harihar for this film), a product of the Film and Television Institute of India, and speculated that his association with *Main Aur Tum* could perhaps have come from "a weak moment" or "sheer desperation."[78]

Thus, NRI films and their associated sourcing practices provided the commercial impetus for many aspiring filmmakers to try out similar narrative patterns in the form of low-budget films (Fig. 22). The transnational circulation of these films helped fashion vernacular productions as well. Glamour cinema and sex education films were already in circulation by the time the NRI films entered the exhibition circuit. The scheme boosted the local production economy and was a historical precedent for soft-porn films, specifically in terms figuring out what would succeed in the market. One recurrent statement I heard from many soft-porn filmmakers was that they considered their films to be a continuation of the "English film" wave. Such statements also evoke the sense of legitimacy that soft-porn filmmakers were attempting to cultivate through their adoption of already existing practices that allowed exploitation films to circulate in Indian exhibition circuits.[79]

ALTERNATIVE INFRASTRUCTURES:
MALAYALI DIASPORIC MEDIASCAPES AND THE GULF

NRI films and their influence on Malayalam filmmakers demonstrate that transnational flows are also at work beyond the perceived centers of national boundaries. The popular imagination of Indian transnationalism has been marked by the dominant presence of westward-bound NRIs. As Madhavi Mallapragada points out, the NRI category emerged in the 1970s and 1990s to become "central to the migrant sensibilities of the diverse communities that are part of the loosely (and problematically) defined 'Indian diaspora in the United States.'"[80] The problematic preeminence of the West in discourses of Indian transnationalism breaks down in the case of regions such as Kerala, where the movement is not merely *not* from the center of the nation-state but also toward a non-Western location such as the Middle East. While Kerala is part of a "southern" Indian regional formation, it is also imbricated in a postcolonial "South Asian" formation. This unsettles the imagination of "regionalism" as something bounded within the Indian states and exposes a "transnational" regionalism based on cultural ties and geographical affinities that point toward a "localization" of the transnational imagination.

This localized transnationalism is evident in Kerala's affinity with the Arabian Sea and its long history of migration and flows with the Middle East (the Gulf) rather than with the West. The Kerala migration survey conducted by the Center for Development Studies (CDS) states that in 2018, 89.2 percent of the total emigrants from Kerala migrated to the Gulf.[81] The oil boom in the late 1960s and the infrastructural developments that followed attracted a substantial amount of migrant blue-collar labor to the Gulf Cooperation Council countries. As early as 1978, there were weekly flights from Trivandrum to Dubai, and illicit trade of contraband between Kerala and Dubai was also reported.[82] This longer history of exchange points to what Inderpal Grewal calls a network of "transnational connectivities," which are by nature uneven, incomplete, and always in flux.[83] Kerala's relationship to the Gulf is marked by an uneven connectivity where the lower-income group of migrants who form the substantial outmigrant category from Kerala are distinct from the upward mobility and return on investment envisaged in the NRI. In essence, the Gulf stands in as the location of "the dream" for the Malayali community. Similar to the "American Dream," this imagination of the Gulf is also fraught with internal contradictions that sometimes challenge and unsettle the picture-postcard imagination of a prosperous elsewhere. But the fact that this dreamscape replaces America (and the West, more broadly) with the Gulf challenges the dominant imagination of transnationalism, which upholds the journey to the West as a symbolic movement toward prosperity.

The emergence of diasporic televisual audiences illustrates how such internationalization is reflected in and through the media. In August 1993, Asianet debuted as the first television-on-air cable transmission. Because they needed imported equipment to set up their cable network and studio, Asianet decided to sell connections to NRIs. Asianet also started selling "Asianet Privilege NRI connections" in 1994, which allowed NRIs to gift an Asianet cable connection to their family based in Kerala, with the transaction being paid in foreign currency. To mobilize a dedicated audience base, the Asianet team also met with diasporic organizations and branches of the UAE Exchange, headed by B. R. Shetty, which had many Malayali employees. By the mid-1990s, Asianet became the first non-British broadcaster in Bahrain for the entire Middle East. The same year, Qatar Cablevision also began to telecast Malayalam content, which was delivered as videocassettes by carriers. Kairali TV, which was formed in 2000, also had a substantial shareholder base of Malayali migrants in the Gulf. When Kairali TV expanded its operations to form Kairali Arabia in 2011, it presented its motivation for the new channel as responding to the need to be "closer to our audience and make programmes [that are] interesting to them."[84]

These developments on the television front had precedents in earlier media history. By the 1980s, "Gulf money" had become a crucial part of the Malayalam cinema circuit. For instance, Abdul Jabbar, a doctor working in the Gulf, financed theaters in Trivandrum, Ernakulam, and Quilon (Kollam), each named after his three daughters.[85] V. B. K. Menon, the producer who headed Marunadan Films (*marunadan* means "one who belongs to a different place"), also distributed Malayalam films in the Gulf. He produced the 1980 film *Vilkanundu Swapnangal* (Dreams to sell; dir. M. Asad), which included scenes shot in the Gulf. The film's promotional material foregrounded how the Gulf features in the diasporic community's assertion of its identity. The text of one promotional poster reads:

> A fertile land for dreams—
> impossible to be numbered
> A desert of dreams, for most,
> dead and buried
> Don't you include among those keeping
> ready to go, wishing to mine gold!
> Lo! And Behold!
> Here comes N.O.C. Sent to you by Malayalees
> Abroad.[86]

Yet the exhibition of Malayalam cinema in the Gulf goes back farther to the 1960s, when film prints were illegally sent from India through carriers. From the 1980s onward, theaters in the Gulf such as Golden Cinema, Galleria Cinema, Dubai Cinema, and Deira Cinema started to screen Malayalam films. Many of these theaters were concentrated in Bur Dubai on the western side of Dubai Creek, a hub for South Asians. Previously known as Plaza Cinema, Golden Cinema was a 1,500-seat family-run business owned by the Galadari brothers. It opened in 1971 and was a popular destination for watching Malayalam, Hindi, and Tamil films.[87] The theater even held Thursday night world premieres ahead of Friday night openings in India that included the traditional festivities associated with film premieres in India, including *chendamelam*, a percussion ensemble performed in South India.

Malayalam cinema in the Gulf in the 1980s catered to migrants who craved a sense of connection with the homeland. Theaters such as the El Dorado in Abu Dhabi, owned by Gulshan, who was a distributor of both Hollywood and Indian films, provided this connection. As they traveled to and from their worksites, migrants often formed floating crowds that intermittently populated spaces of transit, and cinema itself began to cater to this transitory aspect. For instance, Kalba theater in Sharjah, also known as Station Cinema, was an open-air cinema close to bus and taxi stations that clearly targeted floating populations of migrant workers. Malayalam films were also screened in theaters such as Rusayl Oman (Oman), Al-Hamra Cinema (Sharjah), Granada Cinema, and the Bahrain City Center, which had talkies that were numbered from one to twenty. A quick survey of Gulf-based newspapers from the 1980s reveals that films from Kerala were

FIGURE 23. An example of UAE newspaper advertisements for films from India at the *Cinemas in the U.A.E.* exhibition, curated by Ammar Al Attar at NYU Abu Dhabi Art Gallery in 2018. Image courtesy Ammar Al Attar.

advertised in Malayalam, which indicates that the theaters expected Malayali audiences (Fig. 23).[88] Distributors from Kerala sent promotional posters, which were stamped with the logo of the theaters where they were screened.

Most of my respondents were nostalgic as they reminisced about what such spaces meant to them. "It was not just the space for socializing with our friends. The space resonated with our experience of watching the films in India," said Mahesh, who was at the last show at the Golden Cinema before it was shut down.[89] Another respondent, Unnikrishnan, recalled that the operator of the Al Hamra theater in Sharjah was from Calicut: "He was our contact person to check out when Malayalam films would be screened. In front of the theater, there would be posters in Malayalam of the latest films or the expected films. For us, theater spaces were places to meet other Malayalis."[90] Yet another respondent, Saju, who now runs his own business in the Gold Souk said: "The only connection we had with our dear and near ones were through letters. The films that we saw in VCDs and in theaters were our only source of connecting to the family."[91] For emigrants like these, cinema—both as film object and theatrical space—offered a connection to home. Thus, cinematic experience, like food and clothing, offers a sensuous, affective link to the idea of home. In the process, cinema is elevated to a heightened form of sociality, marked by an active awareness of cinema as a sign of home. Malayalam cinema provided both localized entertainment as well as emotional comfort to scores of Malayali workers who stayed and worked in the Gulf, away from Kerala for years on end. Needless to say, "cinema" here includes popular mainstream films as well as B-grade features and soft-porn as popular commodities that traveled through their own unique channels, both official and underground.

SOFT-PORN AS DIASPORIC SOCIALITY

In the early 2000s, many laborer camps in Dubai screened Malayalam soft-porn films to workers as part of their Friday night entertainment. This had precedents in earlier screenings in the 1970s and 1980s. For instance, in the 1970s, *Kaamsastra* (dir. Prem Kapoor, 1975), which was publicized as a "sex-education family romance," was screened at the Plaza Cinema. *Kaamsastra* was a pedagogic film that advocated an open attitude toward sexuality. The film was not well-received upon its release in India. For instance, a response in *The Times of India*'s reader's forum accused it of advising married women to emulate prostitutes to satisfy the lust of their perverted husbands, in addition to including depictions of rape and masturbation, leaving the reviewer to wonder, "What else can be shown in blue films which are banned by the government?"[92] In contrast to reviewers like this who found it "obscene," my respondents in the Gulf were liberal and open to the film's message. Reminiscing about film-watching during his early years of unemployment in the Gulf, Saju recounted that watching *Kaamsastra*'s depiction of "tabooed relations and fantasy scenes provided a semblance of normalcy" in an otherwise precarious situation.[93] Films that were received in India as trash or as peddling in sensational scenes under the guise of sex education accrued a different value in a diasporic space. Although *Kaamsastra* is not a Malayalam soft-porn film, it set the stage for the kind of all-male diasporic sociality that would later allow such films to thrive.

Sony Betamax and the home video format established a transnational market for porn films that operated largely through rental parlors. *Adult Video News*, published by employees of Movies Unlimited, a Philadelphia-based distributor, was available in video parlors in Dubai and Kerala in the 1980s. The reduced magnification, distortions, "noise," and progressive deterioration of image quality in videos were not seen as a problem but as encapsulating the very experience of watching porn.[94] In addition to the availability of sex films on video in the Gulf, agents traded in soft-porn films and expanded their markets beyond India by using an ingenious mode of distribution to reach out to the diasporic Malayali male audience based in the Middle East. The major obstacle in the export of these films was the customs check at airports, which entailed a stringent monitoring system for counterfeit media. In the DVD era that coincided with the rise of soft-porn, some agents bypassed customs checks by using women who were traveling to join their families as carriers and by using master DVDs that stored the illicit films under home video content.[95] The women who brought pornographic material to the Gulf were mostly kept in the dark about the content hidden on the DVDs and even about the fact that they were being used to transport illegal media content so that the details were not exposed to anyone outside the close-knit network.

Different distribution systems coexisted with the smuggling of DVDs. Blue films also reached the migrant community through dish-enabled television subscription services, which had sex-specific channels. But the prohibitive prices of these channels deterred many from subscribing to them, even though many respondents mentioned that there were hotels that had pay-per-view options. Sometimes material also made its way accidentally, as when cleaning staff on ships picked up CDs discarded by the sailors. In the late 1990s, at the peak of the soft-porn boom, such films became available on discs sold in areas such as Naif in Deira. These included the streets next to the West Hotel or the now closed Jesco Supermarket, which sold CDs for five dirhams (approx. $1.36).[96] As a hub where male migrants sought out female company, Naif was seen as a space of guilty pleasures and clandestine deals, and although the popularity of CDs and DVDs has dwindled with the ubiquity of online streaming, the impact of such soft-porn DVDs can still be seen there in other forms of visual culture. During my field visits, visiting cards for massage parlors left on car windows or strewn on the roadside were a daily sight. Today, these massage parlors still carry traces of soft-porn cinema in more ways than one (Fig. 24).

Although the UAE government has banned suggestive advertisements for massage parlors, and reports about prospective customers being duped into visiting these places and subsequently robbed and assaulted are rife, my call to a parlor in Naif yielded unexpected results. Perched amid coffee parlors run by African migrants, the place was more like a small, one-unit room that arranged services depending on the client's preferences and the sex worker's willingness to meet them. Upon calling, I was asked if I wanted a lesbian escort for my stay in Dubai. When it became clear that what I needed was not a sexual service but to talk about sexual services, my Ethiopian contact was more than happy to oblige. She even introduced me to a few Indian escorts who spoke to me in detail about the sexual fantasies of Indian men in Dubai and their experiences in encountering soft-porn outside the alleys close to their parlor.

Nada, who is in her mid-forties, came to Dubai from Kerala in the early 2000s. She recounted to me that when she started off as a sex worker in 2004, there were days when she was approached by clients not for sex but out of the sheer need for company in an alien land. As in the adult motel rooms that brought adult video into the confines of private space, sexual intimacy was bound up with the experience of sharing space with a stranger. She stated: "The tropes of sexual fantasies they have were mostly spin-offs from the soft-porn films—like using seductive

MIGRATION, MEDIA, AND SOFT-PORN   137

FIGURE 24. Sample of visiting cards distributed in the Deira and Bur Dubai areas. A card at bottom right features the image of Sunny Leone (see chapter 3). Author's personal collection.

charms to vocalize the masculinity of the man or to enact the *bhabhi* (sister-in-law) fantasy. Some even wanted us to read out Malayalam erotic fiction to help them masturbate."⁹⁷ My conversations at the laborer camps in Sonapur in the outskirts of Dubai also focused on the unmet sexual needs of the largely South Asian migrant population and the circulation of Bangladeshi and Indian porn films that helped them to come to terms with their repressed sexual needs. Here, ethnic identification and a mutual awareness of their citizenly alterity bring migrants and sex workers together in an unlikely corporeal solidarity, in which the idea of "the pornographic" is distilled into sexual practices and informal spaces that supplement belonging. In this light, media artifacts and the everyday practices and consciousnesses they enable can be understood as vernacular formations that mediate a transnational economy routed through informality.

This informality stands in contrast to—and outside of—the bilateral connections and flows that follow official state agendas, and the NRI imagination of Indian transnationalism that is mainly marked by a westward journey into perceived neoliberal prosperity. Soft-porn's informal networks of production within Indian territories are paralleled by equally informal and underground channels of circulation and absorption outside of the country. This traffic in contraband media objects and desires enables Kerala's expatriate population in the Gulf to reconstruct a sense of a home when they are far away from it. If we understand these consumption practices as constituting a media public, then soft-porn's media public can be also said to constitute a "transnational public."

CONCLUSION

Both Gulf migrants and the target NRI community envisioned in the NRI scheme form the larger nonresident Indian community, but they are separated by a significant power differential. Although the NRI scheme was suggested and facilitated through a formalized, institutionalized realm, soft-porn circulated in the Gulf through pirate circuits that developed informally and provided coping mechanisms for migrant communities to survive in precarious labor conditions. In this chapter, I have addressed how the idea of the alternative transnational can help elucidate regional formations and the practices by which different stakeholders who are situated outside the boundaries of the nation-state forge connections with one another.

In vernacularizing cinema's forms and possibilities, and in engendering mutations in the global flows of media and culture, Malayalam soft-porn offers alternative ways of imagining the global. This allows for a reconsideration of the region and the various ways in which it has been used by the diasporic communities to consolidate identities and navigate structures of belonging. This is but one stage in the story; the emergence of digital and internet-enabled media has opened up even more avenues for mediating belonging. Even with its trappings of geolocation and national regulations, the global spatiality of the internet has allowed for different flows and migrations of media objects. Soft-porn, a form that is "dead" in the industrial sense of the term, enjoys an afterlife in the many fragments of audiovisual and textual artifacts floating on the internet.

5

(Dis)Appearances

Digital Remediations of Soft-Porn in the Contemporary

Although soft-porn fizzled out as a production category by the mid-2000s, its symbolic value as a remnant of the celluloid era persists in the single-screen theater circuit in both provincial and metropolitan cities. This lingering presence mobilizes an affective economy through an array of nostalgic remembrances in filmic representation, art, and digital forms. These manifestations, which I call "(dis)appearances," function as an ensemble of references that present a composite, but hazy re-presentation of soft-porn. Such spectral evocations work through assemblages of memorial work that diffuse soft-porn's affective resonances through fragmented sensorial and temporal registers. In this chapter, I explore the continued re-emergences of soft-porn in cultural objects and public discourse.

The pit stops in this journey include B-circuit film exhibition in Kolkata and Mumbai, soft-porn fragments in pornographic websites, and remediations of soft-porn in online micro-celebrity culture. Tracing both the shift to the digital and the displacement of soft-porn's perceived popularity to other cultural forms, I explain how soft-porn cinema reappears in different guises in contemporary screening practices. Through a study of films and other contemporary digital media, I locate a wide range of artifacts that mobilize the cultural memory of soft-porn as a temporal and generic marker. In so doing, I not only identify a soft-porn stylistic effect in contemporary media, but also a "soft-porn affect" that mobilizes affective, memorial, and sensual registers. Contemporary happenings and objects are sometimes labeled "soft-porn" because they activate a range of affective registers shared with the raw, textural, and somatic qualities of soft-porn cinema.

THE DISPERSED AFTER-PRESENCE OF SOFT-PORN IN CONTEMPORARY B-CIRCUIT EXHIBITION

Soft-porn film exhibition in India is now mostly limited to B-circuit theaters, which rely on reruns of older films because they cannot afford to purchase new releases and on geographical proximity to transit areas to attract audiences to such theaters. In the era of multiplex theaters and malls that cater to upscale audiences, soft-porn exhibition is often limited to single-screen theaters. In theaters outside Kerala, soft-porn appears as part of discounted package deals of South Indian films dubbed in Hindi. These theaters function as fringe cinematic territories that allow transgressive desires to be channeled through categories that are labeled as coming from elsewhere.

This is evident in the exhibition of these films in single-screen theaters in metropolitan cities such as Mumbai and Kolkata, where they are at once localized as "Madrasi" films and conflated with erotic English films imported from the US and Europe. For example, a Malayalam soft-porn film like *Virgin Lady* could be part of the same billing as an English-language erotic film like *Body* (Fig. 25). Both Mumbai and Kolkata are thriving metropolitan cities that have seen the rise of urban shopping malls, designer boutiques, and multiplexes under the sway of a neoliberal economy. However, older single-screen theaters often exist alongside the shiny objects of a new India, evoking a heterotopic world distinct from the pleasures of neoliberal consumption. Many theaters located adjacent to Falkland Road, an erstwhile entertainment district in Mumbai during the British regime, house *dargahs* (shrines) in their premises. As Madhushree Dutta writes, "It is quite a common sight to find an eager audience paying obeisance at the darghas moments before rushing to catch an x-rated film."[1] Located in marketplaces, spaces of bus and train transit, and red-light districts, theaters such as Silver Talkies and New Roshan in Mumbai and Bhawani Theatre and Pradip Cinema in Kolkata routinely show Malayalam soft-porn and erotic cinema. Catering to a mostly working-class audience, these last remnants of the era of single-screen theaters are battling for survival amid depleting profits and reduced viewership.

Located at Tollygunge, Kolkata's Bhawani Theatre does not have a boundary wall and spreads to the main road, which also houses a few roadside eateries. There are four shows—12:15 p.m., 3 p.m., 6 p.m., and 8:45 p.m.—and each seats no more than fifteen or twenty patrons. Spandan, a fellow academic and my Kolkata guide, was my translator for the ticket collectors and managers. When we arrived at Bhawani during my fieldwork in 2018, the theater was screening *Pati Ya Premi* (Husband or lover; dir. V. R. K. Prasad, 1999). My outsider status stood out too much in Kolkata, and the ticket collector at Bhawani initially refused to let me in for the noon show, directing me to come for the 3 p.m. show, as the ones at noon were "not meant for women." I was duly warned by ticket collectors and managers that I could be mistaken for a sex worker, and the theater personnel were worried

DIGITAL REMEDIATIONS OF SOFT-PORN   141

FIGURE 25. List of films pasted outside Pradip Cinema, Kolkata. Photo by author.

about my "safety." After some cajoling, the manager finally gave in, buying Spandan's description of my "unique research interests," but with the clear instruction that I would be called and allowed to enter fifteen minutes after the film started. As I made my way into the cinema hall amid middle-aged men who were curious about my intentions, Spandan waved at me from one dark side of the hall. He had been asked to sit close to the exit, as the manager wanted us to leave the cinema immediately after the show was over. Luckily for us, noon screenings were mostly soft-porn from South India. The tickets for the balcony seats were forty rupees (approx. $0.62) and rear stall seats were thirty-five rupees (approx. $0.54)—substantially lower prices than the 180–250 rupee price (approx. $2.82–$3.92) range for tickets charged in Kolkata multiplexes. By the time we entered, the previous screening was over, and the next film, *Naya Gupt Gyan* (New secret knowledge; dir. D. V. S. Reddy, 1999), a soft-porn rip-off of the highly successful

FIGURE 26. The poster of *Naya Gupt Gyan* at the entrance of Bhawani Theatre in Kolkata. Photo by author.

sex education film *Gupt Gyan* (dir. B. K. Adarsh, 1974), was playing.[2] *Naya Gupt Gyan* turned out to be a remix of footage assembled from Malayalam films starring Silk Smitha that included excerpts of cut-pieces sourced from various time periods, alongside other material, some of which resembled homemade amateur porn. Despite the jerky movements and poor quality that marked the cut-pieces, they were seamlessly edited, and peppy background music provided a connective tissue that brought them together.

The most notable of the exhibition strategies used in Bhawani was the outright redaction of contentious material that could invite disapprobation from the middle-class neighborhood. The poster featured the actress Reshma's upper body had been redacted, in the process removing the explicit sexual parts—in this case, her breasts, which had been colored over with a sharpie (Fig. 26). Such editing leaves a trace of the process on the object: the deleted or blackened portion is surrounded by clear text or images, inviting the viewer to imaginatively hypothesize about the redacted content.[3] In contexts where redaction becomes expected, filmmakers (and, in this instance, exhibitors) voluntarily eliminate sections without doing violence to the meaning of the image by drawing attention to its potential (but suppressed) sexual energy. According to S. V. Srinivas, posters advertising sex films "turn the act of censorship into a promise," as blackening exposed parts of the body featured in the posters is routinely performed by theatre owners.[4] This conceptualization was clear in the manager's explanation of why the poster had been redacted: "The posters supplied by the distributors were too explicit and we were worried about the negative publicity since the theater is close to residential quarters. So, we toned it down. But it works, doesn't it? See the gaze of the passersby and how they are stealing a quick glimpse at the actress."[5]

Clearly, redaction aligned with the respectability politics of urban space, where such theaters coexist with middle-class neighborhoods or otherwise public areas. The same respectability politics also impacted my own reception as a female researcher in these spaces, which were, ironically, peddling sexually titillating images of women. During most of my fieldwork, my presence in single-screen theaters screening soft-porn films was met with a mix of curiosity, skepticism, and anxiety. My experience in Kolkata was marked by a sense of déjà vu, because my previous fieldwork in Bombay had led to similar situations. These theaters are marked either as all-male spaces or as spaces where only certain kinds of women could be made visible. When I did my first survey of single-screen theaters in Bombay, I was allowed access to the interior of Silver Talkies with my partner only after convincing the manager that I was married and that if anything happened inside the theater, we would take responsibility for it. Elsewhere, though, policemen on patrol raised concerns about my presence in the sex workers' quarters at Kamathipura. In 2017, this involved being stopped at a police aid post for many hours, until my friend Dipti called the station to furnish surety for me. Interestingly, the inspector had detained me at the station for my own safety.

The red-light district of Kamathipura in Bombay has a unique relationship with theaters that screen soft-porn films. Like Kolkata's Bhawani Theatre and Pradip Cinema, Bombay's Silver Cinema (Fig. 27) has been a regular haunt of migrant laborers and sex workers due to its low ticket prices and proximity to the quarters of construction workers. The shows scheduled for August 27, 2014, were publicized as a "special show" because it was Eid al-Fitr, the day that marks the end of the holy fasting month of Ramadan.

A poster of a film titled *Miss Dirty* was perched on a wooden board on the sidewalk opposite the quarters where sex workers stayed. Next to the handwritten text "Eid Mubharak" (Eid wishes), the Hindi text on the poster read, "Love doesn't recognize age, caste, class, or social status" (author's translation). Having noted the poster's tag "Top Sexy Drama" and the film's "Adult" certification unambiguously exhibited, I was surprised to see the image of Silk Smitha alongside the title *Miss Dirty* and curious to know if the film had any relationship to Milan Luthria's *The Dirty Picture*. Expecting a good turnout owing to the holiday, the theater management had decided to screen a re-release of a 1990 film starring Silk Smitha, *Reshma Ki Jawani* (Malayalam title: *Layanam*, dir. Thulasidas), but the image used

FIGURE 27. Entrance and box office of Silver Talkies, Mumbai. Photo by author.

was from a different film titled *Ratilayam* (dir. P. Chandra Kumar; Fig. 28), a 1983 film which was re-released in Hindi as *Gumrah Jawani* in 1988. It turned out that Silver Talkies had retitled the promotional poster outside to reference *The Dirty Picture*, hoping to draw in a bigger crowd (Fig. 29), inadvertently creating a Silk Smitha assemblage curated from multiple, almost replaceable images from various films. The manager had ingeniously incorporated references to *The Dirty Picture* to give the Silk Smitha vehicle a new lease on life. He told me, "We don't have enough money to convert the theater to digital format, but we can evoke the same sensations that *The Dirty Picture* evoked in the audience. Why waste time on the fake?"[6]

This idea of "the fake" is striking and returns us to questions of cinema's virtuality, as Silk Smitha no longer exists as a real living body but only as a cinematic

FIGURE 28. Original lobbycard for *Ratilayam*, retitled here as *Gumrah Jawani*. Author's personal collection.

image. As an embodiment of screen pleasures, the *madakarani* of soft-porn cinema is always already virtual—that is, she exists in a cinematic or fantasy space separate from the physical space of the viewer. Thus, even when the real bodies of actresses such as Silk Smitha are gone, they continue to appear in cinematic spaces—film magazines, posters, and theaters such as Silver Talkies—as real, "not fake" bodies. This resurgence is made possible through the technological mediation of the cinematic apparatus, which includes the paraphernal apparatuses of print and digital spaces. In September 2023, Silk Smitha reemerged in a brief snippet in the trailer of the Tamil film *Mark Antony* (dir. Adhik Ravichandran)—not in the flesh, but as a computer-generated body. The move was received harshly, with criticisms ranging from the inappropriate sexualization of women to the use of digital technology and artificial intelligence to objectify the dead.[7] However, both the computer-generated imagery (CGI) and the critical responses to it point toward the continued negotiations between agency, visibility, and control of cinematic bodies. Although not the same as Smitha's reappearance in the Silver Talkies poster, the CGI incident is part of the same cinematic continuum and lends credence to Giuliana Bruno's assertion that cinema resembles cemeteries in that it is "home to residual body images" and "inhabit[s] multiple points in time and collapse[s] multiple places into a single place."[8] By mapping soft-porn's return in such diverse spaces, we can begin to trace the shadowy routes through which its

FIGURE 29. Poster of *Reshma Ki Jawani* at Silver Talkies. Photo by author.

imagination circulates as affect. I turn now to look at additional dispersed sites where these residual images are revived, including contemporary cinematic representation and social media.

SOFT-PORN'S RESURGENCE IN MAINSTREAM MALAYALAM CINEMA

In the recent past, several mainstream films have reminisced on soft-porn as a marker of the celluloid era. Films such as *Classmates* (dir. Lal Jose, 2006), *Kanyaka Talkies* (dir. K. R. Manoj, 2013), *Ore Mukham* (Same face; dir. Sajith Jagadnathan, 2016), *Pavada* (Skirt; dir. G. Marthandan, 2016), *Parava* (Birds; dir. Soubin Shahir, 2017), *Rosapoo* (Rose; dir. Vinu Joseph, 2018), and *Super Deluxe* (dir. Thiagarajan Kumararaja, Tamil, 2019) evoke a range of themes such as male bonding, teenage fascination with soft-porn actresses, and soft-porn production practices, in the process activating the interests of soft-porn's original audience base. In this section, I explore four of these films—*Rosapoo, Kanyaka Talkies, Super Deluxe*, and *Pavada*—to show the different tonalities of memory that surface in these films' explorations of soft-porn cinema.

Rosapoo centers on the misadventures of two male protagonists, Shanu (Biju Menon) and Ambrose (Neeraj Madhav), who, after a series of entrepreneurial failures, embark on a career in adult film production and try to make a soft-porn movie titled *Rosapoo*. The film narrativizes the boom in soft-porn as an aftereffect of the financial crisis of the 1990s. Despite the money and labor that go into the film's production, Shanu and Ambrose ultimately end up in debt because the shrewd production executive pockets the profits accrued from the distribution rights. Although a fictional tale, *Rosapoo* draws from and demystifies popular narratives of soft-porn film production (Fig. 30). The film's opening credits are accompanied by a peppy song and intermittent gasps of orgasmic moaning, a popular aural presence in soft-porn films of the 1990s. These references to soft-porn work both at the narrative and affective levels. The introductory scene of the actress Laila, otherwise referred to as "Laila *thatta*" (*thatta* is a term for a middle-aged woman used by the Muslim community), exemplifies the film's involvement of different modalities, including direct references to the real people behind the making and casting of these films. In positioning Laila as the face of soft-porn cinema, the film presents her as an analog for Shakeela. For instance, Laila's refusal to work with the production executive who has "made six films for the price of one" (author's translation) is a reference to the duplication of Shakeela's shots in multiple films, which, as Shakeela told me in one of our interviews, was an "unscrupulous way of discounting labor" that led to the demise of soft-porn.[9] The sequence introducing Laila also invokes the memory of "English soft-porn" films made by the director U. C. Roshan, who worked in the first decade of the 2000s. Roshan penned his films' dialogue in English as a strategy to bypass rigid censorship codes. In response to Ambrose's query about why soft-porn films were made in half-baked English and not in any other Indian language, the production executive explains: "If it is in Malayalam, the censor board will cut everything off. The filmmakers can have an easy go if the films are in English."

Faced with the possibility of being ostracized from his family and community because of his association with soft-porn films, Ambrose is advised to change his name to A. M. Rose—a reference to soft-porn cinema's economy of fictitious names and identities. This specific naming strategy connects back to specific case of A. T. Joy, a soft-porn director in the first decade of the 2000s who had to change his name to Joy Anthony in 2014 to recast his reputation in the industry as a serious filmmaker. *Rosapoo* also pays homage to soft-porn film, making the otherwise eclipsed memory of these films visible. For instance, Shanu and Ambrose appear in a fantasy sequence as Adam and Eve, invoking P. Chandrakumar's *Aadyapaapam*

FIGURE 30. Casting call of *Rosapoo*. The mention of "Good Looking FAT LADY" is a direct reference to the buxom heroines of soft-porn films. Posted on Twitter, July 6, 2017, by Thameens Films (@Thameensfilms), with the caption "#Rosapoo casting call at #Chennai. July 12th @shibuthameens #BijuMenon #SunnyWayne #VinuJoseph."

(1988). Titles of other prominent films are changed, with enough similarities retained to allow identification; for instance, *Kinnarathumbikal* is changed to *Kiloyolathumbikal*, in homage to its status as the harbinger of the soft-porn wave.

In contrast to the stereotype of soft-porn actresses as willing participants in casting-couch arrangements, *Rosapoo* pictures the heroine Reshmi as having to constantly fight the crew's attention and demands for sexual service. *Rosapoo* climaxes with a sequence that shows news reports of Reshmi's arrest following the murder of a director and his friend—an act of self-defense after the director assaults her. An unnamed man emerges from the crowd to protect her; fuming with anger, he urges the crowd not to mistake the actress's screen image with her real self. However, as the film ends, it is revealed to the audience that this sequence is actually the climax of a new film that Ambrose has directed—Reshmi's name being retained in the film within the film. This slippage between the "real" Reshmi of *Rosapoo*'s narrative and the "fictional" Reshmi of the film-within-the-film collapses actress and character. This device evokes very real events in Kerala, especially given that the name Reshmi echoes the name of the real soft-porn starlet Reshma, whose arrest, interrogation, and consequent case of online slut-shaming I examined in chapter 3. If the real Reshma's humiliation at the hands of the police and the crowd that gathered to jeer her was typical of mob mentality, the film's insertion of the fictional Reshmi's life was recuperative, especially given the timing of *Rosapoo*'s release in 2017, a period marked by urgent questions about the gendered nature of the Malayalam film industry.[10] After this scene outside the courthouse, the film's final sequence depicts a film crew celebrating the successful release of their new film. Shanu and Ambrose receive a video clip by text that shows footage of Ambrose directing Reshmi during a foreplay scene, demonstrating what to do. As the two flabbergasted filmmakers stare at each other, the frame freezes and music begins to play. Refusing narrative resolution, this ending leaves the audience wondering whether this footage will now circulate as a scandalous "porn" video, of the variety that is often tagged "Indian" or "MMS" porn on pornographic websites.[11] Rather than being expressed in language, this open-ended conclusion assumes that the audience's public memory is constituted by the raw textural details of media material such as leaked videos, exposés, MMS porn, and fragments extracted from full films that form the topology of India's erotic mediascape.

K. R. Manoj's 2013 film *Kanyaka Talkies* (Virgin talkies) provides an even earlier instance of incorporating soft-porn cinema's memory. Based on P. V. Shajikumar's short story "18+" (originally published in *Madhyamam* in 2011 and then in book form in 2013), *Kanyaka Talkies* looks back at soft-porn exhibition, the cultures of its circulation, and the different modes of interaction it provoked in the marginal space of B- and C-circuit theaters. "18+" drew on the vicissitudes of Kanyaka Talkies, a real theater based in the district of Kasaragod that screened soft-porn films in the 1990s. The film depicts theater culture in the rural hinterlands as strikingly different from the film-viewing experience offered at A-circuit cinema halls. In the film's narrative, Yakoob, newly returned from the Gulf, decides to set up Kanyaka Talkies in the remote area of Kuyyali in the 1980s. This story references the nouveau riche Gulf emigrants who invested their surplus money in soft-porn films and built a quasi-fictitious mode of film production by hiding their identities as financial backers. Yakoob's initial foray into the film business is portrayed as something innocent, and it is only when the initial prospects of film exhibition give way to heavy financial setbacks that he is forced to turn to soft-porn to make up his losses. Thus, the Kanyaka Talkies theater, which is initially portrayed as screening "family films," becomes a space exclusively for men that draws viewers from all ages. Whereas the theater affords men a sense of male sociality, women look down on it as a sign of moral depravity. After a series of family tragedies resulting from this depravity, Yakoob shuts down the theater and hands it over to the diocese.

A transmedia mode of storytelling undergirds the production of *Kanyaka Talkies* and brings together varied artifacts associated with the memory of soft-porn films. The most immediate is Shaji Kumar's "18+," the short story that inspired the film.[12] In his story, Kumar also reflects on the wider disappearance of theaters that closed or were converted into other spaces. In fact, some of these soft-porn theaters were converted into churches; one in the district of Wayanad serves as a real-life reference for Kanyaka Talkies. Despite this conversion, memories of the theater's soft-porn days refuse to die, and their spectral presence comes to haunt the space. The priest, Father Michael, who is tasked with motivating the believers to strengthen their faith, encounters strange and inexplicable happenings: mass is disrupted by an unseen third party, and moans of lovemaking evoke repressed desires and stir doubts about his capacity to withstand sinful thoughts. Elements of scattered memories associated with soft-porn films resonate in a wide ensemble of stock sounds that suggest seduction and orgasm. This soundtrack creates a parallel world that collapses time as Father Michael hears the actresses whisper from their past into his present. An acknowledgment in the closing credit sequence proclaims that sounds were sampled and layered from preexisting tracks "to create greater awareness about the marginal areas in the history of Indian cinema."

This sonic encounter reanimates the exhibition practices of soft-porn films by using the cut-piece's logic of interruption. The priest's aural hallucinations begin at unexpected moments and venues, just as the cut-piece or *thundu* arrives in the cinematic experience at unanticipated moments. *Kanyaka Talkies*'s reliance on the soundtrack to create the erotic landscape aligns with what Michel Chion calls "audio-vision," a quality that temporalizes the image by creating a "feeling of imminence and expectation."[13] Affirming that sound is more than an additive element, *Kanyaka Talkies* strategically restructures the soundscape to link "the pastness of the recorded event with the presentness of the viewing."[14]

Kanyaka Talkies also mines the liminal space that houses the discarded stuff of the theater—the projection room is retained as a warehouse when the building is renovated. This warehouse reflects what Anthony Vidler calls the "architectural

FIGURE 31. The Silk Smitha image from Lal's installation used in *Kanyaka Talkies*. Image courtesy Priyaranjan Lal.

uncanny"—spaces that blur "the boundaries of the real and the unreal in order to provoke a disturbing ambiguity, a slippage between waking and dreaming."[15] Except for flashback scenes that show its former use as a projection room, the interior of the warehouse is shown only at the end of the film, although shots of its locked doors recur in scenes with the priest. Crucially, Father Michael believes he can achieve closure from his hallucinatory sensations by accessing the abandoned projection room. Like a shaman facilitating contact with the netherworld in an exorcism ritual, Yakoob facilitates this encounter with the past: the doors open after he arrives, and with them the possibility of redemption appears. When they enter, Father Michael and Yakoob find a monumental image of Shakeela projected on the wall. Beams of light are shown projecting out of the actress's visage, such that she appears to be returning the audience's unilateral gaze, like a demigoddess answering her worshipers' prayers.[16] Another shot shows Father Michael's face framed by strips of celluloid, as if to suggest that soft-porn cinema itself has been haunting him all along. A multimedia projection of animated images follows, with Shakeela and the faces of other sex sirens like Silk Smitha, Reshma, Maria, and others alternately appearing on a figure riding a horse—the faces change as the horse gallops along. Evoking Eadweard Muybridge's photography, the galloping horse stands in for the history of cinema while the changing faces allude to soft-porn's forgotten or abandoned female stars (Fig. 31).[17]

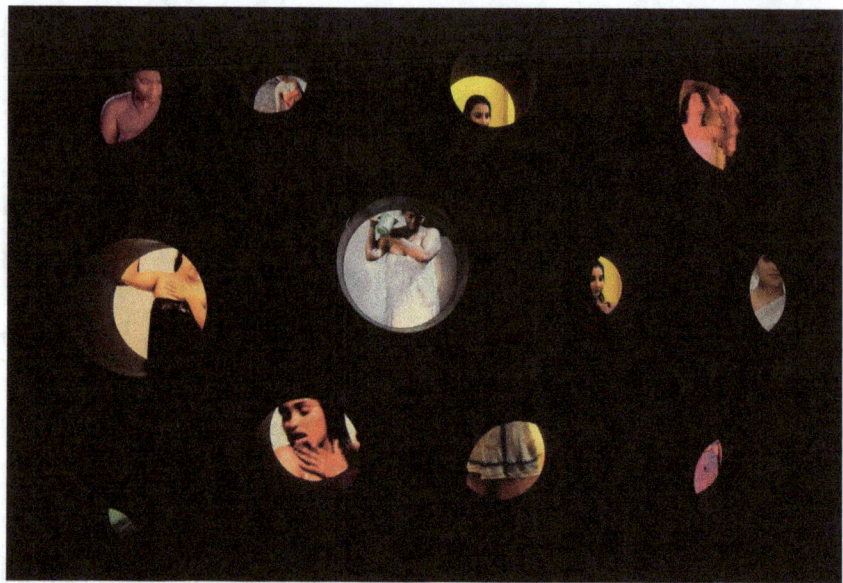

FIGURE 32. The bathing scenes installation used in *Kanyaka Talkies*. Image courtesy Priyaranjan Lal.

Commissioned for the film, this multimedia projection was developed by the graphic designer Priyaranjan Lal as part of a larger project titled *Kuliyum Mattu Scenukalam* (Shower and other scenes) that was part of the 100-Day Artist Cinema section, curated by the film critic C. S. Venkiteswaran and exhibited at the Kochi-Muziris Biennale 2015. According to Lal, "The installations were conceptualized as a timely intervention to counter the neat narratives which structure the history of Malayalam cinema."[18] Another installation in the project showcases a hundred bath scenes from various soft-porn films that are viewed through peepholes, as if to emphasize the voyeuristic fantasy associated with these films (Fig. 32). The number 100 featured prominently because it was the Indian film centenary, and Lal wanted the installation to serve as a reminder of soft-porn's relegation to the dustbin of cinema history. The exhibition used a large cube with peepholes replicating the form of traveling bioscopes, which were popular in India during the celluloid era.[19] Within the film itself, this sequence forms part of the dreamlike space of the theater where the memories of soft-porn cinema are encountered by the characters.

Along with the scene with the galloping horse, this metapicture—to use W. J. T. Mitchell's term for pictures-within-pictures—parses soft-porn's relationship with star-texts.[20] The actresses associated with these films were hyper-visible (as opposed to the anonymous production and distribution staff), but most had very short shelf lives. By fusing this precarious star image with a peephole effect,

Lal's installation invites the audience to reflect on a film culture that has vanished along with the B-circuit theaters that supported it. Within the film, the image is self-referential. A shot of the central peephole reveals a bathing scene from a soft-porn shoot that appears earlier in the film; the static images in the surrounding peepholes are from other older soft-porn films. As an installation piece, the image is already a separate visual artifact that is nested within the film sequence, and the installation in turns nests other film sequences within itself, forming what Mitchell describes as a special category of metapictures marked by "an inside-outside structure that is continuous, without breaks or demarcations or duplications."[21] Another installation featured the faces of *madakarani* from Malayalam cinema on cylindrical posts that were lit from inside. The multitude of faces peppering the installations—many of starlets like Jyothi Lakshmi and Sadhana who had short stints in the soft-porn industry—suggests a long history of sexualized fantasies related to women actresses, of which Shakeela is only a part. Although the installation was publicized as being commissioned as part of *Kanyaka Talkies*, only parts of it were used in the film. In this sense, Lal's work functions as a complementary artistic conversation with the film—a facet of its ficto-critical and transmedial storytelling, with some passages of *Kuliyum Mattu Scenukalam* punctuating the narrative of *Kanyaka Talkies*. These installations and multimedia images depart from the original short story, in which images of Shakeela and other specific actresses are not so central to the narrative. In "18+," the priest only hears the voices of actresses and the soundtrack of soft-porn films, and the story is not invested in the inner workings of the film industry as such. Contrastingly, the installation's visually disruptive effect works to the narrative's advantage, as it highlights the absurd, dreamlike condition of the theater space. Both within and outside the film, the installation forces viewers to consider the conditions of power and social norms that make up film spectatorship. By functioning as a "double vision . . . a double voice and a double relation between language and visual experience," it forces viewers to see, acknowledge, and remember.[22]

Although *Kanyaka Talkies* sutures its account of the fate of soft-porn theaters through references to many "real" soft-porn theater spaces, including the theater in Wayanad that was later converted to a church, the projection room and equipment of S. P. Theatre in Trivandrum was used in the film to specifically stand in for the soft-porn theater. As in the fictional Kanyaka Talkies, the crisis of the 1990s forced Gladys, the owner, to start screening soft-porn. By June 2014, when I visited, it had been converted first into a venue for Pentecostal prayer services and then into a wedding hall. The real space of S. P. Theatre thus uncannily mirrors the fate of the film's fictional theater, as both became spaces of religious and social congregation.

Gladys had no idea that *Kanyaka Talkies*'s plot closely echoed the history of many theaters of the time, including his own. Shakeela's photograph in the projection room of S. P. Theatre was prominently used as publicity material for *Kanyaka*

FIGURE 33. Shakeela's image in the projection room in S. P. Theatre. Photo by author.

Talkies. Gladys was more than happy to share the photo album that documented the theater's varied phases. One photograph included the same Shakeela image. Referring to this photo as from his "Shakeela phase," Gladys showed it to me as evidence that her image had been part of the theater's topography for a long time (Fig. 33). Thus, the physical space of S. P. Theatre takes the form of a palimpsest, with multiple layers of uses, motivations, and experiences etched into its skin.

Super Deluxe, a 2019 Tamil-language film directed by Thiagarajan Kumararaja, uses a similar set of strategies to represent soft-porn. The film paints a poignant portrait of a soft-porn actress as she embraces her identity as an actress and refuses to be cowed by the humiliation or exploitation associated soft-porn work. The film explores a group of teenage boys' aborted attempt to watch a porn film and the aftereffects of the revelation that the actress in the film, Leela, is the mother of one of the boys, Sura. Upon seeing his mother on-screen, Sura gets into an aggressive confrontation with the other boys in which he accidentally stabs himself. His main worry is that everyone seems to have known about his mother's involvement in soft-porn and may already have seen intimate images of her. The concluding sequence, in which Leela opens up to Sura about her stint in soft-porn films, is a rare representation of a soft-porn actress speaking about her autonomy and the need to assert her agential possibilities to explore her desires. When Sura asks if she was duped into acting in these films, Leela says:

> I knew what these films were. I wanted to act . . . and I acted. I acted both in *Amman* films (religious films) as well as porn films. It all depends on how the audience want to see what is in front of them. . . . There are lakhs of people who watch porn, but only four people who act in it. Why do we shun the actors and forgive the viewers?

Leela's assertion of her agency unsettles the sense of victimhood forced upon her. In a joking repartee, Sura's friend tells him that porn stars such as Shakeela and Sunny Leone have normalized their involvement in the industry so much that being a soft-porn actress no longer entails immediate ostracism.

Despite such narratives, some films continue to demonize the soft-porn industry. *Super Deluxe*'s empowering narrative stands in stark contrast to the 2016 film *Pavada*, for example. *Pavada* is about the making of a fictional film, also titled *Pavada*, and castigates soft-porn production practices for delegitimizing the labor of the production unit. After the director suddenly dies in the middle of shooting the film-within-the-film, the production executive reshoots and interpolates it with sexually explicit bits so that it can be circulated as a soft-porn film. Although the film turns out to be a success, the people associated with it endure harsh consequences: faced with constant heckling, the producer quits his vocation as a professor, and the lead actress Sicily leaves the village fearing ostracism. The film explores the producer's meeting with the actress's son years later, when the production executive-turned-producer announces the re-release of *Pavada* as the first adult film in 3D format. In a last-ditch effort to stop its re-release, the producer and the actress's son are forced to retrace the film's history, which includes tracking down the production unit members who were part of the original film. Although they rally in support of the dispersed crew members, they encounter many setbacks as they attempt to secure a legal injunction against the re-release.

A satellite TV channel that is interested in airing the story offers what seems like the only option at salvation: bringing back the dupe (body double) who had acted in these films knowing what it involved. Even though they manage to track her down, on realizing that she has moved on to have a family that is perhaps unaware of her previous work as an extra, they decide not to follow up on the request to clear the air. With no other option, Sicily, the original film's heroine, is forced to seek legal recourse. She appears in a court scene and faces a humiliating cross-examination from the opposing lawyer, who compares her to a profiteer exploiting her victimhood for compensation. Sicily pitches her appeal to stop the re-release as a mother's request not to allow her son to see risqué images of her. In contrast, her lawyer likens Sicily's plight to the kind of forceful exposure that men enact by publicizing female colleagues' phone numbers and drawing nudes of women who have rejected them on the walls of public urinals. In this way, the film situates Sicily's specific violation within a longer history of gendered and sexual violence. It also presents the exploitative strategies and unscrupulous dealings associated with soft-porn as part of the operative logic of production executives, whose sole motive is to make profitable deals with no consideration for the lives and dignity of the people involved. But in so doing, it ascribes to the stereotype of soft-porn as a negative form that signals the denigration of moral values and societal norms. Unlike *Kanyaka Talkies* or *Rosapoo, Pavada* is moralistic at best, depicting the production executive as the core of everything that is morally wrong about the consumption of sexual media.

"MALLU HOT SEX" (OR MALAYALAM SOFT-PORN GOES DIGITAL)

While mainstream films turn to the soft-porn era for its citational capital, other manifestations of citational practice have emerged in current Malayalam media, used for varying ends. In this section, I explore such noncinematic reverberations of the soft-porn wave in the landscape of digital media production and consumption. During the heyday of the soft-porn wave, incorporating Shakeela's presence could give a film that had tanked at the box office a new lease on life, and many production executives believe that unused shots of her were recycled into other films without her awareness or consent.[23] In a strange way, soft-porn films themselves began to exist as fragments, reflecting the ontology of the cut-piece phenomenon on which they thrived. In 2018, my interest in *thundu* came full circle when I had an opportunity to view some fragments of Malayalam soft-porn films on a Steenbeck at the University of Southern California's Hugh M. Hefner Moving Image Archive. These fragments were brought to the archive by film buff and archivist David Farris, who had been collecting films of all varieties for his now-defunct Shabistan Film Archive project, which sought to preserve film material from across South Asia. Farris had collected the material from distributors and exhibitors in B-circuit theaters in India, many of whom had gone out of business and kept the film cans in storage facilities and old factories. One of the reels that Farris brought with him was labeled "Misc Indian Ladies"—a name Farris himself scrawled on the artifact to describe what he called a cut-piece reel and to distinguish it from other reels that included trailers, newsreels, and dailies (Fig. 34). He had acquired the reel from a distributor based in Karnataka who was willing to sell him the material for 20 rupees (approx. $0.30) per can.

Although I could identify one of the actresses as Reshma, the reel otherwise consisted of diverse fragments from various unidentifiable sources, and included scenes of bathing, female masturbation, foreplay, and so on. Even though it was but a single reel, "Misc Indian Ladies" was marked by the cut-piece's logic of surprise, with each turn on the Steenbeck promising the unannounced eruption of something new to see and hear. The reel also displayed the fragmentary nature of Malayalam soft-porn films, which themselves could become cut-piece

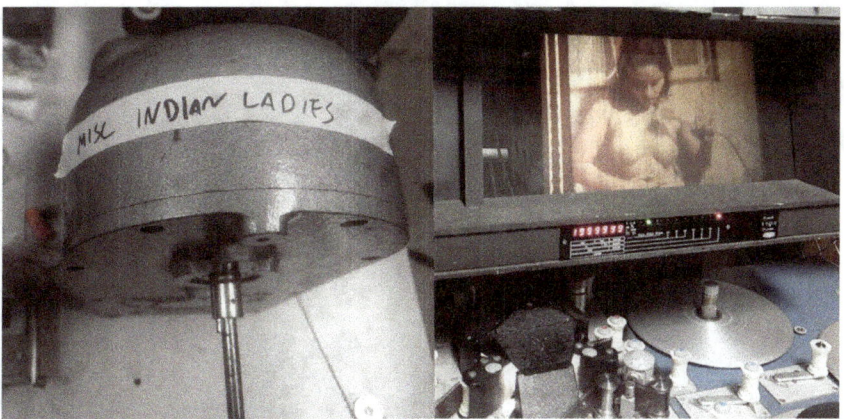

FIGURE 34. The label "Misc Indian Ladies" (on the left) and cut-piece showing an unidentified actress in a bath scene (on the right). Photo by author.

fragments once they were extracted from their parent film and inserted into a different one. The cut-piece's status as a floating sign of "soft-porn-ness" that can attach itself to other narratives and give rise to new meanings is also duplicated in the arena of pornographic websites. Like "Misc Indian Ladies," fragments of soft-porn found on pornographic websites such as Pornhub and XVideos are often anonymous but exude a distinct soft-porn-ness through tags such as "Mallu Sex," "Mallu Hot Aunty," or "Mallu Hot Scene" ("Mallu" being short for "Malayali" or "Malayalam").

Tags and labels such as these function through an imprecise citational practice based on the approximation of the cinematic region whence these bits may have come.[24] Clips of Malayalam soft-porn films on XVideos and Pornhub are routinely misattributed or not attributed at all. For instance, one Shakeela clip uploaded on Pornhub in 2016 appears with the title "Shakeela Uncensored Hot Movie Scene" (Fig. 35).[25] The only identifiable referent here is Shakeela; the film's title is not mentioned and, for all practical purposes, is not even important in the overall scheme of this digital display. What is important, however, are the "related videos" that appear on the side and below the video player, some with film titles included, although most are unattributed. The viewer of the page is presented with an array of short clips with titles such as "Shakeela Enjoing with Young Man hot sence [sic]," "Shakeela With Man in Bedroom," "shakeela mallu aunty," "Mallu Aunty Romantic Bed Hot Scene Reshma Affair," and "Reshma seducing a boy." This placement of videos next to other suggested videos that are related to (or labeled as) Malayalam soft-porn makes the parent film less important than the overall imagination that structures this constellation of videos. The video clip loses its indexical relationship to a particular film and becomes part of an idea of

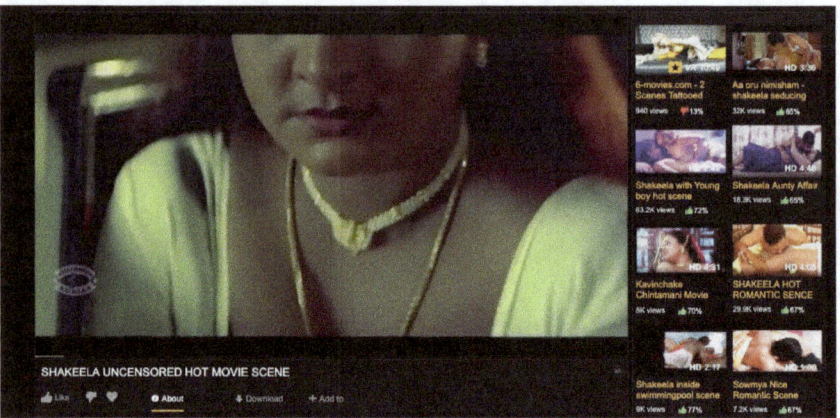

FIGURE 35. A screenshot from an online porn site.

Malayalam soft-porn, manifested here as an algorithmically generated webpage. Each individual video matters less than the endless labyrinth of videos that exist with similar tags,[26] and names such as Shakeela and Reshma pop up in relation to each other without a cohesive narrative about Malayalam soft-porn tying them together. In the universe of tags and metadata, these videos exist in relation to one another prior to being uploaded, and this "offline" knowledge about Malayalam soft-porn informs their online presence without necessarily naming them as such. Searching these pornographic websites with keywords such as "South Indian" or "Mallu" turns up these fragments of Malayalam soft-porn films alongside amateur and homemade porn that is tagged similarly. For instance, on one search result page on XVideos, a fragment from a Reshma film titled "Desi Mallu Indian Porn-Reshma hot" appears next to an amateur video titled "mallu aunty hot blowjob and top riding."[27] Another clip on XVideos is titled "Soumya Full Nude and Other Mallu Sex Scenes Compilation," echoing Farris's "Misc Indian Ladies" reel.[28] Both individual clips and search pages replicate the logic of cut-piece reels such as the one Farris showed me.

Inserting the categorical labels of the "Mallu Aunty bits" or "Hot South Indian bits" into digital space manifests a nostalgic impulse, for these phrases and figures belong to the era of celluloid, and their insertion into the digital playground testifies to their persistence as stubborn residues of the soft-porn era. Their coexistence alongside more recent amateur material—for example, a leaked amateur spy-cam video in a bathroom alongside a Shakeela bathing scene, both shown in a search on XVideos with the term "mallu bath"[29]—further demonstrates that an abstract idea of Malayalam soft-porn informs the uploading and tagging practices of both, and that the nostalgic temporality of Malayalam soft-porn and the contemporariness of amateur porn videos are intrinsically intertwined.

In addition to porn sites, online streaming platforms are another avenue through which soft-porn films circulate in the present, as for instance, on Eros Now, an Indian subscription-based over-the-top platform, owned by Eros International Plc, which was the first VHS distributor in India. Many soft-porn films on the platform—for example, *Aa Oru Nimisham* starring Shakeela and Roshni (see introduction)—are tagged by the platform with the keywords "mature," "mystery," and "romance." Even though I had watched this film as a theatrical release in Kerala and on a DVD, the streaming experience was unique. The emergence of adult platforms like Nueflix and Kooku that cater to sexual content during the COVID-19 pandemic contributed to new forms of organizing explicit media. This led to stacking soft-porn films from the 1990s and 2000s as featured content along with mainstream films. Interestingly, the soft-porn films uploaded on streaming platforms offer us a way of analyzing the formal features of soft-porn films, as these films often lack singular, unaltered texts and are mutable depending on the venues in which they are projected.

Most of the soft-porn films on these streaming platforms are between 90 and 110 minutes long, and they feature fantasy sequences that involve foreplay, deep kissing, and rubbing of bodies and thighs that last up to five minutes. These sequences often reappear with slight variations in execution, with a new set of actors. In each repetition, foreplay and sexual stimulation are followed by a bath sequence, which retains the sound of moaning and sexual ecstasy as a sound bridge. Due to the length, and the strategic combination of long shots, medium shots, and close-ups, these sequences can easily be excerpted and exist autonomously as sex clips—indeed, they are designed to do so. The films' editors also mark points of entry and exit for splicing in *thundu* reels. For instance, a sequence from *Aa Oru Nimisham* contains a zoom in and a cutaway to the image of two birds kissing, which then returns to the sex scene. Such strategies are reminiscent of editing techniques in mainstream Indian cinema, as well. For instance, Madhav Prasad writes about how prohibition is negotiated in cinema by showcasing public confirmation of a private act by showing the heroine emerge from outside the frame with a series of visual suggestions confirming sex, as, for example, crumpled clothes.[30] Similarly, Lalitha Gopalan writes that the depiction of the female body in Indian film is equivalent to coitus interruptus—"a cinematic technique that is most visible when the camera withdraws just before we see a sexually explicit scene."[31] However, soft-porn films go a step beyond this. Instead of withdrawing from the sex act and merely suggesting it through interruption and substitution, soft-porn films use similar tactics like mainstream cinema to mark out where sex can be reinstated into visibility. As seen in the example of *Aa Oru Nimisham* (and this can be extended to other soft-porn films), strategic coverage shots are an editor's way of signaling to projectionists that these are sequences where sex shots or *thundu* can be creatively played with.

Whereas pornographic and streaming websites collapse past and present through the operation of tagging and metadata, social media presents a slightly different manifestation of the soft-porn unconscious. Since the advent of social media in the early 2000s, groups who post adult meme content using an accelerated circulation of sexually suggestive material have appeared online. Many Facebook groups like Kamakeli" (Sex play), "Mace Naughty Trolls," and "Malayalam Naughty Trolls 18+" actively invoke soft-porn films and use images of actresses such as Shakeela or Reshma as their profile pictures, mobilizing thousands of followers with cross-platform reach.[32] Memes are colloquially called "trolls" on these pages. These digital objects are watermarked with the name of the uploader to assert some kind of authorship—an interesting practice given that memes are typically "authorless" and circulate without direct authorial referents. "Trolling" on these pages is quite different from the popular use of the term *troll*, which implies intentionally unsettling or disrupting viewers to elicit a response for the troll's own amusement. Although the "adult trolls" on these fan pages use provocative language, they share more with memes, which place text and image side by side to tease out incongruences. Such adult troll groups are communities of subcultural users who share an investment in the themes and content that populate these groups.[33]

The now-defunct Facebook page Kamakeli described itself as a vibrant interactive space for "Pleasure, Experience, and Enjoyment" (*Anubhuthi, Anubhavam, Asvadanam*), where community members converse through "likes and comments."[34] Kamakeli's tagline on its cover picture—a page catering to "Mallu Non-veg trolls"[35]—played with the binary pure/impure ("non-veg" implying the carnal) to carve out a space to freely express "impure" or socially nonnormative thoughts. Shakeela appeared on the Kamakeli page in two different avatars (Fig. 36). Her image from her debut film *Play Girls* served as the group's profile image for a period—it was changed on August 14, 2019—and an image of her making a thumbs-up sign, a shot featured in many soft-porn films, appeared on a page that lays out community policy.[36] This page featured photographs of legs under "Kamakeli Hot Hotter Hottest." Here, the silhouette of a supine woman was superimposed over the feet. This focus on women's legs recalls the publicity poster of *Avalude Ravukal* (Her nights, 1978), the massive popularity of which triggered a wave of erotic films in the 1980s.

These pages regularly feature activities or "contests," including competitions for *Kamakeli Kamarani* (sex queen), in which group members vote for "contestants" in the form of profiles of mainstream Malayalam actresses. The images are sanitized and the sexual charge is added through written text, which allows pages to bypass Facebook regulations for offensive images (until they are eventually banned). Trolls on such pages tend to use two different inscription modes—one image-dominant and one text-dominant. In the first mode, trolls use images that directly reference soft-porn films or contentious scandals and thereby invite community members to make intertextual connections between the referenced images and the sexual context. In the second mode, trolls take advantage of the disconnect between text and image, drawing visual references from Malayalam cinema

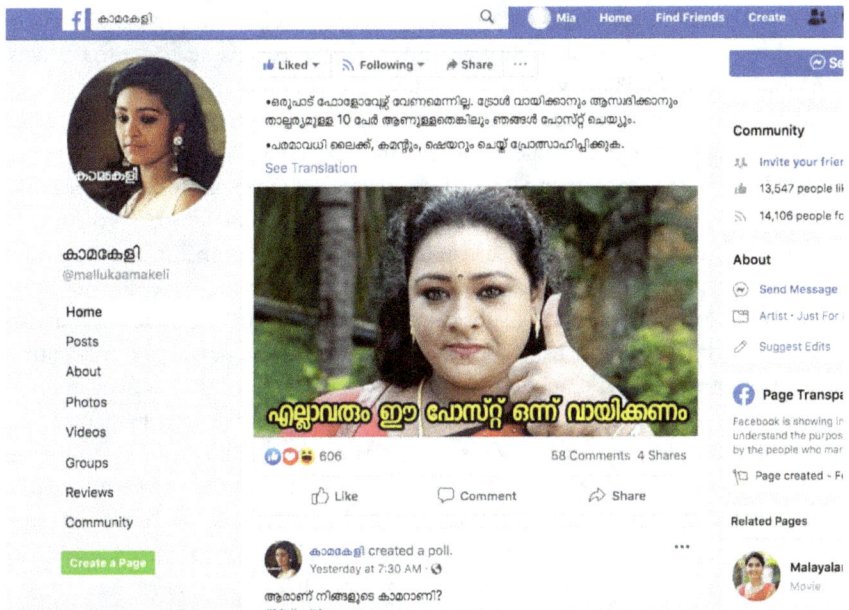

FIGURE 36. Screenshot from *Kamakeli* showing two different images of Shakeela featured on the home page.

or television—often using images that do not have any direct sexual connotation but whose meaning changes drastically when taken out of context and juxtaposed with sexually explicit Malayalam text. This insertion of written text functions like *thundu*, breaking the flow of intended meaning and transforming the object and its meaning by editing. This shock effect exposes the inscription of normative gendered practices and inserts mainstream actors into compromised sexual scenarios that were already part and parcel of the erotic literary tradition. Often, the text is also marked by an asterisk (*) to elide its explicit meanings, in keeping with the use of asterisks in explicit text on social media. Intergenerational love mediated via "Aunty" or *chechi* figures was an oft-repeated theme in the Kamakeli memes. These figures include the "Gulf wife" deprived of conjugal intimacy, female teachers who lure male students into sexual rendezvous, and sexual liberationist female figures who reject marriage. Although these memes ostensibly endow female figures with sexual autonomy, the power invested in these purported figures is transitory—they proclaim a false sense of gender equality by concretizing masculinist modes of performance and misogynistic powers of display.

Adult troll pages coexist with other emergent digital phenomena, including social media micro-celebrities who use such spaces to carve out their fanbases. For instance, California-based Malayali social media influencer Mini Richard, whose

Facebook page has more than 2.5 million followers (as of 2023), strategically mobilizes the demand for sexualized images and markets products that cater to her fans. Richard created the Hugs & Kisses Foundation in 2014 and began using her social media pages to direct her Facebook followers to be prospective patrons of the charity. When she started her profile in Patreon in 2013, the initial pricing tiers were $1, $10 and $25; but she soon found that her users were willing to pay for exclusive package for $25—this was increased first, to $100 and later to $250, for topless pictures.

Richard's social media presence uses the creator-fan relationship as an interface between different platforms including Facebook, Instagram, Patreon, and OnlyFans, with the last two offering subscribers even more direct contact with artists through its tiered levels of access, some of which includes a personal contact number.[37] Her images often emulate the visual and gestural codes of soft-porn films. While some photographs highlight her thighs, navel, and neck, others include performances of role-play (such as dressing up as a schoolgirl or teacher) and even seem to reenact sequences from soft-porn films. She has also curated online photo series that show her in different phases of undress, such as her "pool" or "sexy sari" series, as well as photographs that mark special occasions, such as Independence Day or religious festivals. The fan comments that appear below these images range from appreciations of her efforts to outright declarations of physical violence. While Richard often ignores such trolls, she responds to positive user comments either with a note of thanks for "generous messages" or with her template response, "Hugs and Kisses from California."[38]

In our conversation, Richard spoke at length about how strangers direct message her, requesting "pictures with boobs" and asking how much she charges for a night. She states:

> There is huge sexual frustration among men that I find in Kerala. Since social media offers anonymity, they feel emboldened to send direct messages. That's when I thought that Patreon might be able to capitalize on the hypocrisy around sexuality in Kerala. My experience in Malayalam cinema has also not been great. Since many of photographs on social media were glamorous, many roles that were offered were on the expectation that I was ready for any "adjustment."[39]

During our conversation, Richard stated that there was a substantial interest in her content from Malayali clients based in the Gulf, whose interest in her stemmed from linguistic and ethnic connections. Many seek her for the vicarious female companion of a "a bold Malayali woman," as she puts it. Reflecting on the factors that might be contributing to her popularity, she adds that her situation as a Malayali in the United States and her marriage to an American might have contributed to the interest Malayali clients have in her, "as in the Malayali imagination, a woman who married outside the community, and that too across race, could very well be wild in bed."[40] My interaction with Mini Richards tied up many loose ends I was trying to unpack with the figure of the *madakarani*. Richards gets requests for customized role-playing inflected by tropes from soft-porn. Some

FIGURE 37. Picture of Mini Richard, featured on her Facebook page. Image courtesy Mini Richard.

clients specifically request her for video performances wearing underskirt, Indian bra, and blouse, referencing the sexualized imagination of rustic women in erotic novels and soft-porn (Fig. 37). Many clients, who appear in the fictitious name on Tango, address her as *chechi*, which again refers to the desire for an older woman, a trend that soft-porn films capitalized on.

While there was pushback against her Patreon and photo series from certain quarters of Malayali society, Richard embraces her bodily agency. She countered a personal attack by filing a defamation suit when moralistic portals such as Karma News alleged that she was "leading an immoral life."[41] She challenges sexual norms by contesting her detractors' focus on her age and their suggestion that middle-aged women should not express their sexuality.[42] Beyond this assertion of individual freedom of sexual expression, what is most interesting about Richard's social media presence is her *mode* of sexual posturing. Platforms do not provide direct bodily access to Richard but rather work through the constant deferral of the possibility of touch. Even in her role-play scenarios, Richard reserves the right to cut off clients if they cross the boundaries to which they have consented. Richard performs as a *madakarani* figure on digital screens in a mode of visual and performative citation that invokes soft-porn cinema's actresses. Her mode of reaching out to fans is a form of constant but palpable "nontouch"—perhaps a digital extension of the screen pleasures offered by the *madakarani*. In this, Richard is not very different from the starlets who formed the core of the soft-porn imaginary, wherein the eroticized body on screen replaced the physical sex act. This replacement of the *act* of sex with *images* of sex in the mediated erotic landscape resonates with Jacques Derrida's proposition that masturbation replaces sex.[43] Even with all their opportunities to comment and chat with her, Richard's fans know that they are physically removed from her. At best, the fans can buy coins on Tango to gift her a crown or a kiss (an emoji that then will be superimposed on her face). Yet despite the impossibility of touch, they not only indulge in but pay for the deferral of touch. In that sense, Richard herself becomes an interface in which soft-porn's fantasies of access and excess resurface. Just as the interface of the cinema screen offers visual and aural pleasure with little direct stimulation of the other senses, Richard's digital body *becomes* the screen. The memory of soft-porn resurfaces through Richard's body as it is rendered by the platform. Simultaneously palpable and distant, this digital body, like the search pages on Pornhub and XVideos, becomes part of a larger assemblage formed by the intersection of different senses, images, and technologies.

CONCLUSION

Thus, even after soft-porn's life cycle as a defined industrial genre is well over, its residual effects stick to media production and consumption practices in the contemporary moment. The *madakarani* of soft-porn cinema slips onto the screens of the present in dispersed and varied ways. What is even more striking is the way that the texts, narratives, and overall public experience of the soft-porn years have led to the rise of a soft-porn unconscious that reproduces the kind of scandalous media publics seen in the *Thaniniram* years (see introduction) within the media formations of the present. Soft-porn, then, lingers as a kind of a bridge that glues media publics of the print era to the digitally saturated, 24/7 news cycle of the present. This soft-porn unconscious is, in some ways, neutral, and its (gendered) political charge depends on who uses the tropes and vocabulary of soft-porn and to what effect. I conclude *Rated A* by examining some ways in which the soft-porn unconscious has reemerged in public discourse and media formations outside of the direct field of the cinematic.

Conclusion

In Praise of Bad Women

The pornographic imagination continues to reverberate in Indian media spheres, long after Malayalam soft-porn films fizzled out as an industrial genre. As I have demonstrated throughout this book, media publics are premised on a contentious relationship with normative social and gender codes, such that the information exchanged in this mediated space is necessarily fraught with interruptions, noise, and deferrals. Making sense of such noise is crucial in understanding how politics, social life, sexuality, and normative gender roles overlap. Memories of soft-porn return not just as cinematic renditions, circulating fragments, and forms of posturing, as seen in the previous chapter, but also permeate imaginations of gender negotiations, as well as gossip and scandal in the public sphere. This recirculation is significant for understanding how gender, sexuality, and media impact media publics in South Asia.

In 2013, Kerala's news cycle went into a tizzy about the "Solar Scandal," in which the energy company Team Solar had duped investors of almost seventy lakh rupees (approx. $117,725) by offering to install solar panels in business and residential buildings. Although financial fraud was at the center of the scandal, more salacious details of the case soon eclipsed it—Saritha S. Nair, one of the entrepreneurs who headed Team Solar, revealed that politicians had demanded sexual services from her in exchange for clearance for the project at various phases. Despite being held without bail and receiving negative publicity for fraud, Nair managed to keep the political establishment and media on tenterhooks. While in prison, she wrote a letter listing the names of the high-profile politicians who sought sexual services from her, categorizing them into abusers and consensual partners. Nair also claimed that she had digital evidence to support her allegations, and Asianet News later released the letter.[1] Although sex scandals involving politicians are not new to Kerala (see the introduction), the Solar scandal was unique in the way it catapulted Nair to celebrity status. Previously, women involved in sex scandals in Kerala were subjected to humiliation and disapprobation, and there was a concerted effort to do the same in this case as well.

The villification of Nair's character becomes immediately clear in light of the sexually explicit videos of her that were leaked online. These videos had multiple entries on pornographic sites such as XVideos, Pornhub, Xhamster, and Redtube, and were edited to different lengths and given different labels and tags collated from multiple sources. The fragmentary nature of the videos allows them to exist simultaneously as separate clips on the same platforms. For instance, on Pornhub, different iterations of the leaked video (all removed now) were labeled "I am Saritha Nair," "SELFY-2," and "INDIAN-Saritha Bhabhi Saree Striping."[2]

Some news sites reported the leak as an instance of "revenge porn" that was meant to silence Nair from calling out the sexual harassment being meted out to her.[3] Here the violation occurs not so much in the act of recording but in the act of online, nonconsensual circulation.[4] Leaks are dispersed processes that move media artifacts out of their intended trajectories of circulation and give way to new sensorial assemblages. According to Wendy Hui Kyong Chun and Sarah Friedland, new networked media are inherently marked by leaking, and leaking media is in turn intricately connected to slut-shaming. They write that the "endemic publicity of the internet . . . blames the user—*her* habits of leaking—for systemic vulnerabilities."[5] Habits of leaking and cultural anxieties merge in the Indian scenario, such that a woman's very character comes to be defined by her being recorded, whether knowingly or not. In Nair's case, these videos were leaked to sabotage her credibility, but she negotiated public discourse around the leak in a way that makes her case unique. She repeatedly asserted that she had the right to capture intimate images of herself and that the leak was an intrusion into her privacy. In this regard, the leaked videos further supported Nair's allegations that the police, who had access to her mobile phone and laptop, acted in collusion with the politicians she had named to leak the videos to tarnish her image.

Although Nair shot the videos on her mobile phone, capturing intimate moments of herself alone, her use of conventions of the selfie and her gaze at the camera framed the videos in a different light. Devoid of vocal sound, the videos visually frame Nair as a pleasure-seeking subject in the act of recording herself. As opposed to the traces of hidden cameras or coercion evident in rape videos, here the camera-wielding subject is actively in control of the images shot. The personal tone of the videos suggests she sent them to people with whom she was consensually intimate. But when the videos were leaked to the public, their symbolic meaning changed, pitching Nair as a "bad woman"—someone willing to strip for public consumption. J. Devika refers to the media's use of the term *peedhanam* (torture) to refer to sexual crime as a "covering effect" that shields middle-class sensibilities from the horror of sexual violence while simultaneously leaving room for titillation.[6] In the case of Nair, however, the media used her claims of sexual abuse as a hook to set up her revelations about the salacious details of the relationships she shared with the politicians she named.

However, although there was a move to portray her in a negative light, Nair was able to turn the tide. She stressed the fact that even though she may have been "unconventional," consent mattered when it came to intimate relationships. Despite her implication in the fraud scheme, her sheer persistence in voicing her complaints and her skill in challenging lawyers and journalists ended up swaying public opinion in her favor. Although she changed her statements and then recanted them multiple times, her larger argument was that justice had to be served, regardless of one's political stature or power. In one interview, Nair stated:

> People might cast me as a bad woman and I don't claim that I have too great a reputation among Malayalis. But my point is that when political integrity is bartered for sex, it would certainly discourage more women from entering into the public mainstream, either as entrepreneurs or as influencers of public opinion. Now Saritha S. Nair has become a key word for everything that is rotten with ambitious women, but we need to dig deep to understand what the conditions are that expect women to compromise from the word go.[7]

Nair's public posturing consolidated her image as a self-made woman capable of withstanding challenges in an unfair patriarchal system. Such posturing aligns with the figure of the *madakarani*, who raises questions about gender and social mobility even as she is steeped in sexual overtones. In press conferences, Nair reiterated the need to consider her not as an *ira* (victim), but as a survivor (*athijeevichaval*). By asserting her identity as the aggrieved party, she used the media's staging of her as a *sadharana stree* (ordinary woman) who was caught in a political tussle because of her gender. When the media cast doubt on Nair's allegations, she responded by aligning her exposé with the #MeToo allegations that had just caught worldwide attention. She stated that her revelations are part of the *thurannu parachil* (exposure/confession) that one must succumb to when all other doors are closed.[8] Throughout the scandal, Nair used *savarna* body aesthetics to her advantage in more ways than one. With her ability to carry herself with the confidence that comes with the symbolic capital afforded by upper-caste origins, Nair was able to mark herself as distinct from previous women who had been caught up in sexual scandals. Further, a Dalit woman would not have had the same access to politicians that Nair had, nor would the media have covered her story in the same way. Her revelations were even likened to those of Kuriyedattu Tatri, a Brahmin woman who named sixty-five men from different castes in her *Smartavicharam* (ritualized trial of a Brahmin women accused of adultery) in 1905.[9]

The Solar scandal was also scripted and produced into a film titled *Solar Swapnam* (Solar dream; dir. Joy Antony, 2014). While the film was not pornographic, it was still mired in significant controversy due to its content. The film was denied permission for release when Biju Radhakrishnan, an accused in the Solar case, filed an injunction against it, claiming that the villainous character of Kartha was a defamatory reference to him. *Solar Swapnam* was directed by the soft-porn film director A. T. Joy, who worked under the pseudonym Joy Antony so that the public would not pick up on his association with soft-porn films. According to the producer Raju Joseph, the film highlighted Malayali society's discriminatory tendencies against women.[10] The main character, a thinly disguised "Haritha Nair" played by actress Pooja, is an ambitious woman and a survivor of child sexual abuse who is ready to fight for social justice causes close to her heart. She is duped by an entrepreneur, Ajay Kartha, who exploits her charms to win over investors and leaves her to take the blame for financial fraud. Despite the film's opening disclaimer that it was fictitious, there is little doubt that *Solar Swapnam* bore direct and intentional resemblance to the Solar scandal, the only change being that it centered on a real estate firm instead of a solar energy company. The film's narrative grants symbolic reprieve to Saritha Nair by portraying her screen twin, Haritha, as a victim of a political game played by powerful men. They include the influential politician-turned-businessman K. R. P., who sexually assaults Haritha, and Kartha, who knows all along that this project was only a smokescreen to gather money. The film concludes with the death of K. R. P., leaving Haritha with an opportunity to run for and be elected as a member of the parliament. Reel life and real life uncannily coalescence here, as Saritha Nair attempted to contest elections in 2019. Ultimately, her candidacy was canceled because Section 8 of the Representation of the People Act does not allow any person convicted in a criminal case to contest elections before completing six years of punishment.[11]

In the context of the leak of Saritha Nair's sexually explicit videos, *Solar Swapnam* itself is undergirded by a soft-porn unconscious. Although *Solar Swapnam* is not a soft-porn film, Saritha Nair's extra-textual aura combines with soft-porn's history of incorporating political scandal either in narrative texts or through cut-pieces. The ensuing reaction of this chemistry (with A. T. Joy as a catalyst) recasts the screen pleasures of the *madakarani* through the medium of Nair. Nair, one could argue, is not merely a *madakarani* but also embodies the disruptive power that the cut-piece wields in public discourse. In the wake of the Solar scandal, Nair emerged as a celebrity, appearing on numerous television talk shows and even acting in two short films (not pornographic), *Gulfukarante Bharya* (The wife of the Gulf emigrant; dir. Joshy Medayil, 2015; Fig. 38) and *Anthyakoodasha* (Anointing of the sick; dir. Kiran Anil Kumar, 2015).[12]

Like Mini Richard, the creator discussed in the previous chapter, Saritha Nair's media posturing recalls the figure of the *madakarani*, especially in her negotiation with patriarchy. Her exposé cast doubts on why the political establishment was so unsettled by her revelations. For instance, in an opinion piece on the Solar scandal, Shajahan Madampat writes:

FIGURE 38. Saritha Nair in *Gulfukarante Bharya*. The screenshot is from a fantasy sequence that shows Tom dreaming that he would get a chance at an intimate relationship with Saritha.

A seductress hell-bent on destroying the lives of respectable men, a woman of loose morals who used her body to rise up the social ladder, a habitual liar, a shameless slut—these are some of the epithets usually marshaled to pejoratively describe the woman.... But our collective notions of morality are so skewed that we miss the forest for the woods, and mistake the victim for the perpetrator. Whether Saritha Nair used her sexuality to twist the system to her favor or the system with its corrupt ways edged her ever so cunningly into a precipice is not even a legitimate question because of the simple reason that it is she who lost everything in the game.[13]

The examples of Mini Richard and Nair demonstrate that media technologies have become central to the mediation of sex and scandals in Kerala's public sphere. This is a continuation of the practices used by film magazines to weave fragmentary narratives around scandals and build group consensus among readers to justify the circulation of speculative narratives because of the sticky situations that the subjects have landed themselves in. This forceful exposure is tantamount to defamation, as sensational media pieces breach privacy by connecting seemingly implausible scenarios that are never factually verified as news reports. As Richard's and Nair's cases suggest, scandal publics are fueled by partial exposure: the scandal's fragmentary nature allows varied narrative possibilities to coexist, creating a thicket of information. Such publics are always gendered, and men have a distinct advantage in pushing the rhetoric in their favor. Women like Richard and Nair counter this system in distinctly new ways by taking agential control of their information and identity even when subjected to viral scrutiny.

Where does all of this leave soft-porn? The genre and its industrial practices now belong to the past. Yet as my discussion has shown, soft-porn transcends the film screen—its screen pleasures (and the complexities thereof) lend themselves to other discourses about sex and gender. In the process, soft-porn itself has become a mise en abyme—it draws from and blends into past forms such as glamour cinema, *painkili*, and sensational reporting, and, at the same time, informs how we understand the relationship between sex, obscenity, and the new media landscape in the present. There are lessons to be drawn from soft-porn, be it the alternative labor practices that were engendered by filmmakers or the forms of dissident gender posturing that the *madakarani* in soft-porn narratives enabled. As I have shown throughout *Rated A*, such forms are also not without their own problems. It was never soft-porn filmmakers' intention to resolve gender issues or the puritanical repression of sexuality. But like any great churning, soft-porn has generated productive force. Although misogyny and sexual violence continue to be issues in cinema—even mainstream cinema—without the soft-porn years, the turning of the tide seen in the Saritha Nair case might have been well-nigh impossible. Thus, even though Malayalam soft-porn genre emerged almost as out of accident and necessity, we would be well served to pay attention to the latticework of its media publics. Writing from the positionality of a feminist media scholar, I have offered a humanistic understanding of the social lives of film genres and how they impact our mediated understanding of sex and gender in the contemporary world. In the preceding chapters, I have used archival and ethnographic research to map the intricacies of pornography as an industry and as a genre, foregrounding the agency of performers and industry professionals. Acknowledging the West-centered approach in porn studies, I have shed some light on the South Asian context, where the definitional boundaries of the pornographic are nebulous at best. Attitudes toward porn today continue to be shaped by various factors, including the persistence of the colonial past in current legal regimes and conservative social norms that complicate the categories of the obscene and the pornographic.

In mapping these narratives, my work has been invested in examining a genre that emerged outside the framework of national cinema and the imagined national cinematic center—Bollywood. Curiously, as this book has shown, Malayalam soft-porn came to define the imagination of "Indian" pornography across the country and in places such as the Middle Eastern Gulf. This foregrounds the ways in which national and transnational infrastructures, on the one hand, and industrial practices and genres, on the other, allow certain kinds of sexual imaginations to circulate across the globe. Thus, this book also offers alternative ways of imagining the categories of the regional, the national, and the transnational.

The alternative transnational imaginations and circuits traversed by soft-porn films have, in fact, been a core focus of this research. As I have shown in the preceding pages, soft-porn films owe their genealogy to a wide variety of local sources such as pulp fiction, yellow magazines, and erotic illustrations, as well as transnational sources such as the American exploitation cinema that began to enter India via the NRI scheme, a lucrative import program initiated in the 1980s. Thus, this import of new forms of sexual fantasy and expression was mediated by larger infrastructural forces that were at work prior to the soft-porn moment that had a marked influence on its development as a genre and form of film practice. In turn, Malayalam soft-porn films themselves are carriers of fantasies across borders, especially to the Middle Eastern Gulf, which has a large migrant South Asian population in the oil and service sectors. The popularity of soft-porn films among the Malayali diasporic communities in the Middle East, primarily (but not exclusively) among blue-collar workers, led to the emergence of a clandestine pirate circuit for the distribution of these films, and in the early 2000s, many laborer camps in Dubai used to screen Malayalam soft-porn films to workers as a part of their Friday night entertainment.

Needless to say, there are many gaps in the stories of soft-porn I have tried to tell—partly because of physical constraints and partly due to the paucity of sources. Nonetheless, by locating the tense negotiations between sexuality, import policy, diasporic circulation, labor issues, and censorship in contemporary India, I have offered a model for understanding film genres outside of screen space. As I have shown, such genres constitute not just industrial formations but entire fields of social relations and gendered imaginaries. I fondly remember a meeting with a respondent, Maniappan, in 2013 during one of my initial visits to Kodambakkam. A publicity agent who had been in the industry for more thirty-five years, Maniappan asked me a question that has haunted me throughout the writing of this book:

> For a project like this, getting the pattern of production by skimming through the ledgers and trade journals is not "deep" enough. You should know the lives of the people whose daily sustenance was linked to the making of these films. Can you write a history of a factory without addressing the labor that made the factory functional?[14]

Although Maniappan may not have been thinking about a mixed-methods approach or about the kind of negotiations between aspirations, hope, and labor that many scholars have written about, his advice was valuable in pushing me to think critically about why this project must be about recovering the narratives of soft-porn personnel as much as it is about mapping the networks that these workers carefully created for sustaining their lives and careers. Although the labor that went into making these films was delegitimized because of the taboos associated with soft-porn, many of these workers were aware that adult film circuits existed elsewhere and that the quest for respectability had driven other adult filmmakers to organize. The founding of the Adult Film Association of America in 1969, which brought distributors and exhibitors together, was a result of the fight against censorship and efforts to cultivate a public that is open to the market these films can provide. I spoke to many soft-porn filmmakers who were familiar with this history of exploitation films and who bemoaned the fact that their efforts to make sexually explicit films would have succeeded had they only been making them elsewhere. Thus, even in the creative freedom with which they experimented, these filmmakers, actors, and technicians constantly remade the genre of soft-porn films as they worked through and improvised regulatory mechanisms to stay afloat in selected distribution platforms. This book is an incomplete but invested story of these changes.

NOTES

INTRODUCTION: SOFT-PORN 101

1. Swapna Mukhopadhyay, *The Enigma of the Kerala Woman: A Failed Promise of Literacy* (New Delhi: Social Science Press, 2007); K. K. Baburaj, *Mattoru Jeevitham Saadhyamaanu* [Another life is possible] (Calicut: Other Books, 2019); Sharmila Sreekumar, *Scripting Lives: Narratives of Privileged Women in Kerala* (Hyderabad: Orient Blackswan, 2009).

2. J. Devika and Mini Sukumar, "Making Space for Feminist Social Critique in Contemporary Kerala," *Economic and Political Weekly* 41, no. 42 (October 21–27, 2006): 4469–75.

3. J. Devika, "Feminism and Late Twentieth-century Governmentality in Kerala, India: Towards a Critical History," in *Feminist Subversion and Complicity: Governmentalities and Gender Knowledge in South Asia*, ed. M. Mukhopadhyay (New Delhi: Zubaan, 2006), 123–46.

4. J. Devika, "Getting beyond the Governmental Fix in Kerala," *Signs: Journal of Women in Culture and Society* 39, no. 3 (2014): 582.

5. V. N. Deepa, "Queering Kerala: Reflections on Sahayatrika," in *Because I Have a Voice: Queer Politics in India*, ed. G. Bhan and A. Narrain (New Delhi: Yoda Press, 2005), 175–96; Nalini Jameela, *Me, Sex Worker: The Autobiography of Nalini Jameela* (Kottayam: DC Books, 2005).

6. Shobha, interview by author, June 5, 2013, Trivandrum.

7. "The Kerala Sex Education Row," *Rediff*, February 16, 2007, https://www.rediff.com/news/2007/feb/16kerala.htm.

8. J. Binuraj, "Abasha Arattukal," *India Today*, October 4, 2000, 38–39.

9. "The Cinematograph (Amendment) Act, 2023," *Gazette of India* (Ministry of Law and Justice, New Delhi), August 4, 2023, https://mib.gov.in/sites/default/files/Gazette%20of%20India%20for%20The%20Cinematograph%20%28Amendment%29%20Bill%202023.pdf.

10. "Film Censorship Norms Relaxed," *Economic Times*, January 12, 1978.

11. Charu Gupta, *Sexuality, Obscenity, Community: Women, Muslims, and the Hindu Public in Colonial India* (New York: Palgrave, 2001), 30–33; 53.

12. "Bombay Calling," *filmindia* 14, no. 4 (April 1948): 12.

13. Manishita Dass, *Outside the Lettered City: Cinema, Modernity, and the Public Sphere in Late Colonial India* (Oxford: Oxford University Press, 2015), 3–4.

14. William Mazzarella, *Censorium: Cinema and the Open Edge of Mass Publicity* (Durham, NC: Duke University Press, 2013), 17.

15. One of the incidents involved the boycott of the film awards by the Minister of State for Sports and Women Margaret Alva, citing her concern about Raj Kapoor's *Ram Teri Ganga Maili* (1985), which won top honors. This boycott came after protests by women's organizations about the "derogatory portrayal of women" in the film. Alva tabled the Indecent Representation of Women (Prohibition) Act in 1986 in the Rajya Sabha.

16. "Sex is the Bane of Malayalam Films," *The Indian Express*, February 16, 1979.

17. Catharine MacKinnon and Andrea Dworkin, eds., *In Harm's Way: The Pornography Civil Rights Hearings* (Cambridge, MA: Harvard University Press, 1998).

18. S. V. Srinivas, *Megastar: Chiranjeevi and Telugu Cinema after N. T. Rama Rao* (New Delhi: Oxford University Press, 2009), 164, 168, 170.

19. Material compiled in *Manushi* 8 (1981), cited in Vimal Balasubrahmanyan, "The Watchdogs: Women Monitor the Media," in *Gender and Censorship*, ed. Brinda Bose (New Delhi: Women Unlimited, 2006), 69.

20. "Soft Porn Film Stopped," *Maharashtra Herald*, September 4, 1983.

21. Balasubrahmanyan, "Watchdogs," 57; Kaumudi News Service, "Against Blue Films," *Film*, September 1983, 31–32.

22. Balasubrahmanyan, "Watchdogs," 65.

23. Nina Kapoor cited in Balasubrahmanyan, "Watchdogs," 65.

24. Tejaswini Ganti, "The Limits of Decency and the Decency of Limits: Censorship and Bombay Film Industry," in *Censorship in South Asia: Cultural Regulation from Sedition to Seduction*, ed. Raminder Kaur and William Mazzarella (Bloomington: Indiana University Press, 2009), 87–122.

25. Sandeep Unnithan, "People Who Were Shopkeepers Are Now Censor Board Members: Vijay Anand," *India Today*, August 5, 2002, https://www.indiatoday.in/magazine/05-08-2002.

26. Brinda Bose, "When the Towel Drops: Sexuality, Censorship, and Cinema," *Seminar*, March 2008, https://www.india-seminar.com/2008/583/583_brinda_bose.htm.

27. Shohini Ghosh, "The Troubled Existence of Sex and Sexuality: Feminists Engage with Censorship," in *Image Journeys: Audio-visual Media and Cultural Change in India*, ed. Christiane Brosius and Melissa Butcher (New Delhi: Sage, 1999), 233–60.

28. Arvind Rajagopal, "Preface," in *The Indian Public Sphere: Readings in Media History*, ed. Rajagopal (New Delhi: Oxford University Press, 2009), xiii.

29. Sanjay Srivastava, "Street, Footpath, Gated Community: On the Cultures of Indian Pornography," in *Sexuality Studies*, ed. Srivastava (New Delhi: Oxford University Press, 2013), 228–53.

30. Gregory Lukow and Steven Ricci, "The 'Audience' Goes 'Public': Intertexuality, Genre, and the Responsibilities of Film Literacy," *On Film* 12 (Spring 1984): 29.

31. Binuraj, "Abasha Arattukal," 38.

32. Warwick Mules, "Media Publics and the Transnational Public Sphere," *Critical Arts: North-South Cultural and Media Studies* 12 (1998): 24–44.

33. Mules, "Media Publics," 24.

34. Jürgen Habermas, *The Structural Transformation of the Public Sphere: An Inquiry into a Category of Bourgeois Society* (Cambridge, MA: MIT Press, 1991), 171.

35. Craig Calhoun, ed., *Habermas and the Public Sphere* (Cambridge, MA: MIT Press, 1992); Nancy Fraser, "Rethinking the Public Sphere: A Contribution to the Critique of Actually Existing Democracy," *Social Text* 25/26 (1990): 56–80; Joan Landes, *Women and the Public Sphere in the Age of the French Revolution* (Ithaca, NY: Cornell University Press, 1988).

36. Geoff Eley, "Nations, Publics, and Political Cultures: Placing Habermas in the Nineteenth Century," in *Habermas and the Public Sphere*, ed. Craig Calhoun (Cambridge, MA: MIT Press, 1992), 325.

37. Michael Warner, *Publics and Counter Publics* (Cambridge, MA: MIT Press, 2002), 413–14.

38. Thomas Blom Hansen, "Whose Public, Whose Authority? Reflections on the Moral Force of Violence," *Modern Asian Studies* 52, no. 3 (2018): 1076–87; Sudipta Kaviraj, "Filth and the Public Sphere: Concepts and Practices about Space in Calcutta," *Public Culture* 10, no. 1 (1997): 83–113; Sandria B. Freitag, *Collective Action and Community: Public Arenas and the Emergence of Communalism in North India* (Berkeley: University of California Press, 1989).

39. Arjun Appadurai and Carol A. Breckenridge, "Editor's Comment" and "Why Public Culture?," *Public Culture* 1, no. 1 (1988): 6.

40. Arvind Rajagopal, "A 'Split Public' in the Making and Unmaking of the Ram Janmabhumi Campaign," in *The Indian Public Sphere: Readings in Media History*, ed. Rajagopal (New Delhi: Oxford University Press, 2009), 207–27.

41. Rajagopal, "A 'Split Public,'" 208.

42. Devika and Sukumar, "Making Space," 4469–75.

43. Udaya Kumar, "Ambivalences of Publicity: Transparency and Exposure in K. Ramakrishna Pillai's Thought," in *The Public Sphere from Outside the West*, ed. Divya Dwivedi and Sanil V (London: Bloomsbury, 2017), 82–83.

44. J. Devika, interview by author, November 29, 2017, Trivandrum.

45. J. Devika, "Memory's Fatal Lure: The Left, the Congress, and 'Jeevan' in Kerala," *Economic and Political Weekly*, 43, no. 30 (July 26, 2008): 13–16.

46. The Touring Gestapo, "Samskaram Virangaladikkunnu" [The culture is shaken], *Thaniniram Film Entertainment Magazine* 5, no. 11 (August–September 1957): 9–99.

47. "Good Books for Entertainment and Knowledge," *Thaniniram Film Entertainment Magazine* 5, no. 11 (August–September 1957): 50.

48. The price for a dozen bedroom photos and intercourse photos were three and three and a half rupees, respectively. *Thaniniram Film Entertainment Magazine* 5, no. 11 (August–September 1957): 63.

49. Rajeev Kumaramkandath, "Sexual Realism? (Hetero)Sexual Excess and the Birth of Obscenity," in (*Hi)Stories of Desire: Sexualities and Culture in Modern India* (Cambridge: Cambridge University Press, 2020), 62.

50. Vaikom Muhammad Basheer, "Sabdangal," in *Basheer Sampoorna Kritikal* [Basheer complete works] (1992; Kottayam: DC Books, 2008), 429.

51. M. R. Chandrasekharan, *Keralathile Purogamana Prastanathinte Charitram* [The history of progressive movement in Kerala] (Calicut: Olive Publications: 1999), 349.

52. Govinda Pillai, "Udathasahityavum Janapriyasahityavum" [High literature and popular literature] in *Janapriya Sahityam Malayalathil* [Popular literature in Malayalam], ed. M. G. Sreekumar (Kottayam: National Book Stall, 2014), 26–27.

53. K. A. Martin, "Ganesh's Exit a 1964 Redux of P. T. Chacko," *The Hindu*, April 3, 2013, http://www.thehindu.com/news/cities/Kochi/ganeshs-exit-a-1964-redux-of-pt-chacko/article4574223.ece.

54. Carmel Christy, *Sexuality and Public Space in India: Reading the Visible* (London and New York: Routledge, 2017).

55. Brian Harvey, *Russia in Space: The Failed Frontier* (London: Springer, 2001).

56. High Court judgment, Joseph@ Baby v. S. I. of Police on January 29, 2005, Order by K. A. Abdul Gafoor and R. Basant, paragraph 10, https://indiankanoon.org/doc/207046.

57. Martin, "Ganesh's Exit."

58. Manjunath Pendakur, *Indian Popular Cinema: Industry, Ideology, and Consciousness* (Cresskill, NJ: Hampton Press, 2003); Navaneetha Mokkil Maruthur, *Unruly Figures: Queerness, Sex Work, and the Politics of Sexuality in Kerala* (Seattle: University of Washington Press, 2019).

59. Advertisement, *The Times of India*, 1978.

60. By our Film Critic, "Sexplosive Film," *The Indian Express*, March 4, 1978.

61. E. V. Sreedharan, telephone interview by author, December 18, 2013.

62. "Avalude Ravukal poster," *Film*, issue 94, 1978.

63. Express News Service, "Film maker Asked to Pay Damage," *The Indian Express*, August 8, 1979.

64. "Malayalam Film seized in Madras," *The Hindu*, September 15, 1978.

65. "Ban on Film Lifted in Kerala Area," *The Times of India*, December 12, 1978.

66. "Censorship," Report on the Working Group on National Film Policy, 1980, in the digital collection, NFAI, Pune, accessed December 2022.

67. Bhrigupati Singh, "Aadamkhor Haseena (The Man-Eating Beauty) and the Anthropology of a Moment," *Contributions to Indian Sociology* 42, no. 2 (2008): 258.

68. "Government Not to Allow Sex on Screen," The International Press-cutting Service, February 6, 1978, in NFAI library, accessed November 2017.

69. Huneed Contractor, "Hindi Soft Porn Films: A Part of the Medium?" *Maharashtra Herald*, January 11, 1990.

70. "Sex is the Bane of Malayalam Cinema."

71. Mary E. John, "Globalization, Sexuality, and the Visual Field: Issues and Non-issues for Cultural Critique," in *The Indian Public Sphere: Readings in Media History*, ed. Arvind Rajagopal (New Delhi: Oxford University Press, 2009), 279.

72. Linda Williams, *Hard Core: Power, Pleasure, and the "Frenzy of the Visible"* (Berkeley: University of California Press, 1989), 41.

73. Williams, *Hard Core*, 8.

74. David Andrews, *Soft in the Middle: The Contemporary Softcore Feature in Its Contexts* (Columbus: Ohio State University Press, 2006), 10, 2.

75. Williams, *Hard Core*, 123.

76. Eithne Johnson, "Excess and Ecstasy: Constructing Female Pleasure in Porn Movies," *Velvet Light Trap* 32 (1993): 37.

77. John Corbett and Terri Kapsalis, "Aural Sex: The Female Orgasm in Popular Sound," *The Drama Review* 40, no. 3 (1996): 102–11.

78. For this analysis, I am indebted to the expertise of Jeff Smith, an expert on film sound and music at the University of Wisconsin-Madison.

79. Andrews, *Soft in the Middle*, 15.

80. Laura Kipnis, *Bound and Gagged: Pornography and the Politics of Fantasy in America* (Durham, NC: Duke University Press, 1998), 123.

81. Williams, *Hard Core*, 6.

82. Monika Mehta, *Censorship and Sexuality in Bombay Cinema* (Austin: University of Texas Press, 2011), 3.

83. Darshana Sreedhar Mini, "The Spectral Duration of Malayalam Soft-porn: Disappearance, Desire, and Haunting," *Bioscope: South Asian Screen Studies* 7, no. 2 (2017): 130.

84. Sreenivasan, "Neela Chitrangal: Maruunna Samvakyangal" (Blue films: Changing equations), *India Today* 12, no. 2 (January 16, 2001): 46–47.

85. Darshana Sreedhar Mini, "Locating the 'B' in B-circuit Cinema," in *Film Studies: An Introduction*, ed. Vebhuti Duggal, Bindu Menon, and Spandan Bhattacharya (Delhi/Kolkata: Worldview Publications, 2022), 319–28.

86. *The Times of India*, November 16, 1984, 2, and March 17, 1978, 2.

87. Siddarth (actor, name changed), in discussion with author, November 12, 2018, Chennai.

88. Tom Gunning, "The Cinema of Attractions: Early Film, Its Spectator, and the Avant-Garde," in *The Cinema of Attractions Reloaded*, ed. Wanda Strauven (Amsterdam: Amsterdam University Press, 2006), 382.

89. Lotte Hoek, *Cut Pieces: Celluloid Obscenity and Popular Cinema in Bangladesh* (New York: Columbia University Press), 2014.

90. Hoek, *Cut Pieces*, 2, 10.

91. Hoek, *Cut Pieces*, 30.

92. Hoek, *Cut Pieces*, 4.

93. A. T. Joy, interview by author, July 22, 2016, Chennai.

94. Roshan, interview by author, June 5, 2010, Trivandrum.

95. Nandu, interview by author, September 10, 2011, Trivandrum.

96. The different thematic categorizations for the feature films include historical, biographical, mythological, devotional, legendary, horror, fantasy, action/thriller, crime, satire, comedy, spoof, and adventure. Mehta, *Censorship and Sexuality*, 14.

97. Anandavalli (member of certification committee), interview by author, July 13, 2016, Chennai.

98. Elena Gorfinkel, *Lewd Looks: American Sexploitation Cinema in the 1960s* (Minneapolis: University of Minnesota Press, 2017), 97.

99. Directors A. T. Joy, Thrikkunnappuzha Vijayakumar, and Dubai Mani, interviews by author, September, July, and August 2013, respectively.

100. Susanna Paasonen, *Carnal Resonance: Affect and Online Pornography* (Cambridge, MA: MIT Press, 2011); Tristan Taormino et al., *The Feminist Porn Book: The Politics of Producing Pleasure* (New York: The Feminist Press at the City University of New York, 2013); Mireille Miller-Young, *A Taste for Brown Sugar: Black Women in Pornography* (Durham,

NC: Duke University Press, 2014); Heather Berg, *Porn Work: Sex, Labor, and Late Capitalism* (Chapel Hill: University of North Carolina Press, 2021).

101. Clarissa Smith and Feona Atwood, "Porn Studies: An Introduction," *Porn Studies* 1, no. 1–2 (2014): 1–6.

102. Miller-Young, *A Taste for Brown Sugar*, vii.

103. Jennifer C. Nash, *The Black Body in Ecstasy: Reading Race, Reading Pornography* (Durham, NC: Duke University Press, 2014), 2–3.

104. Vijeta Kumar, "S for Silk Smitha," *Rum Lola Rum* (blog), April 12, 2020, https://rumlolarum.wordpress.com/2020/04/12/s-for-silk-smitha.

105. Jenny Rowena, "The 'Dirt' in the Dirty Picture: Caste, Gender, and Silk Smitha," *Round Table India*, December 17, 2012, http://roundtableindia.co.in/index.php?option=com_content&view=article&id=5283:the-dirt-in-the-dirty-picture-caste-gender-and-silk-smitha&catid=119:feature&Itemid=132; Manju Edachira, "Anti-caste Aesthetics and Dalit Interventions in Indian Cinema," *Economic & Political Weekly* 55, no.38 (September 19, 2020): 47–53; Shyma P., "The Caste of Casting: Thilakan and 'Backward' Articulations in Malayalam Cinema," *BioScope: South Asian Screen Studies* 13, no.2 (2022): 154–75.

106. Tejaswini Ganti, *Producing Bollywood: Inside the Contemporary Hindi Film Industry* (Durham, NC: Duke University Press. 2012); Clare M. Wilkinson-Weber, *Fashioning Bollywood: The Making and Meaning of Hindi Film Costume* (London: Bloomsbury Academic, 2014).

107. Vicki Mayer, *Below the Line: Producers and Production Studies in the New Television Economy* (Durham, NC: Duke University Press, 2011), 5.

108. Neepa Majumdar, *Wanted Cultured Ladies Only! Female Stardom and Cinema in India, 1930s–1950s* (Champaign: University of Illinois Press, 2009); Kiranmayi Indraganti, *Her Majestic Voice: South Indian Female Playback Singers and Stardom, 1945–1955* (New Delhi: Oxford University Press, 2016); Usha Iyer, *Dancing Women: Choreographing Corporeal Histories of Hindi Cinema* (London: Oxford University Press, 2020).

109. Usha Iyer, "Stardom Ke Peeche Kya Hai? / What is behind the Stardom? Madhuri Dixit, the Production Number, and the Construction of the Female Star Text in 1990s Hindi Cinema," *Camera Obscura* 30, no. 3 (2015): 129–59.

110. Purnima Mankekar, *Screening Culture Viewing Politics: An Ethnography of Television, Womanhood, and Nation in Postcolonial India* (Durham, NC: Duke University Press, 1999), 103; Kamala Visweswaran, *Fictions of Feminist Ethnography* (Minneapolis: University of Minnesota Press, 1994), 139.

111. Amy Flowers, *The Fantasy Factory: An Insider's View of the Phone Sex Industry* (Philadelphia: University of Pennsylvania Press, 1998).

112. Peter Alilunas, *Smutty Little Movies: The Creation and Regulation of Adult Video* (Berkeley: University of California Press, 2016), 29; Eric Schaefer, "The Problem with Sexploitation Movies," *Iluminace* 3 (2012): 151.

113. Alilunas, *Smutty Little Movies*, 30.

114. Andrews, *Soft in the Middle*, 185.

115. Allyson Nadia Field, "Editor's Introduction: Acts of Speculation," *Feminist Media Histories* 8, no. 3 (2022): 2.

116. Roshan, interview.

1. *MADAKARANI*: THE SCREEN PLEASURES OF THE SEX SIREN IN MALAYALAM CINEMA

1. Tom Brown and Belen Vidal, eds., *The Biopic in Contemporary Film Culture* (New York: Routledge, 2014).
2. "Extras," *Film Mirror* 28, no. 1 (January 1, 1989): 25–26.
3. Uma Chakravarti, *Gendering Caste: Through a Feminist Lens* (Calcutta: Stree, 2003).
4. Debashree Mukherjee, *Bombay Hustle: Making Movies in a Colonial City* (New York: Columbia University Press, 2020), 142; Kunnukuzhi S. Mani, *P. K. Rosy: The Mother of Malayalam Cinema* (Trivandrum: Mythri Books, 2019), 23; Anirban K. Baishya, "Revisiting Assamese Cinema," MPhil diss., Jawaharlal Nehru University, 2013.
5. Ruth Vanita, *Dancing with the Nation: Courtesans in Bombay Cinema* (London: Bloomsbury 2018), 41.
6. Lens Eye, "A Hard Day's Starlet," *The Times of India*, October 9, 1988.
7. Madhuja Mukherjee, *Voices of the Talking Stars: Women of Indian Cinema and Beyond* (New Delhi: Sage, 2017).
8. Durba Mitra, *Indian Sex Life: Sexuality and the Colonial Origins of Modern Social life* (Princeton, NJ: Princeton University Press, 2020), 50.
9. "Cinemalokam," *Cinemamasika* 2, no. 9 (1940): 33.
10. *Anasashyam* [Immorality], special issue, *Cinemamasika* (September 1948): 95.
11. "Athum Itum: Cinematharangalude rahasya jeevithareeti (This and that: The secret life of cine stars)," *Cinema Masika* 1, no. 1 (October 11, 1946): 66.
12. "Film Extra in Eve's Garb," *filmindia* 14, no. 4 (April 1948): 55.
13. "Sultanas in Sex Trade," *filmindia* 14, no. 7 (July 1948): 10–11.
14. TNM Staff, "Director Omar Alleges Trailer Launch Cancelled As Mall Didn't Want Shakeela As Guest," *News Minute*, November 19, 2022, https://www.thenewsminute.com/article/director-omar-alleges-trailer-launch-cancelled-mall-didn-t-want-shakeela-guest-170123.
15. Prabha Kotiswaran, *Dangerous Sex, Invisible Labor: Sex Work and the Law in India* (Princeton, NJ: Princeton University Press, 2011).
16. Announcement of "Chuvannatheruvil Veenadinjavar" (Those trapped in redlight streets), *Nana*, 1974, accessed from the loose-bound volume at Appan Thampuran library, Thrissur, September 14, 2013.
17. Anjali Arondekar, *Abundance: Sexuality's History* (Durham, NC: Duke University Press, 2023), 3.
18. "Extras," *Film Mirror*.
19. Jane M. Gaines, *Pink-Slipped: What Happened to Women in Silent Film Industries* (Champaign: University of Illinois Press, 2018); Shelley Stamp, *Lois Weber in Early Hollywood* (Berkeley: University of California Press, 2015); Erin Hill, *Never Done: A History of Women's Work in Media Production* (New Brunswick, NJ: Rutgers University Press, 2016); Maggie Hennefeld, *Specters of Slapstick and Silent Film Comediennes* (New York: Columbia University Press, 2018).
20. Shiv Visvanathan, "The Dirty Picture: Free, Sexual and Female," *Firstpost*, December 6, 2011, http://www.firstpost.com/entertainment/the-dirty-picture-free-sexual-and-female-148161.html.

21. A. Srinivasa Rao, "Silk Smitha Wasn't Dirty At All, Says Brother," *India Today*, December 13, 2011, http://indiatoday.intoday.in/story/silk-smitha-the-dirty-picture-brother/1/163431.html.

22. Gaurav Malani, "It Was Awkward Discussing Necklines and Hemlines with Vidya Balan: Milan Luthria," *The Times of India*, December 1, 2011, http://timesofindia.indiatimes.com/entertainment/bollywood/news-interviews/Vidya-Balan-has-a-unique-sex-appeal-Milan-Luthria/articleshow/10932269.cms?referral=PM.

23. Malani, "It Was Awkward."

24. Ashish Rajadhyaksha, "The 'Bollywoodization' of the Indian Cinema: Cultural Nationalism in a Global Arena," *Inter-Asia Cultural Studies* 4, no. 1 (2003): 25–39.

25. Taniya Talukdar, "'Dirty Picture' Chose Men: Milan Luthra," *Daily News and Analysis*, April 11, 2011, http://www.dnaindia.com/entertainment/report-dirty-picture-chose-me-milan-luthria-1530653.

26. Nandhu Sundaram, "The Man Who Found Silk Smitha: Vinu Chakravarthy Reminded Us of the Classicism in Cinema," *News Minute*, April 28, 2017, http://www.thenewsminute.com/article/man-who-found-silk-smitha-vinu-chakravarthy-reminded-us-classism-cinema-61116; Vicki Lalwani, "Ekta Kapoor Slams Silk Smitha's Boyfriend," *The Times of India*, February 21, 2011, https://timesofindia.indiatimes.com/entertainment/hindi/bollywood/news/Ekta-slams-Silk-Smithas-boyfriend/articleshow/7538035.cms.

27. Jenny Rowena, "The 'Dirt' in the *Dirty Picture*: Caste, Gender, and Silk Smitha," *Round Table India*, June 17, 2012, https://www.roundtableindia.co.in/the-dirt-in-the-dirty-picture-caste-gender-and-silk-smitha.

28. Jenny Rowena, The 'Dirt' in The Dirty Picture: Caste, Gender and Silk Smitha—Part 2," *Dalitweb*, October 8, 2012, https://www.dalitweb.org/?p=106.

29. Yogesh Maitreya, "Indian Film and the Dalit Identity: Perariyathavar Is the Cinema that a Caste-society Needs to Become Humane," *Firstpost*, July 15, 2020, https://www.firstpost.com/art-and-culture/indian-film-and-the-dalit-identity-perariyathavar-is-the-cinema-that-a-caste-society-needs-to-become-humane-8598221.html.

30. Drawing from the writings of Mahatma Jyotiba Phule (1827–1890), Iyothee Thass (1845–1914), and Bhimrao (Babasaheb) Ambedkar (1891–1956), Ambedkarite filmmakers foreground the Dalit-Bahujan movement's efforts to show how social, cultural, and historical contexts shape subjectivities and advocate for democratizing social and intellectual life by reclaiming narratives. Mapping the incipient ways caste structures uphold rigid social stratification through hereditary status, endogamy, and social barriers sanctioned by custom, law, or religion, Ambedkarite filmmakers shed light on the lack of conversation on caste in Indian cinema by drawing attention to the exclusion faced by marginalized communities by relying on narratives that can reflect the experiences of the caste-oppressed communities.

31. Susan Gubar, *Racechanges: White Skin, Black Face in American Culture* (New York and Oxford: Oxford University Press, 1997), 38.

32. Shailaja Paik, *The Vulgarity of Caste: Dalits, Sexuality, and Humanity in Modern India* (Stanford, CA: Stanford University Press, 2022), 1–2.

33. Ranjani Mazumdar, *Bombay Cinema: An Archive of the City* (Minneapolis: University of Minnesota Press, 2007), 86.

34. Erumeli Paremeshwaran Pillai, *Malayala Sahityam kalakhattangalilude* [Malayalam literature through different stages] (1996; Kottayam: DC Books, 2013), 129.

35. "The Sex Stories of Zeenat: The Story of Sex Worker Zeenat," *Fire* (January 2009): 32.

36. http://www.firemagonline.com/445/?ok.

37. K. N. Shaji (one of the co-founders of *Fire* magazine), interview by author, November 12, 2017.

38. The city of Madras was officially renamed Chennai in 1996. I use Madras when the accounts I cite refer directly to it or were written before 1996. For all other purposes, I use the name Chennai.

39. Vazhoor Jose, who had worked with *Nana* in the 1980s, went on to become a publicity agent for film production companies and is still much sought-after for public relations work in the Malayalam cinema industry.

40. "Grab the Opportunity that Beckons You," *Nana*, October 1986, 13.

41. Although the journalist is not in the frame, the details carrying his identity and mode of procuring images are emblazoned on the actual photographs. However, the individual journalist is not credited in these articles—usually, the byline is "Madras Correspondent."

42. Ariella Azoulay, *The Civil Contract of Photography* (New York: Zone Books, 2008), 15.

43. Rarichan (personal collector), in discussion with author, April 15, 2013.

44. Anil (name changed), interview by author, April 3, 2012.

45. In the 1970s and 1980s, *Nana* and *Chitrabhumi* carried special issues in remembrance of actors like Satyan, Adoor Bhasi, and Prem Nazir; actresses like Rani Chandra, Vijayashree, Rani Padmini, and Silk Smitha; directors like John Abraham and Padmarajan; and producers like Kunchacko.

46. "Alden Whitman, Dead at 76; Made an Art of Times Obituaries," *New York Times*, September 5, 1990, http://www.nytimes.com/1990/09/05/nyregion/obituary-alden-whitman-is-dead-at-76-made-an-art-of-times-obituaries.html.

47. "Rani Padmini: Remembering the Tragedy: Lives Destroyed in the Mad Rush for Fame," *Chitrabhumi*, November 2–8, 1986, 14–17.

48. "Only Five People to Witness Rani Padmini's Funeral," *Chitrabhumi*, November 9–15, 1986, 26–28; "Story of Indira as the Actress' Mother," *Chitrabhumi*, November 9–15, 1986, 27.

49. "Rani Padmini," 15.

50. "Rani Padmini," 14.

51. "In Search of the Mysteries Behind the Double Murders," *Nana*, November 1986, 8–15.

52. "Need Male Support," *Chitrabhumi*, December 7–12, 1986, 29.

53. Kakkanadan, "Malayala Films in Gulf Dweeps," *Nana*, December 16, 1973, 10–11.

54. "Why Did I Decide Not to Act in Udaya Films?" *Nana*, December 2, 1973, 13–14.

55. "Udaya Files Defamation Suit against Nana and Vijayashree," *Nana*, December 23, 1973, 36.

56. "Udaya Files Defamation Suit," 36.

57. "Isn't This Too Much" and "Ponnapuramkotta and Gayatri," *Nana*, April 1973, 1, 13. The reference to toddy business was seen as objectionable to Krishnaswamy, the managing director of *Nana*, as many *abkari* (the selling or manufacture of liquor) businessmen

had donned the mantle of film producers. Hence, an apology for the use of this reference appeared in the "Correction" column in the next issue of *Nana*.

58. *Chithrabhumi* featured the film in a quiz years later in 2001, asking readers to identify its title based on this specific scene, which showcased the moment signaling the fall of Vijayashree-Udaya relations. "Movie Quiz," *Chithrabhumi*, January 28–February 3, 2001, 35.

59. K. V. S. Elayath. "Fight to Finish," *Nana*, January 10, 1987, 39.

60. Elayath, "Fight to Finish," 38–40.

61. Jayaraj, Bombay, "Vijayashree Allergy," Readers Page, *Nana*, December 16, 1973, 29.

62. "What Do You Want? An Interview or a Confession?" *Nana*, December 16, 1973, 9.

63. K. V. S. Elayath, "Wartime Preparations for the Second Phase of Battle," *Nana*, January 3–10, 1987, 38–40.

64. K. N. Shaji Kumar, *Cinemamangalam*, "When She Was Left All Alone" (Published as part of a series on the life of Smitha titled *Nishashalabham* [Nocturnal butterfly]), April 8, 2013, 17; and "The Multifarious Roles Smitha Enacted" (part of the same series), May 27, 2013.

65. Paul Zacharia, "Silk Smitha's Story was of Brutal Economics and Sexual Politics of the Southern Film Industry," *The Times of India*, October 10, 2011, https://timesofindia.indiatimes.com/india/Silk-Smithas-story-was-of-brutal-economics-and-sexual-politics-of-the-southern-film-industry/pmredirectshow/10298000.cms.

66. "Smitha Wanted to Become an Actress like Savithri," *Chitrabhumi*, October 6, 1996.

67. A. C. Srihari, "Smithayude Maranam: Oru Flashback" [Smitha's death: A flashback], in *Vishudda Smitha* [Virtuous Smitha], ed. Shivakumar Kankol (Kannoor: Spectrum, 1997), 5–7; Shivakumar Kankol, "Oru Atmahatyanandara Kuruppu" [A Post-suicide note] in Kankol, *Vishudda Smitha*, 11–14.

68. See "Silk Smitha of *The Dirty Picture* Booked for Obscenity," *India Today Online*, December 8, 2011, http://indiatoday.intoday.in/story/silk-smitha-of-the-dirty-picture-booked-for-obscenity/1/163294.html; Rao, "Silk Smitha Wasn't 'Dirty' at All."

69. K. Aswathy, "Silk Smitha Revamped," *New Indian Express*, April 19, 2013, http://www.newindianexpress.com/entertainment/malayalam/2013/apr/19/silk-smitha-revamped-469534.html.

70. Jon Lewis, *Hard-Boiled Hollywood: Crime and Punishment in Postwar Los Angeles* (Oakland: University of California Press, 2017), 34–35.

71. Christopher Hamlin, "Forensic Facts, the Guts of Rights," in *Global Forensic Cultures*, ed. Ina Burney and Hamlin (Baltimore: Johns Hopkins University Press, 2019), 6.

72. Hamlin, "Forensic Facts," 7.

73. Giuliana Bruno, *Streetwalking on a Ruined Map: Cultural Theory and City Films of Elvira Notari* (Princeton, NJ: Princeton University Press, 1993), 271, 272–74.

74. Caroline Osella and Filippo Osella, "Young Malayali Men and Their Movie Heroes," in *South Asian Masculinities: Context of Change, Sites of Continuity*, ed. Radhika Chopra, Filippo Osella, and Caroline Osella (New Delhi: Women Unlimited, 2004), 224–61.

75. Darshana Sreedhar and Vinu Abraham, "When Ghosts Come Calling: Re-'projecting' the Disappeared Muses of Malayalam Cinema," in *Sarai Reader 09: Projections*, ed. Shveta Sarda and Raqs Media Collective (New Delhi: CSDS, 2013), 336–45.

76. "Oormakalile Nayikamar, Madhuri: The Lost Heroine," *Rastradeepika Cinema*, April 13, 2013, 20.

77. Lens Eye, "A Hard Day's Starlet."

2. WAITING FOR KODAMBAKKAM:
ECONOMIES OF WAITING AND LABOR IN TINSEL TOWN

1. Ghassan Hage, Introduction to *Waiting*, ed. Hage (Carlton: Melbourne University Press, 2009), 3.

2. Debashree Mukherjee, *Bombay Hustle: Making Movies in a Colonial City* (New York: Columbia University Press, 2020), 4.

3. Hage, *Waiting*, 97–98.

4. Monica Minnegal, "The Time Is Right: Waiting, Reciprocity, and Sociality," in Hage, *Waiting*, 90.

5. Vincent Wasco describes political economy as "the study of social relations, particularly the power relations that mutually constitute the production, distribution and consumption of resources." Vincent Wasco, *The Political Economy of Communication* (London: Sage, 2009), 2.

6. Michel Foucault and Jay Miskowiec, "Of Other Spaces," *Diacritics* 16, no. 1 (Spring 1986): 24.

7. Priya Jaikumar, *Where Histories Reside: India as a Filmed Space* (Durham, NC: Duke University Press, 2019), 8.

8. Jaikumar, *Where Histories Reside*, 3.

9. Giuliana Bruno, *Atlas of Emotions: Journeys in Art, Architecture, and Film* (New York: Verso, 2002), 6.

10. Ranjani Mazumdar, *Bombay Cinema: An Archive of the City* (Minneapolis: University of Minnesota Press, 2007), xxxv.

11. Mazumdar, *Bombay Cinema*, 4–5.

12. Hirokazu Miyazaki, *The Method of Hope: Anthropology, Philosophy, and Fijian Knowledge* (Stanford, CA: Stanford University Press, 2004), 14.

13. Shenoy's reference to the "visa" in this context suggests the Malayali migration to the Gulf Cooperation Council regions that started in the 1960s.

14. Shanti Kumar, "Mapping Tollywood: The Cultural Geography of 'Ramoji Film City' in Hyderabad," *Quarterly Review of Film and Video* 23, no. 2 (2006): 129–38.

15. *Project Cinema City*, ed. Madhusree Dutta, Kaushik Bhaumik, and Rohan Shivkumar (New Delhi: Tulika Books, 2013).

16. David Harvey, "Space as a Key Word," Paper for Marx and Philosophy Conference, May 29, 2004, Institute of Education, London, http://frontdeskapparatus.com/files/harvey2004.pdf.

17. Chithra Madhavan, "Ancient Shrines of Kodambakkam," *The Hindu*, January 2, 2003, http://www.thehindu.com/thehindu/mp/2003/01/02/stories/2003010200790300.htm.

18. *Chennai: Memory Chips* (Chennai: Legacy Publications, 2000), 52.

19. For a detailed account on the films made by Vijaya Vauhini and Prasad studios during this volatile period and their impact on Madras-based studios, see Swarnavel Eswaran Pillai, *Madras Studios: Narrative, Genre, and Ideology in Tamil Cinema* (New Delhi: Sage, 2015).

20. Theodore Baskaran. "Cinema Houses in Chennai" in *The Unhurried City: Writings on Chennai*, ed. C. S. Lakshmi (New Delhi: Penguin Books, 2004), 80.

21. Sashi Nair, "An Anthem for Chennai as Kodambakkam Celebrates," madrasmusings.com, September 1–15, 2009, http://madrasmusings.com/Vol 19 No 10/otherstories.html—story4.

22. P. K. Sreenivasan, *Kodambakkam: Black and White* (Thrissur: Current Books, 2013), 10.

23. Sashi Nair, "Madras Week: Capturing the Spirit of Ghoda Bagh, Films of 1960s–70s Shot in Kodambakkam Studios," sashinair.blogspot.com, August 24, 2009, http://sashinair.blogspot.com/2009/08/madras-week-capturing-spirit-of-ghoda.html.

24. Sreenivasan, *Kodambakkam*, 15.

25. Manikandan (production manager), in discussion with author, August 23, 2013.

26. Mathews (production manager), in discussion with author, September 30, 2013.

27. Udaya was started in Alappuzha by Kunchacko as Udaya Pictures in 1942. Merryland was started by P. Subrahmanyam in 1950 in Nemom.

28. The main production houses then were Chandrathara Productions and Associate Productions, both based in Madras.

29. Sreenivasan, *Kodambakkam*, 200.

30. P. David, *Framekulkappuram: Oru Cinema Still Photographerude Atmakatha* (Beyond frames: The autobiography of a still photographer) (Thrissur: Current Books, 2011), 8.

31. Hage, Introduction to *Waiting*, 3.

32. David, *Framekulkappuram*, 10.

33. Sabeena Gadhihoke, "The Art of Capturing Stillness: Cinema Lobby Cards," *Marg: A Magazine of the Arts* 68, no. 3 (2017): 108–9.

34. David, *Framekulkappuram*, 33.

35. M. T. Vasudevan Nair, *Chitratheruvukal* [Film streets] (Thrissur: Current Books, 2010), 99–105.

36. Nair, *Chitratheruvukal*, 182–83.

37. "Sex in Delhi Halls," *Maharashtra Herald*, August 8, 1983.

38. K. S. Gopalakrishnan (director), in discussion with author, November 23, 2013. Films such as *Lekhayude Maranam Oru Flashback* (The death of Lekha, a flashback; dir. K. G. George, Malayalam, 1983) address the issue of women who came to Kodambakkam in search of a career.

39. Film script of *Goodbye to Kodambakkam*, NFAI, Pune.

40. "Avalude Ravukal," *Chitrakarthika*, December 4, 1977, 34.

41. Foucault, "Of Other Spaces," 24.

42. Raveendran (production manager), in discussion with author, September 1, 2017.

43. Tejaswini Ganti, *Producing Bollywood: Inside the Contemporary Hindi Film Industry* (Durham, NC: Duke University Press, 2012); Anand Pandian, *Reel World: An Anthropology of Creation* (Durham, NC: Duke University Press, 2015).

44. Partipan and Raghavan, in discussion with author, June 16, 2013.

45. For details, see Internet Movie Database, *Aayiram Chirakulla Moham*, https://www.imdb.com/title/tt0353153/?ref_=nv_sr_2. Accessed June 3, 2018.

46. Ramanathan (technician), in discussion with author, May 2, 2013.

47. "Malayalacharithtam," https://www.malayalachalachithram.com/movie.php?i=2197.

48. The editor of the first Malayalam talkie, *Balan*, was known in film circles as "Stock Shot Varghese." When he fell into poverty in the 1960s, he supported his large family by going to studios and labs to sell shots of thunder, lightning, and wild animals. The jungle

films of the 1980s used many of the stock shots from Varghese, and shots featuring jungle would appear as part of erotic sequences.

49. Maniappan (distributor), in discussion with author, September 23, 2013.

50. As Kamala Govindan, one of the rare women *painkili* novelists, said: "The distinction between high and low brow taste seems to be there only in Kerala. When my novels were translated to Kannada, it is the mainstream publishers who approached me for rights. In Kerala, one has to fight a tough battle if one happens to be writing in one of the 'Ma weeklies.' Even the co-operative of writers in Kerala, *Sahitya Pravarthaka Sahakarana Sangham* were not too keen to publish novels that were first serialized in these magazines." P. K. Sreenivasan, "Painkali Novelists: Those who Sell of Dreams," *India Today*, June 23–July 7,1980, 46.

51. P. K. Sreenivasan (journalist), in discussion with author, September 26, 2013.

52. These magazines were also called "Kottayam weeklies," because most of them were based in and around Kottayam. In the 1980s, each issue contained parts from more than eight serialized novels. Each of the novels had a minimum of twenty-five chapters, and most of the novelists were juggling more than three to four novels at a time. Sreenivasan, "Painkali Novelists," 44.

53. Mohan Manimala, https://www.facebook.com/artist.mohanan.

54. Sreenivasan, "Painkali Novelists," 45.

55. Narasimhan (production manager), in discussion with author, September 23, 2013.

56. The film's title had to be tweaked because there was already a Malayalam film called *Aadipapam* (dir. K. P. Kumaran, 1979). Most internet search results today, as well as the entries for *Aadyapaapam* in IMDb and YouTube, carry the spelling "Adipapam" instead of the original, correct spelling.

57. *Aadyapaapam* also inaugurated the steel-business owner R. B. Choudary's stint as a producer. Choudary made a few more films along the same lines, like *Layanam* (dir. Thulasidas, 1989), and soon became one of the most successful producers and distributors in South India.

58. Sukumar is now one of the leading cinematographers in the Malayalam film industry.

59. P. Chandrakumar (director), in discussion with author, October 27, 2013, Trivandrum.

60. Jason Pine, *The Art of Making Do in Naples* (Minneapolis: University of Minnesota Press, 2012), 8.

61. Craig Jeffrey, *Timepass: Youth, Class, and the Politics of Waiting in India* (Stanford, CA: Stanford University Press, 2010), 63.

3. EMBODIED VULNERABILITIES: PRECARITY AND BODY WORK

1. Ella Harris and Mel Nowicki, "Cultural Geographies of Precarity," *Cultural Geographies* 25, no. 3 (2018): 387.

2. Kathleen Kuehn and Thomas F. Corrigan, "Hope Labor: The Role of Employment Prospects in Online Social Production," *The Political Economy of Communication* 1, no. 1 (2013): 10.

3. Kuehn and Corrigan, "Hope Labor," 21.

4. Ernst Bloch, *The Principle of Hope*, translated by Neville Plaice, Stephen Plaice, and Paul Knight (1959; Cambridge, MA: MIT Press, 1995), 1:253.

5. For more details on the strategic positioning by workers engaged in precariously placed jobs, see Heather Berg, *Porn Work: Sex, Labor, and Late Capitalism* (Chapel Hill: University of North Carolina Press, 2021); Kate Fortmueller, *Below the Stars: How the Labor of Working Actors and Extras Shapes Media Production* (Austin: University of Texas Press, 2021).

6. Michel Foucault, *Discipline and Punish: The Birth of the Prison*, translated by Alan Sheridan (1978; New York: Random House, 1995).

7. Michael Curtin and Kevin Sanson, "Introduction," *Precarious Creativity: Global Media, Local Labor*, edited by Curtin and Sanson (Oakland: University of California Press, 2016), 5.

8. Lauren Berlant, *Cruel Optimism* (Durham, NC: Duke University Press, 2011), 24.

9. Darshana Sreedhar Mini, "Cinema and the Mask of Capital: Labor Debates in the Malayalam Film Industry," *Studies in South Asian Film and Media* 11, no 2 (2020): 173–89.

10. Thrikkunnappuzha Vijayakumar, in conversation with author, July 2013.

11. Directors A. T. Joy, Dubai Mani, and Vijayakumar, in conversation with author, September 15, 2013, August 19, 2013, and July 15, 2013, respectively.

12. Sreedhar Pillai, "Magic on the Wane," *The Hindu*, August 23, 2002, http://www.hindu.com/thehindu/fr/2002/08/23/stories/2002082300170100.htm.

13. Sreedhar Pillai, "Malayalam Films: The Smut Glut," *India Today*, May 15, 1986, http://indiatoday.intoday.in/story/soft-porn-boom-hits-commercial-cinema-in-kerala-like-a-bolt-from-the-blue/1/348454.html.

14. Kuppuswamy (manager), in discussion with author, August 17, 2013.

15. Roshni Nair, "Shakeela, the Woman Who Inspired Genres without Ever Doing Porn," *DnaIndia*, December 5, 2017, https://www.dnaindia.com/lifestyle/report-shakeela-the-woman-who-inspired-genres-without-ever-doing-porn-2112421.

16. Similar systems are also reflected in more global examples, such as those in Nollywood. Jade Miller, "Labor in Lagos: Alternative Global Networks," in Curtin and Sanson, *Precarious Creativity*, 146–58; Brian Larkin, *Signal and Noise: Media, Infrastructure, and Urban Culture in Nigeria* (Durham, NC: Duke University Press, 2008).

17. Vijayakumar, discussion.

18. Sreekumar (distributor), in discussion with author, July 30, 2013.

19. Sreenivasan, "Neela Chitrangal: Maruunna Samvakyangal" [Blue films: Changing equations], *India Today*, January 16, 2001, 46–47.

20. Only a few directors, such as A. T. Joy, used their real names. Other pseudonyms included Jayadevan, RDX, RJ, Charles, S. P. Sankar, Krishna Chandra, Shajahan, P. Thomas, B. John, Alexander, and so on.

21. Nanda Kumar, interview by author, June 14, 2019, Abu Dhabi.

22. "Around the Studios: Ponnil Kulicha Rathri," *The Indian Express*, December 12, 1978. Clippings in NFAI, Pune, accessed on August 12, 2016.

23. C. S. Venkiteswaran, "Shakeela, Chila Thundu Chintakal" [Shakeela: A few thought pieces], in *Udalinte Tharasancharangal* [The circulation of the star body] (Kottayam: DC Books, 2011), 101–11; G. P. Ramachandran, *Malayalam Cinema: Desam, Bhasha, Samskaram* [Malayalam cinema: Region, language, and culture] (Thiruvananthapuram: The State Institute of Languages, Kerala, 2009).

24. Joy, discussion.

25. Vijayakumar, discussion.
26. Thankachan (producer), in discussion with author, March 5, 2014.
27. Linda Ruth Williams, *The Erotic Thriller in Contemporary Cinema* (Bloomington: Indiana University Press, 2005), 333.
28. Arun Ram, "The Raw Deal," *India Today*, July 1, 2002.
29. Curtin and Sanson, "Introduction," 5.
30. Richard Dyer, *Heavenly Bodies: Film Stars and Society* (London: Routledge, 2004), 5, 6.
31. Judith Butler, *Precarious Life: The Powers of Mourning and Violence* (London: Verso, 2004), xii.
32. Shakeela, *Atmakatha* [Autobiography] (Calicut: Olive Publications, 2013), 138.
33. Jayabharati, who started her film career in the late 1960s, was one of the few Malayalam actresses who was able to portray sensual roles in mainstream Malayalam cinema without being castigated as a second-rate actress. For instance, *Itha Ivide Vare* (dir. I. V. Sasi, 1977) and *Rathinirvedham* (dir. Bharatan, 1978) solidified her as someone whose body emblematized an erotic charge to the narrative.
34. Sreekumar, in conversation with the author, February 25, 2014.
35. In 2000, R. Jay Prasad had other television serials and film projects in the works, all of which ceased abruptly with the success of *Kinnarathumbikal*. Although *Kinnarathumbikal* renewed Shakeela's career and helped the producers recoup their earlier loss, it was a loss for Prasad on many counts. He could neither return to his previous associate position nor take up new projects, because the film cast him in ignominy. Unlike other directors, like U. C. Roshan, who realized the potential market for soft-porn and strategically made films that could stand them in good stead in the distribution front, Prasad bid good-bye to filmmaking altogether for the next fifteen years. Even though another soft-porn film, *Manjukalapakshi* (Cold-weather bird; 2000), was credited in his name, he was not officially part of the project. The practice of sourcing excess shots from various soft-porn films to create a pastiche effect may have been why Prasad's name was used as a trademark that signified authenticity for soft-porn. However, his comeback film in 2015, *Manikyam*, failed to draw attention at the box office. R. J. Prasad (director), in discussion with author, January 13, 2019.
36. Prasad, discussion.
37. M. G. Radhakrishnan, "Porn Again," *India Today*, June 26, 2000.
38. Prasad, discussion.
39. R. Ayyappan, "Sleaze Time, Folks!" *Rediff*, January 24, 2001, http://www.rediff.com/entertai/2001/jan/24mallu.htm, accessed April 10, 2014.
40. Malayalam Dialogues (@kiduquotes), "Eda mone. Thettu cheyyathavar arada? (Shakeela-Kinnarathumbikal)," Twitter, August 19, 2013, 10:02 AM, https://twitter.com/kiduquotes/status/369474386450845698?lang=en.
41. "SUPER SCENE SUPER DIALOGUE FROM UNIVERSAL STAR SHAKEELA "Thettu cheyyathavar aarundeda mone"," March 20, 2011, YouTube (no longer accessible).
42. "Kinnarathumbikal (2000): The LOST Trailer," December 30, 2015, YouTube (no longer accessible).
43. David Andrews, *Soft in the Middle: The Contemporary Softcore Feature in Its Context* (Columbus: Ohio State University Press, 2006), 2.

44. For a detailed account of the contested telecast, see Radhakrishnan Ratheesh, "Soft Porn and the Anxieties of the Family," in *Women in Malayalam Cinema: Naturalizing Gender Hierarchies*, ed. Meena Pillai (Hyderabad: Orient Blackswan, 2010), 194–220.

45. Deepa Nisanth, Facebook, January 21, 2017, https://www.facebook.com/deepa.nisanth/posts/632242393649127, accessed August 5, 2017.

46. Shakeela, *Atmakatha*, 71 (my translation).

47. The word *chechi* also played out interestingly in Bigg Boss Kannada, one of the South-Indian variants of Big Boss, the Indian franchise of the Big Brother format. The press conjectured that one of the male contestants' refusal to address Shakeela as *chechi* was due to the double entendre behind the word; "Rohit Turns Shakeela Down," *The Times of India*, July 3, 2014, http://timesofindia.indiatimes.com/entertainment/kannada/movies/news/Shakeela-wants-to-take-Rohit-to-her-house/articleshow/37706245.cms.

48. P. A. G. Nair, "Kamadikyam Enthukondu" [What's the reason for excessive sex drive?], *Chitrakarthika*, January 16–19, 1977, 29–30.

49. For an account of the Savita Bhabhi phenomenon, see Anirban Baishya and Darshana Sreedhar Mini, "Transgressions in Toonland: Savita Bhabhi, Velamma, and the Indian Adult Comic," *Porn Studies* 7, no. 1 (2020): 115–31.

50. Jhilmil Motihar, "In the Dock," *India Today*, October 11, 2008, http://indiatoday.intoday.in/story/In+the+dock/1/17382.html.

51. Sreedhar Pillai, "Smut Glut," *The Hindu*, August 8, 2002, http://www.thehindu.com/thehindu/mp/2002/08/08/stories/2002080800160200.htm.

52. The News Minute, "Moralistic Porn: Sex Shows on Tamil TV channels Will Amaze You," *The Quint*, November 5, 2016.

53. Netflix India, "Shakeela's Driving School Ft. @ShelVines & Chippy Devassy | Sex Education | Malayalam Sketch," September 22, 2023, YouTube, 5 min., 43 sec., https://www.youtube.com/watch?v=n1XvbSWXpg8.

54. "Malayalam Soft Porn Actress Shakeela to Direct a Malayalam Movie 'Neelakurinji Poothu,'" *Asianetnews*, January 20, 2013, https://www.youtube.com/watch?v=4HwBHhbF6p8.

55. Shyam P. V., "Soft-porn Star Shakeela Plans a Big Entry," *The Times of India*, December 18, 2012, http://timesofindia.indiatimes.com/entertainment/malayalam/movies/news/Soft-porn-star-Shakeela-plans-a-big-reentry/articleshow/17674550.cms.

56. "Romantic Target Trailer Launch—Shakeela, Syed Afzal," February 23, 2015, YouTube, 5 min., 49 secs., https://www.youtube.com/watch?v=iv8m2h1cEqg.

57. "Shakeela Was NOT a Porn Star: First Look of Biopic Starring Richa Chadha Out," *India Today*, November 1, 2018, https://www.indiatoday.in/movies/regional-cinema/story/shakeela-biopic-first-look-richa-chadha-1379998-2018-11-01.

58. HT Correspondent, "Shakeela Biopic First Look Inspired by Silk Smitha's Film Ms Pamela," *Hindustan Times*, November 26, 2018, https://www.hindustantimes.com/bollywood/shakeela-biopic-first-look-inspired-by-silk-smitha-s-film-ms-pamela/story-nsEYiI7UucrJ8ilkpSTQ9O.html.

59. Bollywood News, "Richa Chadha's First Look In Shakeela Biopic Is Inspired by Late Southern Actress Silk Smitha, Here's Why," *timesnownews*, November 26, 2018, https://www.timesnownews.com/entertainment/news/bollywood-news/article/richa-chadhas-first-look-in-shakeela-biopic-is-inspired-by-late-southern-actress-silk-smitha-heres-why/321036.

60. DN, "Then, Don't Sideline Transgenders: Shakeela's Fiery Speech at Madurai," *The Dhinamani*, June 27, 2015.

61. DN, "Then, Don't Sideline Transgenders."

62. Tupur Chatterjee, "'I Am a Porn Star!' Sex and Sunny Leone Unlimited in Bollywood," *Porn Studies* 4, no. 1 (2017): 50–56.

63. "Cinema Abhinayavum Vivatham Niranja Jeevithavum [Film acting and controversial life]," *Janakeeya Kodathi* [People's court], 24 News, Part 1, July 21, 2019, YouTube, 53 min., 6 secs., https://www.youtube.com/watch?v=uZkb5GUA7_A.; and Part 2, July 29, 2019, YouTube, 42 min., 1 sec., https://www.youtube.com/watch?v=Hk-jMZ6-FJU.

64. Usha Iyer, *Dancing Women: Choreographing Corporeal Histories of Hindi Cinema* (London: Oxford University Press, 2020), 40.

65. @nagpspk1, Twitter, August 17, 2017 (no longer accessible).

66. Harsha Raj Gatty, "Porn-stars are Part of Pop Culture, Says Owner of Kerala's Very Adult Bus for Teens," *News Minute*, July 3, 2018, https://www.thenewsminute.com/article/porn-stars-are-part-pop-culture-says-owner-kerala-s-very-adult-bus-teens-84098.

67. Radhakrishnan, "Soft Porn and the Anxieties of the Family," 194–220.

68. The Malayalam film industry wields a patriarchal and heavy-handed sense of exclusivity in managing its production practices as a male-centric system. Male stars and their availability decide the production schedule and the selection of the co-actresses. Actresses are paid much less than actors, and this has been continuing as an unquestionable practice despite unionization in the film industry.

69. "Soft Porn Film Stopped," *Maharashtra Herald*, September 4, 1983.

70. Shaji (actor), in discussion with author, September 19, 2013. Shaji also mentions that the "normal" industry practice was for the cast to sign a contract and then they would receive an advance. The rest of the fee would be paid after dubbing to ensure that the cast remained faithful to the dubbing schedule before committing to other projects. In Shakeela's case, the day-to-day basis of payment was a radical departure from an entrenched industrial standard.

71. Settu Shankar, "Police Arrest Reshma for Flesh Trade!" Filmibeat.com, December 24, 2007, https://www.filmibeat.com/malayalam/news/2007/reshma-flesh-trade-241207.html.

72. "Reshma at Police Station," March 2, 2008, YouTube, 5, min., 12 secs., https://www.youtube.com/watch?v=dFlzu1S9pnw.

73. Shankar, "Police Arrest Reshma for Flesh Trade!"

74. As opposed to the labored aspects of sex work, it was framed as "prostitution" throughout Reshma's interrogation and the newspaper reportage.

75. Itimes, "Tragic Life of Indian Porn Star Reshma," *Indiatimes*, May 18, 2015. https://www.indiatimes.com/lifestyle/self/tragic-life-of-indian-porn-star-reshma-277078.html?picid=1274977.

76. Itimes, "Tragic Life of Indian Porn Star Reshma," *Indiatimes*, May 18, 2015. https://www.indiatimes.com/lifestyle/self/tragic-life-of-indian-porn-star-reshma-277078.html?picid=1274977.

77. Wendy Hui Kyong Chun and Sarah Friedland, "Habits of Leaking: Of Sluts and Network Cards," *differences: A Journal of Feminist Cultural Studies* 26, no. 2 (2015): 1.

78. Bhanu, *Dupe* (Kottayam: DC Books, 2010), 5, 7–8.

79. Shakeela (actress), in discussion with author, July 14, 2016.

80. Bhanu, *Dupe*, 56.

81. In 2002, the Hindi film *Ek Chhotisi Love Story* (dir. Shashilal Nair, 2001) was mired in controversy when the identity of the body double was revealed, leading to numerous salacious reports. The actress Manisha Koirala alleged that she had not been provided adequate knowledge about the nude scenes shot with a body double. Jessica Choksi, the body double, also made a public appearance and refuted the director's claims that the continuity sequences shot with her conformed exactly with the script. She was appalled by the negative publicity she received due to the spat between the director, Shashilal Nair, and Koirala, during which Nair revealed her identity.

82. Rosalind Gill and Andy Pratt, "In the Social Factory? Immaterial Labour, Precariousness, and Cultural Work," *Theory, Culture & Society* 25, no. 7–8 (2008): 3.

83. Louise Waite, "A Place and Space for a Critical Geography of Precarity?" *Geography Compass* 3, no. 1 (2009): 412–33.

84. A. T. Joy (director), telephone interview by author, September 12, 2018.

4. THE ALTERNATIVE TRANSNATIONAL: MIGRATION, MEDIA, AND SOFT-PORN

1. Nitin Govil, *Orienting Hollywood: A Century of Film Culture between Los Angeles and Bombay* (New York: NYU Press, 2015), 3.

2. Elizabeth Ezra and Terry Rowden, *Transnational Cinema: The Film Reader* (London: Routledge, 2006), 2.

3. Will Higbee and Song Hwee Lim, "Concepts of Transnational Cinema: Towards a Critical Transnationalism in Film Studies," *Transnational Cinemas* 1, no. 1 (2010): 18.

4. Govil, *Orienting Hollywood*, 190–91.

5. Toby Miller et al., *Global Hollywood* (Berkley: University of California Press, 2002).

6. Mette Hjort, "On the Plurality of Cinematic Transnationalism," in *World Cinema: Transnational Perspectives*, ed. Nataša Durovicová and Kathleen Newman (London: Routledge/American Film Institute Reader, 2010), 12–13.

7. Inderpal Grewal and Caren Kaplan, *Scattered Hegemonies: Postmodernity and Transnational Feminist Practices* (Minneapolis: University of Minnesota Press, 1994).

8. Jigna Desai, *Beyond Bollywood: The Cultural Politics of South Asian Diasporic Film* (Routledge: New York, 2004), 182–83.

9. Ashish Rajadhyaksha, "The 'Bollywoodization' of the Indian Cinema: Cultural Nationalism in a Global Arena," *Inter-Asia Cultural Studies* 4, no. 1 (2003): 25–39.

10. Andrew Higson, "The Concept of National Cinema," *Screen* 4, no. 30 (1989): 41.

11. Pushkar Banakar, "Korean, English Movies Welcome in Manipur, Bollywood is Not," *New Indian Express*, November 4, 2018, http://www.newindianexpress.com/thesundaystandard/2018/nov/04/korean-english-movies-welcome-in-manipur-bollywood-is-not-1893901.html.

12. Ravi Vasudevan, "Geographies of the Cinematic Public: Notes on Regional, National, and Global Histories of Indian Cinema," *Journal of the Moving Image* 9 (2010): 95.

13. Gayatri Gopinath, *Unruly Visions: The Aesthetic Practices of Queer Diaspora* (Durham, NC: Duke University Press, 2018), 5.

14. "Soft Porn Film Stopped," *Maharashtra Herald*, September 4, 1983.

15. "Officials to Review 'Soft porn' Films," *The Times of India*, November 8, 1983.

16. C. Unnikrishnan, "Soft-porn Films Being Screened Again," *The Indian Express*, July 20, 1983.

17. Vimal Balasubrahmanyan, "The Watchdogs: Women Monitor the Media," in *Gender and Censorship*, ed. Brinda Bose (New Delhi: Women Unlimited, 2006), 65.

18. "Officials to Review 'Soft porn' Films."

19. Ravi Kottarakkara, interview by author, September 12, 2013, Chennai.

20. Tina Sara Anien, "Another Dubbed Film Released," *Deccan Herald*, March 8, 2019, https://www.deccanherald.com/metrolife/another-dubbed-film-released-722217.html; The Competition Commission of India is a statutory body within the Ministry of Corporate Affairs that is responsible for enforcing the Competition Act of 2002, which, following economic liberalization in 1991, promotes competition and private enterprise in India.

21. The South Indian states led agitations against the imposition of Hindi language as the national language. The ban on dubbing has allowed Kannada producers to buy the film rights of successful "other language" films and remake them in Kannada.

22. Peter Alilunas, *Smutty Little Movies: The Creation and Regulation of Adult Video* (Berkeley: University of California Press, 2016), 13.

23. Ravi Sundaram, "Revisiting the Pirate Kingdom," in *Postcolonial Piracy: Media Distribution and Cultural Production in the Global South*, ed. Lars Eckstein and Anja Schwarz (London: Bloomsbury, 2014), 36.

24. Shaukat, interviews by author, April 25 and 26, 2023, Dubai.

25. Narayanan, interview by author, January 19, 2019, Calicut.

26. Narayanan, interview.

27. *The Sex Education Encyclopedia* (Kottayam: Moral Books, 1978).

28. Thampy, interview by author, June 15, 2019, Abu Dhabi.

29. Dan Herbert, *Videoland: Movie Culture at the American Video Store* (Berkeley: University of California Press, 2014), 62.

30. Issac, interview by author, January 18, 2019, Calicut.

31. Wahab, interview by author, November 15, 2018, Abu Dhabi.

32. Kathyrn C. Hardy, "Constituting a Diffuse Region: Cartographies of Mass-mediated Bhojpuri Belonging," *BioScope: South Asian Screen Studies* 6, no. 2 (2010): 145.

33. See, e.g., the case of Indian films imported into the Soviet Union by Soveksportfil'm in the 1950s. These films were often accompanied by advice literature aligned with Soviet ideology but often circulated beyond the pedagogical rhetoric of the state, allowing viewers to reflect on the contradictions of its dominance in dictating consumer tastes. Sudha Rajagopal, *Indian Films in Soviet Cinemas: The Culture of Movie-Going After Stalin* (Bloomington: Indiana University Press, 2008).

34. Ashok Row Kavi, "Indian Film Industry the Biggest Purveyor of Black Money in the Country," *India Today*, February 28, 1978, https://www.indiatoday.in/magazine/cover-story/story/19780228-indian-film-industry-the-biggest-purveyor-of-black-money-in-the-country-822900-2014-05-06#ssologin=1#source=magazine.

35. Several legal judgments have addressed the issue of film subsidies, contesting the income-tax department's claims that subsidies should be included as taxable income in the form of revenue receipts and not be seen on nontaxable capital receipts. See, e.g., Commissioner of Income-Tax v. Udaya Pictures (P) Ltd on June 26, 1996 (Kerala High Court); V. N. Sarpotdar v. Dy. Cit on December 12, 2000; and Jagapathy Art Pictures v. Commissioner of Income-Tax on April 15, 1998 (Madras High Court).

36. Govil, *Orienting Hollywood*, 81.

37. The residences raided included those of the actors Raj Kapoor, Vyjayantimala, Prem Nath, Mala Sinha, and Rajindranath, and the music directors Shankar and Ravi. *The Hindu*, August 25, 1964.

38. Govil, *Orienting Hollywood*, 82.

39. "IMPEC to Control Film Export," *The Times of India*, March 5, 1979.

40. "IMPEC Stand Causes Big Drop in Film Export," *Screen*, February 3, 1978.

41. The balance of payment is a statement that records all economic transactions between entities in one country and the rest of the world within a stipulated period. These transactions include remittances; import and export of goods, services, and capital; and transfer payments such as foreign aid. It is used to highlight a country's competitive strengths and weaknesses, and helps in achieving balanced economic-growth. Will Kenton, "Balance of Payments in Global Transactions: Why Does It Matter?," *Investopedia*, September 24, 2023, https://www.investopedia.com/terms/b/bop.asp.

42. External payment crisis refers to a situation in which the external debt accrued through essential imports or services cannot be paid and results in the devaluation of the nation's currency when foreign investors withdraw their investments.

43. "Advertisement for Aksai VS-23," *Filmfare* 37, no. 13 (1988): n.p.

44. Farida Batool Syeda, "New Media, Masculinity, and Mujra Dance in Pakistan," PhD diss., SOAS, University of London, 2015, 71.

45. Tom O' Regan, "Remembering Video: Reflections on the First Explosion of Informal Media Markets through the VCR," *Television & New Media* 13, no. 5 (2012): 383–98.

46. R. Srinivasan, "The Hi-tech Smugglers," *The Times of India*, September 29, 1991, 18.

47. Srinivasan, "Hi-tech Smugglers," 18.

48. "Save Film Industry from Video Piracy," *Deccan Chronicle*, January 14, 1986.

49. Chacko, interview by author, April 25, 2023, Dubai.

50. "S. Indian Film Industry Call to End Video Piracy," *Business Standard*, December 12, 1986.

51. Jagannath Dubashi, "Video: The Piracy Plague," *India Today*, September 15, 1984.

52. Despite the promulgation of the Tamil Nadu Exhibition of Films on Television Screen through Video Cassette Recorders and Cable Television Network (Regulation) Act of 1984, which the Tamil Nadu government intended to control video piracy, the Tamil Nadu Film Industry Protection Council initiated widespread protests in 1986 because the act had not been implemented. This act was replaced by the central government's Cable Television Network (Regulation) Act of 1995.

53. For instance, Tara Singh & Sons, one of the clearance agents for the NRIs based in Bombay, helped execute paperwork for clearance once the consignment reached the airport.

54. The numbers break down as follows: twelve out of fifty-three films submitted in 1985; twenty-eight out of ninety-four submitted in 1986; five out of forty-one submitted in 1987; ten cases were pending and one withdrawn (*The Times of India*, 1988).

55. "The Porn Brokers," *The Indian Express*. Clippings in NFAI, Pune, accessed, August 12, 2016.

56. Reddi, interview by author, June 11, 2019, Chennai.

57. "Porn Brokers."

58. Ramesh (name changed), interview by author, August 12, 2013, Chennai. He had retired from the Prasad lab after working there for about thirty years.
59. "Porn Brokers."
60. "Protests Grow over Obscenity," *Sunday Observer*, July 20, 1986.
61. "45 NRI Films Denied Certificates," *The Times of India*, June 17, 1988; Amrita Malik, "The Great Soft Porn Hard to Sell," *Statesman*, September 5, 1987.
62. M. Rahman, "Film Producers Boycott Censor Board, Stop Sending Films for Certification," *India Today*, February 28, 1986.
63. "NRI Films," *The Indian Express*, April 30, 1988. Clippings in NFAI, Pune, accessed August 12, 2016.
64. "50 p.c. NRI Films Rejected: NFDC Chief," *The Times of India*, May 5, 1988.
65. Shenoy (name changed, retired staff of NFDC), interview by author, July 2, 2017, Mumbai.
66. "Import of NRI films Not To Be Banned," no date. Clippings in NFAI, Pune, accessed October 30, 2017.
67. "Probe into IMPEC Affairs Urged," no date. Clippings in NFAI, Pune, accessed August 12, 2016.
68. "Porn Brokers."
69. "Advertisement," *Film Information*, September 7, 2002. 3.
70. *Film Information*, 3. Samhita Sunya, *Sirens of Modernity: World Cinema via Bombay* (Berkeley: University of California Press, 2022), 175.
71. Kevin Hefferman, "Seen as a Business: Adult Film's Historical Framework and Foundations," in *New Views of Pornography: Sexuality, Politics, and the Law*, ed. Lynn Comella and Shira Tarrant (Westport, CT: Praeger, 2015), 42.
72. Sai (pseudonym; former employee at the Exports Division, NFDC), interview by author, July 22, 2016, Bombay.
73. *Sex and the Animals* (dir. Harold Hoffman, 1969), 96 min.
74. "Porn Brokers."
75. "Porn Brokers."
76. Ratan Bhatia, "Sexyclopedia," *Sunday Observer*, July 30, 1987, 1.
77. Ratan Bhatia, "Sexyclopedia," *Sunday Observer*, July 30, 1987, 1.
78. Untitled clipping in the digital collections, NFAI library, accessed August 12, 2013.
79. Patel (film exhibitor), interview by author, November 12, 2018, Mumbai.
80. Madhavi Mallapragada, "Home, Homeland, Homepage: Belonging and the Indian American Web," in *Reorienting Global Communication: India and China Media Beyond Borders*, ed. Michael Curtin and Hemant Shah (Urbana: University of Illinois Press, 2006), 67.
81. S. Irudaya Rajan, K. C. Zachariah, and Ashwin Kumar, "Large-Scale Migration Surveys: Replication of the Kerala Model of Migration Surveys to India Migration Survey 2024," in *India Migration Report 2020: Kerala Model of Migration Surveys*, ed. Irudaya Rajan (Oxford: Routledge, 2020), 1–22.
82. N. K., "Blue in the Red," *The Times of India*, January 12, 1997, 17.
83. Inderpal Grewal, *Transnational America: Feminisms, Diasporas, Neoliberalisms* (Durham, NC: Duke University Press, 2005), 23.

84. Pia Heikkila, "Kairali TV to Build on Hit Show with Gulf," *The National*, October 26, 2011, https://www.thenational.ae/business/kairali-tv-to-build-on-hit-show-with-gulf-channel-1.563576.

85. Sreedhar Pillai, "Kerala Goes through Frenetic Theatre Boom Fueled by Gulf Money," *India Today*, November 15, 1982, https://www.indiatoday.in/magazine/indiascope/story/19821115-kerala-goes-through-frenetic-theatre-boom-fuelled-by-gulf-money-772359-2013-07-30.

86. N.O.C. refers to No Objection Certificate, a term used to refer to the travel document. Sebastian Thejus Cherian, "Filmic Imagination and UAE's Social History through the Lens of Malayalam Cinema of the 1980s," paper presented at the Film and Visual Media in the Gulf: Images, Infrastructures, and Institutions Connecting Africa, The Middle East, South Asia, and the World, October 28–30, 2018, NYU Abu Dhabi Institute.

87. In 2011 it was taken over by Indian film distributors A. P. International and Ayngaran International and renamed Golden Cinema. In 2013, Golden Cinema hosted a free screening of the Tamil film *Aarambam* (dir. Vishuvardhan, 2013) for 1,500 laborers from the ETA Group as a part of Dubai International Film Festival. Chris Newbould, "Dubai loses a piece of history as Golden Cinema prepares to close; Uttama Villain is theatre's last film," *The National News*. April 29, 2015. When Golden Cinema was shut down in May 2015, the last film to be screened was the world premiere of *Uttama Villain*, starring Kamal Hassan. With this closure, UAE lost its last stand-alone cinema house. Interestingly, sections of the auditorium's seating were salvaged and used in Cinema Akil, one of Dubai's first art house cinemas, which was opened on Alserkal Avenue. "Cinema Akil: Dubai's first arthouse cinema," *Whatson*, November 15, 2018, https://whatson.ae/2018/11/cinema-akil-dubais-first-arthouse-cinema.

88. Ammar Al Attar and Dale Hudson, "Interview with Ammar Al Attar on Cinemas in the UAE Exhibition," in *Reorienting the Middle East: Film and Digital Media Where the Persian Gulf, Arabian Sea, and Indian Ocean Meet*, ed. Dale Hudson and Alia Yunis (Indianapolis: Indiana University Press, 2024), 102–20.

89. Mahesh, interview by author, November 28, 2018, Abu Dhabi.

90. Unnikrishnan, interview by author, January 18, 2019, Calicut.

91. Saju, interview by author, June 18, 2019, Dubai.

92. M. P. Chawla, "It's Pandering to the Sex starved, Not Sex Education," *The Times of India*, July 7, 1975.

93. Saju, interview.

94. Lucas Hilderbrand, *Inherent Vice: Bootleg Histories of Videotape and Copyright* (Durham, NC: Duke University Press, 2009).

95. Saju, interview.

96. Chellappan, interview by author, June 22, 2019, Dubai.

97. Nada, interview by author, June 21, 2019, Dubai.

5. (DIS)APPEARANCES: DIGITAL REMEDIATIONS OF SOFT-PORN IN THE CONTEMPORARY

1. Madhusree Dutta, "Popular Cinema and Public Culture in Bombay," *Seminar*, 2014, https://www.india-seminar.com/2014/657/657_madhusree_dutta.htm.

2. For a historical account of the production and censorship tussles over *Gupt Gyan*, see Monika Mehta, *Censorship and Sexuality in Bombay Cinema* (Austin: University of Texas Press, 2011).

3. Peter Galison, "Blacked-out Spaces: Freud, Censorship, and the Reterritorialization of Mind," *British Journal for the History of Science* 45, no. 2 (2012): 237.

4. S. V. Srinivas, *Megastar: Chiranjeevi and Telugu Cinema after N. T. Rama Rao* (New Delhi: Oxford University Press, 2009), 168.

5. Manohar (manager of Bhawani Theatre), interview by author, December 17, 2017, Kolkata.

6. Teslim (manager of Silver Talkies), interview by author, August 27, 2014, Mumbai.

7. TNM Staff, "Vishal's Mark Anthony Faces Criticism for 'Reviving' Silk Smitha through CGI and Objectifying her," *The News Minute*, September 8, 2023, https://www.thenewsminute.com/tamil-nadu/vishals-mark-anthony-faces-criticism-for-reviving-silk-smitha-through-cgi-and-objectifying-her.

8. Giuliana Bruno, *Atlas of Emotion: Journeys in Art, Architecture, and Film* (New York: Verso, 2002), 147.

9. Shakeela, interview by author, July 10, 2019, Chennai.

10. This episode also resonates with an actor's assault and kidnapping of a Malayalam actress in 2017, which triggered demands for safer working spaces for women.

11. Anirban Baishya, "Pornography of Place: Location, Leaks, and Obscenity in the Indian MMS Porn Video," *South Asian Popular Culture* 15, no. 1 (2017): 57–71.

12. Shaji Kumar, telephone interview by author, June 15, 2014.

13. Michael Chion, *Audio-vision: Sound on Screen* (New York: Columbia University Press, 1994), 5.

14. Donato Totaro, "Gilles Deleuze's Bergsonian Film Project: Part 2," *Offscreen* 3, no. 3 (1999), http://offscreen.com/view/bergson2.

15. Anthony Vidler, *The Architectural Uncanny: Essays in the Modern Unhomely* (Cambridge, MA: MIT Press, 1992), 11.

16. Christopher Pinney refers to the image's sensory quality as "corpothetics." He defines *darshan* as the mutuality of "'seeing and being seen,'" where vision is mobilized as part of a unified sensorium. Christopher Pinney, *Photos of the Gods: The Printed Image and Political Struggle in India* (London: Reaktion Books, 2004), 9.

17. Priyaranjan Lal, interview by author, January 8, 2015.

18. Lal, interview.

19. Sudhir Mahadevan, "Traveling Showmen, Makeshift Cinemas: The Bioscopewallah and Early Cinema History in India," *Bioscope* 1, no. 1 (2010): 27–47.

20. W. J. T. Mitchell, *Picture Theory: Essays on Verbal and Visual Representation* (Chicago: University of Chicago Press, 1994).

21. Mitchell, *Picture Theory*, 42.

22. Mitchell, *Picture Theory*, 68.

23. A. T. Joy, Thrikkunnappuzha Vijayakumar, and Dubai Mani, interviews by author, September 2013, July 2013, and August 2013, respectively.

24. Lotte Hoek, "When Celluloid Pornography Went Digital: Class and Race in the Bangladeshi Cut-piece Online," *Porn Studies* 7, no. 1 (2019): 97–114.

25. "Shakeela Uncensored Hot Movie Scene," uploaded by Unknown, *Pornhub*, 2016, https://www.pornhub.com/view_video.php?viewkey=ph56aa245376786.

26. Anirban Baishya and Darshana Mini, "Figuring the Aggregated Aunty: Metadata and South Asian Aunties," *Text and Performance Quarterly* 42, no. 3 (2021): 315-31.

27. "Desi Mallu Indian Porn-Reshma hot." XVideos, 4 mins.

28. "Soumya Full Nude and Other Mallu Sex Scenes Compilation," uploaded by Gemborn16, XVideos, 21 min., 3 sec., https://www.xvideos.com/video46365669/soumya_full_nude_and_other_mallu_sex_scenes_compilation.

29. https://www.xvideos.com/?k=mallu+bath.

30. Madhav Prasad, "Cinema and Desire for Modernity," *Journal of Arts & Ideas* 25-26 (December 1993): 71-86.

31. Lalitha Gopalan, *Cinema of Interruptions: Action Genres in Contemporary Indian Cinema* (New Delhi: Oxford University Press, 2002).

32. "Kamakeli," https://www.facebook.com/mallukaamakeli; "Mace Naughty Trolls," https://www.facebook.com/macetrolls; "Malayalam Naughty Trolls," https://www.facebook.com/mntrolls.official, accessed October 12, 2019.

33. Whitney Phillips, *This is Why We Can't Have Nice Things: Mapping the Relationship between Online Trolling and Mainstream Culture* (Cambridge, MA: MIT Press, 2015); Limor Shifman, *Memes in Digital Culture* (Cambridge, MA: MIT Press, 2014).

34. Admin, "Kamakeli," Facebook, August 4, 2019, https://www.facebook.com/mallukaamakeli/photos/a.420293595070699/724912547942134/?type=3&theater, accessed October 12, 2019.

35. Admin, "Kamakeli," Facebook, August 11, 2019, https://www.facebook.com/mallukaamakeli/photos/p.728894330877289/728894330877289/?type=1&theater, accessed October 12, 2019.

36. Admin, "Kamakeli," Facebook, August 4, 2019, https://www.facebook.com/mallukaamakeli/photos/a.419330448500347/724939527939436/?type=1&theater, accessed October 12, 2019.

37. Mini Richard, Patreon, https://www.patreon.com/MiniRichard, accessed October 12, 2019.

38. The grooming of such a fanbase has now evolved to monetizing the popularity of her images to support her charity, the Hugs & Kisses Foundation. Richard announced that likes on her page would be matched with monetary investments in her charity. The money from the charity goes to beneficiaries in Kerala who need financial support.

39. Mini Richard, telephone interview by author, July 9, 2019.

40. Mini Richard, telephone interview by author, September 24, 2023.

41. Mini Richard, Facebook, July 27, 2019, https://www.facebook.com/ActressMiniRichard/photos/a.453090944723541/2710542132311733/?type=3&theater, accessed October 12, 2019.

42. "Mini Richard in Indiavision Good Morning Keralam," *India Vision*, December 2, 2018, https://www.youtube.com/watch?v=JaYAXPW-puE.

43. Jacques Derrida, "The Dangerous Supplement," in *Of Grammatology*, translated by Gayatri Chakravorty Spivak (Baltimore: Johns Hopkins University Press, 2016 [1974]), 153-71.

CONCLUSION: IN PRAISE OF BAD WOMEN

1. TNM Staff, "Saritha Nair's Explosive Letter Alleges that C. M. Oomen Chandy Sexually Abused Her," *News Minute*, April 3, 2016, https://www.thenewsminute.com/article/saritha-nair-s-explosive-letter-alleges-cm-oommen-chandy-sexually-abused-her-41122.

2. "I Am Saritha Nair," Pornhub, 2014, https://www.pornhub.com/view_video.php?viewkey=1820080872; "SELFY-2," Pornhub, 2014, https://www.pornhub.com/view_video.php?viewkey=1932781015; "INDIAN-Saritha Bhabhi Saree Striping," Pornhub, 2014, https://www.pornhub.com/view_video.php?viewkey=672775064.

3. TMN, "Saritha Nair's Leaked Videos—Another Case of 'Revenge Porn'?" *News Minute*, February 24, 2015, https://www.thenewsminute.com/news/saritha-nair-s-leaked-videos-another-case-revenge-porn-23273.

4. Ashad Ashraf, "A Dark Trade: Rape Videos for Sale in India," *Al Jazeera*, October 31, 2016, https://www.aljazeera.com/indepth/features/2016/10/dark-trade-rape-videos-sale-india-161023124250022.html.

5. Wendy Hui Kyong Chun and Sarah Friedland, "Habits of Leaking: Of Sluts and Network Cards," *differences: A Journal of Feminist Cultural Studies* 26, no. 2 (2015): 3.

6. J. Devika, "Being 'In-translation' in a Post-colony: Translating Feminism in Kerala State, India," *Translation Studies* 1, no. 2 (2008): 190.

7. Mathrubhumi News, "Saritha Nair Interview, Mathrubhumi News," October 11, 2017, YouTube, 23 min., 40 sec., https://www.youtube.com/watch?v=VM4sbfsrLIs.

8. Mathrubhumi News, "Saritha Nair Interview."

9. Manorama News, "Saritha Nair and Oomen Chandy | Vayil Thonniyathy | Manorama News," October 15, 2017, YouTube, 22 min., 9 sec., https://www.youtube.com/watch?v=vNu5T7CMXSg.

10. Gayathry V. Pillai, "Saritha Nair Threatens Solar Swapnam's Producer!" *Filmibeat*, June 13, 2014, https://www.filmibeat.com/malayalam/news/2014/saritha-s-nair-threatens-producer-solar-swapnam-movie-145416.html.

11. Express News Service, "Kerala Solar Scam-Accused Saritha Nair's Election Dreams Suffers Total Eclipse," *The Indian Express*, April 7, 2019, http://www.newindianexpress.com/states/kerala/2019/apr/07/kerala-solar-scam-accused-saritha-nairs-election-dream-suffers-total-eclipse-1961216.html.

12. *Gulfukarante Bharya* (dir. Joshy Medayil, 2015), *Dailymotion*, 14 min., 54 sec., https://www.dailymotion.com/video/x2e3vy3; *Anthyakoodasha* (dir. Kiran Anil Kumar, 2015), Facebook, 41 min, 35 sec., https://www.facebook.com/watch/?v=2124303337688306.

13. Shajahan Madampat, "One Woman & Many Powerful Men," *Outlook*, April 6, 2016, https://www.outlookindia.com/website/story/one-woman-many-powerful-men/296798.

14. Maniappan (publicity agent), in discussion with author, March 22, 2013.

BIBLIOGRAPHY

ARCHIVES

AKG Center Library, Trivandrum, India
Appan Thampuran Library, Thrissur, India
Chittira Thirunal Grandashala, Trivandrum, India
Kerala University Library, Kerala, India
Mathrubhumi Archives, Calicut, India
National Film Archive of India (NFAI), Pune, India
The Nehru Memorial Museum and Library, New Delhi, India

NEWSPAPERS AND MAGAZINES

Business Standard
Chitrabhumi
Chitrakarthika
Cinemamangalam
Cinemamasika
Crossfire
Deccan Chronicle
Deccan Herald
Deepika
Dhinamani
Film
Filmfare
filmindia
Film Information
Film Mirror
Gulf Today
Hindu
Honeymoon Guide
India Today
The Indian Express
Indian Techonomist: Bulletin
Maharashtra Herald
Nana
Rastradeepika Cinema
Screen
Statesman
Sunday Observer
Thaniniram Film Entertainment magazine
The Times of India

BOOKS, JOURNAL ARTICLES, DISSERTATIONS, AND REPORTS

Al Attar, Ammar, and Dale Hudson. "Interview with Ammar Al Attar on Cinemas in the UAE Exhibition." In *Reorienting the Middle East: Film and Digital Media Where the Persian Gulf, Arabian Sea, and Indian Ocean Meet*, edited by Dale Hudson and Alia Yunis, 102–20. Indianapolis: Indiana University Press, 2024.

Alilunas, Peter. *Smutty Little Movies: The Creation and Regulation of Adult Video*. Berkeley: University of California Press, 2016.

Andrews, David. *Soft in the Middle: The Contemporary Softcore Feature in Its Context*. Columbus: Ohio State University Press, 2006.

Appadurai, Arjun, and Carol A. Breckenridge. "Editor's Comment" & "Why Public Culture?" *Public Culture* 1, no. 1 (1988): 1–9.

———, eds. *Consuming Modernity: Public Culture in a South Asian World*. Minneapolis: University of Minnesota Press, 1995.

Arondekar, Anjali. *Abundance: Sexuality's History*. Durham, NC: Duke University Press, 2023.

Azoulay, Ariella. *The Civil Contract of Photography*. New York: Zone Books, 2008.

Baburaj, K. K. *Mattoru Jeevitham Saadhyamaanu* [Another life is possible]. Calicut: Other Books, 2019 (2008).

Baishya, Anirban K. "Revisiting Assamese Cinema." MPhil diss., Jawaharlal Nehru University, 2013.

———. "Pornography of Place: Location, Leaks, and Obscenity in the Indian MMS Porn Video." *South Asian Popular Culture* 15, no. 1 (2017): 57–71.

Baishya, Anirban K., and Darshana Sreedhar Mini. "Translating Porn Studies: Lessons from the Vernacular." *Porn Studies* 6, no. 3 (2020): 1–11.

———. "Figuring the Aggregated Aunty: Metadata and South Asian Aunties." *Text and Performance Quarterly* 42, no. 3 (2021): 315–31.

Balasubrahmanyan, Vimal. "The Watchdogs: Women Monitor the Media." In *Gender and Censorship*, edited by Brinda Bose, 56–73. New Delhi: Women Unlimited, 2006.

Basheer, Vaikom Muhammad. "Sabdangal." In *Basheer Sampoorna Kritikal* [Basheer complete works], 417–55. Kottayam: DC Books, 1992.

Baskaran, Theodore. "Cinema Houses in Chennai." In *The Unhurried City: Writings on Chennai*, edited by C. S. Lakshmi, 75–84. New Delhi: Penguin Books, 2004.

Berg, Heather. *Porn Work: Sex, Labor, and Late Capitalism*. Chapel Hill: University of North Carolina Press, 2021.

Berlant, Lauren. *Cruel Optimism*. Durham, NC: Duke University Press, 2011.

Bhanu, Surayya. *Dupe*. Kottayam: DC Books, 2010.

Bloch, Ernst. *The Principle of Hope*. Vol. 1. Translated by Neville Plaice, Stephen Plaice, and Paul Knight. Cambridge, MA: MIT Press, 1995. First published in 1959.

Bose, Brinda, ed. *Gender and Censorship*. New Delhi: Women Unlimited, 2006.

Brown, Tom, and Belen Vidal, eds. *The Biopic in Contemporary Film Culture*. New York: Routledge, 2014.

Bruno, Giuliana. *Streetwalking on a Ruined Map: Cultural Theory and City Films of Elvira Notari*. Princeton, NJ: Princeton University Press, 1993.

———. *Atlas of Emotion: Journeys in Art, Architecture, and Film*. New York: Verso, 2002.

Burney, Ina, and Christopher Hamlin, eds. *Global Forensic Cultures*. Baltimore, MD: Johns Hopkins University Press, 2019.

Butler, Judith. *Precarious Life: The Powers of Mourning and Violence*. London: Verso, 2004.

Calhoun, Craig, ed. *Habermas and the Public Sphere*. Cambridge, MA: MIT Press, 1992.

Chakravarti, Uma. *Gendering Caste: Through a Feminist Lens*. Calcutta: Stree, 2003.

Chandrasekharan, M. R. *Keralathile Purogamana Prastanathinte Charitram* [The history of progressive literature in Kerala]. Calicut: Olive publications, 1999.

Chatterjee, Tupur. "'I Am a Porn Star!' Sex and Sunny Leone Unlimited in Bollywood." *Porn Studies* 4, no. 1 (2017): 50–56.

Chennai: Memory Chips. Chennai: Legacy Publications, 2000.

Chion, Michael. *Audio-vision: Sound on Screen*. New York: Columbia University Press, 1994.

Christy, Carmel. *Sexuality and Public Space in India: Reading the Visible*. London: Routledge, 2017.

Chun, Wendy Hui Kyong, and Sarah Friedland. "Habits of Leaking: Of Sluts and Network Cards." *differences: A Journal of Feminist Cultural Studies* 26, no. 2 (2015): 1–28.

Corbett, John, and Terri Kapsalis. "Aural Sex: The Female Orgasm in Popular Sound." *The Drama Review* 40, no. 3 (1996): 102–11.

Curtin, Michael, and Kevin Sanson, eds. *Precarious Creativity: Global Media, Local Labor*. Oakland: University of California Press, 2016.

Dass, Manishita. *Outside the Lettered City: Cinema, Modernity, and the Public Sphere in Late Colonial India*. Oxford: Oxford University Press, 2015.

David, P. *Framekulkappuram: Oru Cinema Still photographerude atmakatha* [Beyond frames: The autobiography of a still photographer]. Thrissur: Current Books, 2011.

Deepa, V. N. "Queering Kerala: Reflections on Sahayatrika." In *Because I Have a Voice: Queer Politics in India*, edited by G. Bhan and A. Narrain, 175–96. New Delhi: Yoda Press, 2005.

Derrida, Jacques. "The Dangerous Supplement." In *Of Grammatology*, translated by Gayatri Chakravorty Spivak, 153–71. Baltimore: Johns Hopkins University Press, 2016 (1974).

Desai, Jigna. *Beyond Bollywood: The Cultural Politics of South Asian Diasporic Film*. Routledge: New York, 2004.

Devika, J. "Feminism and Late Twentieth-century Governmentality in Kerala, India: Towards a Critical History." In *Feminist Subversion and Complicity: Governmentalities and Gender Knowledge in South Asia*, edited by M. Mukhopadhyay, 123–46. New Delhi: Zubaan, 2006.

———. "Being 'In-translation' in a Postcolony." *Translation Studies* 1, no. 2 (2008): 182–96.

———. "Memory's Fatal Lure: The Left, the Congress, and 'Jeevan' in Kerala." *Economic and Political Weekly* 43, no. 30 (July 26, 2008): 13–16.

———. "Getting beyond the Governmental Fix in Kerala." *Signs: Journal of Women in Culture and Society* 39, no. 3 (2014): 580–84.

Devika, J., and Mini Sukumar. "Making Space for Feminist Social Critique in Contemporary Kerala." *Economic and Political Weekly* 41, no. 42 (October 21–27, 2006): 4469–75.

Dutta, Madhusree, Kaushik Bhaumik, and Rohan Shivkumar, eds. *Project Cinema City*. New Delhi: Tulika Books, 2013.

Dyer, Richard. *Heavenly Bodies: Film Stars and Society*. London: Routledge, 2004.

Edachira, Manju. "Anti-caste Aesthetics and Dalit Interventions in Indian Cinema." *Economic and Political Weekly* 55, no. 38 (September 19, 2020): 47–53.

Eley, Geoff. "Nations, Publics, and Political Cultures: Placing Habermas in the Nineteenth Century." In *Habermas and the Public Sphere*, edited by Craig Calhoun, 289–339. Cambridge, MA: MIT Press, 1992.

Erwer, Monica. "Challenging the Gender Paradox: Women's Collective Agency in the Transformation of Kerala Politics." PhD dissertation, Goteborg University, 2003.

Ezra, Elizabeth, and Terry Rowden. *Transnational Cinema: The Film Reader*. London: Routledge, 2006.

Field, Allyson Nadia. "Editor's Introduction: Acts of Speculation." *Feminist Media Histories* 8, no. 3 (2022): 1–7.

Flowers, Amy. *The Fantasy Factory: An Insider's View of the Phone Sex Industry*. Philadelphia: University of Pennsylvania Press, 1998.

Fortmueller, Kate. *Below the Stars: How the Labor of Working Actors and Extras Shapes Media Production*. Austin: University of Texas Press, 2021.

Foucault, Michel. *Discipline and Punish: The Birth of the Prison*. Translated by Alan Sheridan. New York: Random House, 1995. First published in 1978.

Foucault, Michel, and Jay Miskowiec. "Of Other Spaces." *Diacritics* 16, no. 1 (Spring 1986): 22–27.

Fraser, Nancy. "Rethinking the Public Sphere: A Contribution to the Critique of Actually Existing Democracy," *Social Text* no. 25/26 (1990): 56–80.

Freitag, Sandria B. *Collective Action and Community: Public Arenas and the Emergence of Communalism in North India*. Berkeley: University of California Press, 1989.

Gadhihoke, Sabeena. "The Art of Capturing Stillness: Cinema Lobby Cards." *Marg: A Magazine of the Arts* 68, no. 3 (2017): 108–13.

Gaines, Jane M. *Pink-Slipped: What Happened to Women in Silent Film Industries*. Champaign: University of Illinois Press, 2018.

Galison, Peter. "Blacked-out Spaces: Freud, Censorship, and the Reterritorialization of Mind." *British Journal for the History of Science* 45, no. 2 (2012): 235–66.

Ganti, Tejaswini. "The Limits of Decency and the Decency of Limits: Censorship and Bombay Film Industry." In *Censorship in South Asia: Cultural Regulation from Sedition to Seduction*, edited by Raminder Kaur and William Mazzarella, 87–122. Bloomington: Indiana University Press, 2009.

———. *Producing Bollywood: Inside the Contemporary Hindi Film Industry*. Durham, NC: Duke University Press, 2012.

Ghosh, Shohini. "The Troubled Existence of Sex and Sexuality: Feminists Engage with Censorship." In *Image Journeys: Audio-visual Media and Cultural Change in India*, edited by Christiane Brosius and Melissa Butcher, 233–60. New Delhi: Sage, 1999.

Gill, Rosalind, and Andy Pratt. "In the Social Factory? Immaterial Labour, Precariousness, and Cultural Work." *Theory, Culture & Society* 25, no. 7-8 (2008): 1–30.

Gopinath, Gayatri. *Unruly Visions: The Aesthetic Practices of Queer Diaspora*. Durham, NC: Duke University Press, 2018.

Gorfinkel, Elena. *Lewd Looks: American Sexploitation Cinema in the 1960s*. Minneapolis: University of Minnesota Press, 2017.

Govil, Nitin. *Orienting Hollywood: A Century of Film Culture between Los Angeles and Bombay*. New York: NYU Press, 2015.

Grewal, Inderpal. *Transnational America: Feminisms, Diasporas, Neoliberalisms*. Durham, NC: Duke University Press, 2005.

Grewal, Inderpal, and Caren Kaplan. *Scattered Hegemonies: Postmodernity and Transnational Feminist Practices*. Minneapolis: University of Minnesota Press, 1994.

Gubar, Susan. *Racechanges: White Skin, Black Face in American Culture*. New York and Oxford: Oxford University Press, 1997.

Gunning, Tom. "The Cinema of Attractions: Early Film, Its Spectator, and the Avant-Garde." In *The Cinema of Attractions Reloaded*, edited by Wanda Strauven, 381–88. Amsterdam: Amsterdam University Press, 2006.

Gupta, Charu. *Sexuality, Obscenity, Community: Women, Muslims, and the Hindu Public in Colonial India*. New York: Palgrave, 2001.

Habermas, Jürgen. *The Structural Transformation of the Public Sphere: An Inquiry into a Category of Bourgeois Society*. Cambridge, MA: MIT Press, 1991.

Hage, Ghassan ed. *Waiting*. Carlton: Melbourne University Press, 2009.

Hansen, Thomas Blom. "Whose Public, Whose Authority? Reflections on the Moral Force of Violence." *Modern Asian Studies* 52, no. 3 (2018): 1076–87.

Hardy, Kathyrn C. "Constituting a Diffuse Region: Cartographies of Mass-mediated Bhojpuri Belonging." *BioScope: South Asian Screen Studies* 6, no. 2 (2010): 145–64.

Harris, Ella, and Mel Nowicki. "Cultural Geographies of Precarity." *Cultural Geographies* 25, no. 3 (2018): 387–91.

Harvey, Brian. *Russia in Space: The Failed Frontier*. London: Springer, 2001.

Harvey, David. "Space as a Key Word." Paper presented at the Marx and Philosophy Conference, Institute of Education, London, May 29, 2004.

Hefferman, Kevin. "Seen as a Business: Adult Film's Historical Framework and Foundations." In *New Views of Pornography: Sexuality, Politics, and the Law*, edited by Lynn Comella and Shira Tarrant, 37–56. Westport, CT: Praeger, 2015.

Hennefeld, Maggie. *Specters of Slapstick and Silent Film Comediennes*. New York: Columbia University Press, 2018.

Herbert, Dan. *Videoland: Movie Culture at the American Video Store*. Berkeley: University of California Press, 2014.

Higbee, Will, and Song Hwee Lim. "Concepts of Transnational Cinema: Towards a Critical Transnationalism in Film Studies." *Transnational Cinemas* 1, no. 1 (2010): 7–21.

Higson, Andrew. "The Concept of National Cinema." *Screen* 4, no. 30 (1989): 36–47.

Hilderbrand, Lucas. *Inherent Vice: Bootleg Histories of Videotape and Copyright*. Durham, NC: Duke University Press, 2009.

Hill, Erin. *Never Done: A History of Women's Work in Media Production*. New Brunswick, NJ: Rutgers University Press, 2016.

Hjort, Mette. "On the Plurality of Cinematic Transnationalism." In *World Cinema, Transnational Perspectives*, edited by Nataša Durovicová and Kathleen Newman, 12–33. London: Routledge/American Film Institute Reader, 2010.

Hoek, Lotte. *Cut Pieces: Celluloid Obscenity and Popular Cinema in Bangladesh*. New York: Columbia University Press, 2014.

———. "When Celluloid Pornography Went Digital: Class and Race in the Bangladeshi Cut-piece Online." *Porn Studies* 7, no. 1 (2019): 97–114. DOI: https://doi.org/10.1080/23268743.2019.1607539.

Imre, Aniko, and Katarzyna Marciniak, eds. *Transnational Feminism in Film and Media*. New York: Palgrave Macmillan, 2007.

Indraganti, Kiranmayi. *Her Majestic Voice: South Indian Female Playback Singers and Stardom, 1945–1955*. New Delhi: Oxford University Press, 2016.

Iyer, Usha. "Stardom Ke Peeche Kya Hai? / What is behind the Stardom? Madhuri Dixit, the Production Number, and the Construction of the Female Star Text in 1990s Hindi Cinema." *Camera Obscura* 30, no. 3 (2015): 129–59.

———. *Dancing Women: Choreographing Corporeal Histories of Hindi Cinema*. London: Oxford University Press, 2020.

Jaikumar, Priya. *Where Histories Reside: India as a Filmed Space*. Durham, NC: Duke University Press, 2019.

Jameela, Nalini. *Me, Sex Worker: The Autobiography of Nalini Jameela*. Kottayam: DC Books, 2005.

Jeffrey, Craig. *Timepass: Youth, Class, and the Politics of Waiting in India*. Stanford, CA: Stanford University Press, 2010.

Johnson, Eithne. "Excess and Ecstasy: Constructing Female Pleasure in Porn Movies." *Velvet Light Trap* 32 (Fall 1993): 30–50.

Kankol, Shivakumar, ed. *Vishuddha Smitha* [Virtuous Smitha]. Kannoor: Spectrum, 1997.

Kaviraj, Sudipta. "Filth and the Public Sphere: Concepts and Practices about Space in Calcutta." *Public Culture* 10, no. 1 (1997): 83–113.

Kipnis, Laura. *Bound and Gagged: Pornography and the Politics of Fantasy in America*. Durham, NC: Duke University Press, 1998.

Kotiswaran, Prabha. *Dangerous Sex, Invisible Labor: Sex Work and the Law in India*. Princeton, NJ: Princeton University Press, 2011.

Kuehn, Kathleen, and Thomas F. Corrigan. "Hope Labor: The Role of Employment Prospects in Online Social Production." *The Political Economy of Communication* 1, no. 1 (2013), 9–25.

Kumar, Shaji P. V. "18+." In *Kidappara Samaram*, 33–44. Calicut: Mathrubhumi, 2013.

Kumar, Shanti. "Mapping Tollywood: The Cultural Geography of 'Ramoji Film City' in Hyderabad." *Quarterly Review of Film and Video* 23, no. 2 (2006): 129–38.

Kumar, Udaya. "Ambivalences of Publicity: Transparency and Exposure in K. Ramakrishna Pillai's Thought." In *The Public Sphere from Outside the West*, edited by Divya Dwivedi and Sanil V, 82–83. London: Bloomsbury, 2017.

Kumaramkandath, Rajeev. "Sexual Realism? (Hetero)Sexual Excess and the Birth of Obscenity." In *(Hi)Stories of Desire: Sexualities and Culture in Modern India*. Cambridge: Cambridge University Press, 2020.

Landes, Joan. *Women and the Public Sphere in the Age of the French Revolution*. Ithaca, NY: Cornell University Press, 1988.

Larkin, Brian. *Signal and Noise: Media, Infrastructure, and Urban Culture in Nigeria*. Durham, NC: Duke University Press, 2008.

Lewis, Jon. *Hard-Boiled Hollywood: Crime and Punishment in Postwar Los Angeles*. Oakland: University of California Press, 2017.

Lukow, Gregory, and Steven Ricci. "The 'Audience' Goes 'Public': Intertexuality, Genre, and the Responsibilities of Film Literacy." On Film 12 (Spring 1984): 29–36.

MacKinnon, Catharine, and Andrea Dworkin, eds. *In Harm's Way: The Pornography Civil Rights Hearings*. Cambridge, MA: Harvard University Press, 1998.

Mahadevan, Sudhir. "Traveling Showmen, Makeshift Cinemas: The Bioscopewallah and Early Cinema History in India." *Bioscope* 1, no. 1 (2010): 27–47.

Majumdar, Neepa. *Wanted Cultured Ladies Only! Female Stardom and Cinema in India, 1930s–1950s*. Champaign: University of Illinois Press, 2009.

Mallapragada, Madhavi. "Home, Homeland, Homepage: Belonging and the Indian American Web." In *Reorienting Global Communication: India and China Media Beyond Borders*, edited by Michael Curtin and Hemant Shah, 60–82. Urbana: University of Illinois Press, 2006.

Mani, Kunnukuzhi S. *P. K. Rosi: The Mother of Malayalam Cinema*. Trivandrum: Mythri Books, 2019.

Mankekar, Purnima. *Screening Culture Viewing Politics: An Ethnography of Television, Womanhood, and Nation in Postcolonial India*. Durham, NC: Duke University Press, 1999.

Maruthur, Navaneetha Mokkil. *Unruly Figures: Queerness, Sex Work, and the Politics of Sexuality in Kerala*. Seattle: University of Washington Press, 2019.

Mayer, Vicki. *Below the Line: Producers and Production Studies in the New Television Economy*. Durham, NC: Duke University Press, 2011.

Mazumdar, Ranjani. *Bombay Cinema: An Archive of the City*. Minneapolis: University of Minnesota Press, 2007.

Mazzarella, William. *Censorium: Cinema and the Open Edge of Mass Publicity*. Durham, NC: Duke University Press, 2013.

Mehta, Monika. *Censorship and Sexuality in Bombay Cinema*. Austin: University of Texas Press, 2011.

Miller, Jade. "Labor in Lagos: Alternative Global Networks." In *Precarious Creativity: Global Media, Local Labor*, edited by Michael Curtin and Kevin Sanson, 146–58. Oakland: University of California Press, 2016.

Miller, Toby, Nitin Govil, John McMurria, and Richard Maxwell. *Global Hollywood*. Berkley: University of California Press, 2002.

Miller-Young, Mireille. *A Taste for Brown Sugar: Black Women in Pornography*. Durham, NC: Duke University Press, 2014.

Mini, Darshana Sreedhar. "The Spectral Duration of Malayalam Soft-porn: Disappearance, Desire, and Haunting." *Bioscope: South Asian Screen Studies* 7, no. 2 (2017): 127–50.

———. "The Rise of Soft-Porn in Malayalam Cinema and the Precarious Stardom of Shakeela." *Feminist Media Histories* 5, no. 2 (April 2019): 49–82.

———. "Cinema and the Mask of Capital: Labor Debates in the Malayalam Film Industry." *Studies in South Asian Film and Media* 11, no. 2 (2020): 173–89.

———. "Locating the 'B' in B-circuit Cinema." In *Film Studies: An Introduction*, edited by Vebhuti Duggal, Bindu Menon, and Spandan Bhattacharya, 319–28. Delhi/Kolkata: Worldview Publications, 2022.

Mini, Darshana Sreedhar, and Anirban K. Baishya. "Transgressions in Toonland: Savita Bhabhi, Velamma, and the Indian Adult Comic." *Porn Studies* 7, no. 1 (2020): 115–31.

Mitchell, W. J. T. *Picture Theory: Essays on Verbal and Visual Representation*. Chicago: University of Chicago Press, 1994.

Mitra, Durba. *Indian Sex Life: Sexuality and the Colonial Origins of Modern Social Life.* Princeton, NJ: Princeton University Press, 2020.
Miyazaki, Hirokazu. *The Method of Hope: Anthropology, Philosophy, and Fijian Knowledge.* Stanford, CA: Stanford University Press, 2004.
Mukherjee, Debashree. *Bombay Hustle: Making Movies in a Colonial City.* New York: Columbia University Press, 2020.
Mukherjee, Madhuja, *Voices of the Talking Stars: Women of Indian Cinema and Beyond.* New Delhi: Sage, 2017.
Mukhopadhyay, Swapna. *The Enigma of the Kerala Woman: A Failed Promise of Literacy.* New Delhi: Social Science Press, 2007.
Mules, Warwick. "Media Publics and the Transnational Public Sphere." *Critical Arts: North-South Cultural and Media Studies* 12 (1998): 24–44.
Nair, Vasudevan M. T. *Chitratheruvukal* [Film streets]. Thrissur: Current Books, 2010.
Nash, Jennifer C. *The Black Body in Ecstasy: Reading Race, Reading Pornography.* Durham, NC: Duke University Press, 2014.
O'Regan, Tom. "Remembering Video: Reflections on the First Explosion of Informal Media Markets through the VCR." *Television & New Media* 13, no. 5 (2012): 383–98.
Osella, Caroline, and Filippo Osella. "Young Malayali Men and Their Movie Heroes." In *South Asian Masculinities: Context of Change, Sites of Continuity*, edited by Radhika Chopra, Filippo Osella, and Caroline Osella, 224–61. New Delhi: Women Unlimited, 2004.
Paasonen, Susanna. *Carnal Resonance: Affect and Online Pornography.* Cambridge, MA: MIT Press, 2011.
Paik, Shailaja. *The Vulgarity of Caste: Dalits, Sexuality, and Humanity in Modern India.* Stanford, CA: Stanford University Press, 2022.
Pandian, Anand. *Reel World: An Anthropology of Creation.* Durham, NC: Duke University Press, 2015.
Pendakur, Manjunath. *Indian Popular Cinema: Industry, Ideology, and Consciousness.* Cresskill, NJ: Hampton Press, 2003.
Phillips, Whitney. *This is Why We Can't Have Nice Things: Mapping the Relationship between Online Trolling and Mainstream Culture.* Cambridge, MA: MIT Press, 2015.
Pillai, Erumeli Parameshwaran. *Malayala Sahityam kalakhattangalilude* [Malayalam literature through different stages]. Kottayam: DC Books, 2013. First published in 1996.
Pillai, Govinda. "Udathasahityavum Janapriyasahityavum" [High literature and popular literature]. In *Janapriya Sahityam Malayalathil* [Popular literature in Malayalam], edited by M. G. Sreekumar, 26–27. Kottayam: National Book Stall, 2014.
Pillai, Swarnavel Eswaran. *Madras Studios: Narrative, Genre, and Ideology in Tamil Cinema.* New Delhi: Sage, 2015.
Pine, Jason. *The Art of Making Do in Naples.* Minneapolis: University of Minnesota Press, 2012.
Pinney, Christopher. *Photos of the Gods: The Printed Image and Political Struggle in India.* London: Reaktion Books, 2004.
Prasad, Madhav. "Cinema and Desire for Modernity." *Journal of Arts & Ideas* 25–26 (December 1993): 71–86.
Rajadhyaksha, Ashish. "The 'Bollywoodization' of the Indian Cinema: Cultural Nationalism in a Global Arena." *Inter-Asia Cultural Studies* 4, no. 1 (2003): 25–39.

Rajagopal, Arvind, ed. *The Indian Public Sphere: Readings in Media History*. New Delhi: Oxford University Press, 2009.

———. "A 'Split Public' in the Making and Unmaking of the Ram Janmabhumi Campaign." In *The Indian Public Sphere: Readings in Media History*, edited by Rajagopal, 207–27. New Delhi: Oxford University Press, 2009.

Rajagopalan, Sudha. *Indian Films in Soviet Cinemas: The Culture of Movie-Going After Stalin*. Bloomington: Indiana University Press, 2008.

Rajan, S. Irudaya, ed. *India Migration Report 2020: Kerala Model of Migration Surveys*. Oxon: Routledge, 2020.

Ramachandran, G. P. *Malayalam Cinema: Desam, Bhasha, Samskaram* [Malayalam cinema: Region, language, and culture]. Thiruvananthapuram: The State Institute of Languages, Kerala, 2009.

Ratheesh, Radhakrishnan. "Soft Porn and the Anxieties of the Family." In *Women in Malayalam Cinema: Naturalizing Gender Hierarchies*, edited by Meena Pillai, 194–220. Hyderabad: Orient Blackswan, 2010.

Report on the Working Group on National Film Policy. 1980. Accessed from NFAI Pune, December 2022.

Schaefer, Eric. *"Bold! Daring! Shocking! True!" A History of Exploitation Films, 1919–1959*. Durham, NC: Duke University Press, 1999.

———. "The Problem with Sexploitation Movies." *Iluminace* 3 (2012): 148–52.

The Sex Education Encyclopedia. Kottayam: Moral Books. 1978.

Shakeela. *Atmakatha* [Autobiography]. Calicut: Olive Publications, 2013.

Shifman, Limor. *Memes in Digital Culture*. Cambridge, MA: MIT Press, 2014.

Shyma, P. "The Caste of Casting: Thilakan and 'Backward' Articulations in Malayalam Cinema," *Bioscope: South Asian Screen Studies* 13, no. 2 (2022): 154–75.

Singh, Bhrigupati. "Aadamkhor Haseena (The Man-Eating Beauty) and the Anthropology of a Moment." *Contributions to Indian Sociology* 42, no. 2 (2008): 249–79.

Smith, Clarissa, and Feona Atwood. "Porn Studies: An Introduction." *Porn Studies* 1, no. 1–2 (2014): 1–6.

Sreedhar, Darshana. "Theorizing Female Same-Sex Sub-Culture: Dissident Voices in 21st-century Kerala." Master's thesis, Center for Studies in Social Sciences, Calcutta, 2011.

Sreedhar, Darshana, and Abraham, Vinu. "When Ghosts Come Calling: Re-'projecting' the Disappeared Muses of Malayalam Cinema." In *Sarai Reader 09: Projections*, edited by Shveta Sarda and Raqs Media Collective, 336–45. New Delhi: CSDS, 2013.

Sreekumar, Sharmila. *Scripting Lives: Narratives of Privileged Women in Kerala*. Hyderabad: Orient Blackswan, 2009.

Sreenivasan, P. K. *Kodambakkam: Black and White*. Thrissur: Current Books, 2013.

Srinivas, S. V. *Megastar: Chiranjeevi and Telugu Cinema after N. T. Rama Rao*. New Delhi: Oxford University Press, 2009.

Srivastava, Sanjay, ed. *Sexuality Studies*. New Delhi: Oxford University Press, 2013.

Stamp, Shelley. *Lois Weber in Early Hollywood*. Berkeley: University of California Press, 2015.

Sundaram, Ravi. "Revisiting the Pirate Kingdom." In *Postcolonial Piracy: Media Distribution and Cultural Production in the Global South*, edited by Lars Eckstein and Anja Schwarz, 29–48. London: Bloomsbury, 2014.

Sunya, Samhita. *Sirens of Modernity: World Cinema via Bombay.* Berkeley: University of California Press, 2022.

Syeda, Farida Batool. "New Media, Masculinity, and Mujra Dance in Pakistan." PhD diss., SOAS, University of London, 2015.

Taormino, Tristan, Constance Penley, Celine Parrenas Shimizu, and Mireille Miller-Young. *The Feminist Porn Book: The Politics of Producing Pleasure.* New York: The Feminist Press at the City University of New York, 2013.

Vanita, Ruth. *Dancing with the Nation: Courtesans in Bombay Cinema.* London: Bloomsbury, 2018.

Vasudevan, Ravi. "Geographies of the Cinematic Public: Notes on Regional, National, and Global Histories of Cinema." *Journal of Moving Image* 9 (2010): 94–117.

Venkiteswaran, C. S. "Shakeela, Chila Thundu Chintakal" [Shakeela: A few thought pieces]. In *Udalinte Tharasancharangal* [The circulation of the star body], 101–11. Kottayam: DC Books, 2011.

Vidler, Anthony. *The Architectural Uncanny: Essays in the Modern Unhomely.* Cambridge, MA: MIT Press, 1992.

Visweswaran, Kamala. *Fictions of Feminist Ethnography.* Minneapolis: University of Minnesota Press, 1994.

Waite, Louise. "A Place and Space for a Critical Geography of Precarity?" *Geography Compass* 3, no. 1 (2009): 412–33.

Warner, Michael. *Publics and Counter Publics.* Cambridge, MA: MIT Press, 2002.

Wasco, Vincent. *The Political Economy of Communication.* London: Sage, 2009.

Wilkerson-Weber, Clare M. *Fashioning Bollywood: The Making and Meaning of Hindi Film Costume.* London: Bloomsbury Academic, 2014.

Williams, Linda. *Hard Core: Power, Pleasure, and the "Frenzy of the Visible."* Berkeley: University of California Press, 1989.

———. *The Erotic Thriller in Contemporary Cinema.* Bloomington: Indiana University Press, 2005.

INDEX

Aadyapaapam (film), 83–84, 84*fig.*, 121, 147, 149, 185nn56,57
Aa Oru Nimisham (film), 24–25, 159
Aarambam (film), 294n87
Abhilasha, 83–84
Abraham, John, 70
adult, 14, 16, 21–22, 84*fig.*; certificate, 85; certification, 143; content, 121; film, 97, 105, 107, 113, 147, 155, 172; magazines, 122; media, 3, 27, 29; meme, 160; platform, 159; rating, 5*fig.*; theater, 6; troll, 161–62; video, 136. *See also* theaters; video
Adult Film Association of America, 172
Adult Video News, 135
Akhtar, Begum, 32
Alilunas, Peter, 29
All India Film Producer's Council (AIFPC), 124, 127
All Kerala Sunny Leone Fans Club, 110
alternative transnational, 117–19, 123, 145, 138, 171
Alva, Margaret, 174n15
Amma, Konniyur Meenakshi, 14
Anand, Vijay, 6
Andhra Pradesh, 21, 55, 67, 94, 112
Andrews, David, 18, 29, 100
Annakutty Kodambakkam Vilikunnu (*Annakutty, Kodambakkam is Beckoning You*) (film), 64
Antharangam (sex education television program), 103
Anthyakoodasha (film), 169

anti-Hindi protests, 67
Anti-Obscenity Forum, 5
anti-obscenity protests, 5, 55, 73–74
anti-pornography activism, 5–6, 19–20, 102
Appadurai, Arjun, 10
Ardharathri (film), 80
Arondekar, Anjali, 35
Asad, M., 70
ashleelam (obscene), 9, 12
ashleela sahityam (obscene literature), 9
ashleelatha, 12; discourses of, 12–16
Asianet (satellite channel), 100, 110, 132, 166–67
aspiration, 7, 28, 32, 42, 46, 58, 64, 90, 172; aspirational economies, 62, 80; aspirational mobility, 36, 60–61
Avalude Ravukal (*Her Nights*) (film), 14–16, 15*fig.*, 74, 120, 160
Ayiram Chirakulla Moham (film), 80
Ayyaneth, 9
Ayyankali Pada, 102

Babu, Ramachandra, 70
Backer, P. A., 70
Bahrain, 121–22, 132–33
Bai, Jaddan, 32
Bai, Rattan, 33
Balaji Telefilms, 37
Balan (film), 70, 184n48
Balan, Vidya, 31, 37–39, 55
Balasubramanyam, Vimal, 6

INDEX

Bangalore, 23, 43, 83
Bangladeshi cut-piece films, 22, 28
Basheer, Vaikom Muhammad, 12; *Nteuppuppaykkoranendarnnu* (short novel), 13; *Sabdangal* (novella), 13
Basu, Nripendra Kumar: *The History of Prostitution*, 33
Begum, Fatima, 32
Berlant, Lauren, 88
bestiality, 50
Bhagat, H. K. L., 119
Bhaktavatsalam, Minjur, 67
Bhanu, Surayya: *Dupe*, 113–15
Bharatan, 47, 53, 93
Bhaumik, Kaushik, 65
Blom Hansen, Thomas, 10
Body (film), 140, 141*fig.*
body-doubling, 35, 88, 106, 113–15, 155, 190n81
Bollywood, 31, 37, 55, 65, 90, 107–8, 118, 120, 122, 171. *See also* Hindi cinema
Bombay. *See* Mumbai
Breckenridge, Carol A., 10
Bruno, Giuliana, 56–57, 145
Butler, Judith, 95

Calcutta, 4, 33, 128
Calhoun, Craig, 10
caste, 1, 26–27, 36; and gender, 38–41, 87; lack of conversation in Indian cinema on, 180n30
CD (compact disc), 3, 122, 134, 136; pirated, 121
celluloid, 23, 128; era of, 139, 146, 152, 158; pornography, 121; strips of, 151; uncertified, 22
Celluloid (film), 58
Censor (documentary film), 16
censorship, 3–10, 14–16, 20–22, 50, 59, 85, 143, 172; activism against, 6; act of censorship as promise, 143; bypassing, 86, 147; institutions of, 91; regulations of, 111, 119, 128; rigid structures of, 88. *See also* film
Center for Development Studies (CDS), 132
center spreads, 58
Central Board of Film Certification (CBFC), 3–4, 6, 15–16, 20, 28, 123, 126–28, 131
Chacko case, 13
Chadha, Richa, 105
Chakravarthy, Vinu, 37
Chandrakumar, P., 52, 63, 80, 83–85, 121, 147
charasundari, 13
Chaubey, Bhupendra, 108
chechi, 54, 55, 101–2, 161, 163, 188n47
chendamelam, 133

Chennai (also Madras), 15, 20, 23, 43–44, 47, 60–74, 117, 120–21, 131, 181n38; Amaravati, 68; film production in, 77; Kodambakkam Bridge, 68; Mosabi, 68; Palm Grove, 68; Periye Gate, 67–68; Pondy Bazar, 68; Raipetta, 68; Raj Home, 68; Rohini, 68; Saligramam, 68, 69*fig.*, 77; Sowcarpet, 68; trans community of, 107–8, 110; Trustpuram, 75; Vadapalani, 68–69, 79. *See also* India; Kodambakkam
child sexual abuse, 108, 169
Chinankath, Rajan, 9
Chion, Michel, 150
Chitrabhumi (film magazine), 9, 44, 47–48, 54, 57, 181n45, 182n58
Chitrakarthika, 41, 102; illustration as a part of "Papathinte Sambalam" in, 42*fig.*
Chitralekha film society, 98
Chitranjali Studio, 21, 99
Choksi, Jessica, 190n81
Chotta Mumbai (film), 102
Choudary, R. B., 52–53, 83, 185n57
Chun, Wendy Hui Kyong, 167
Cinemamangalam (film weekly), 58
Cinema Marte Dum Tak (docuseries), 89
Cinemamasika (film magazine), 34, 44
cinematic wait-time, 60–65, 90
Cinematograph Act (1952), 3, 6, 125
Cinematograph (Amendment) Act (2023), 3
Cinemavarika (film magazine), 34
Cinerama (film magazine), 44
Cine Voice (film magazine), 73
cine-workers, 7, 27, 61, 82, 87–93, 115. *See also* film
citizen journalists (the Gestapo), 12
civil society activism, 1, 5
Classmates (film), 146
Climax (film), 55–56
Competition Commission of India, 121, 191n20. *See also* India
computer-generated imagery (CGI), 145
condoms, 2, 129. *See also* safe-sex practices
continuity albums, 29, 58, 72, 72*fig.*
Corbett, John, 19
Corrigan, Thomas, 87
corruption, 4, 6, 11
courtesans, 33
Crazy Lady (film), 119
crime, 11–12, 63; thriller, 82
Crime (men's magazine), 2, 42–43, 102
Crossfire (adult magazine), 122
cut-pieces, 22–24, 28, 156–58, 76, 114, 142, 150, 156–58, 157*fig.*, 169. *See also* soft-porn films

Dalit-Bahujan movement, 38–39, 180n30
Dalits, 1, 11, 38–39, 168; violence and sexualization imposed on women of the, 103, 168
Dalit Web, 38–39
Dandavate, Pramila, 5
dargahs, 140
Dass, Manishita, 4
David, P.: *Beyond Frames: The Autobiography of a Cinema Still Photographer*, 71–72, 74
Delhi, 74, 119; Malayalam Film Society in, 6; Odeon cinema hall in, 119; Plaza Cinema in, 5, 16
Delhi Malayalee Association of Mayur Vihar, 119–20
Delhi Media Group, 6
Dennis, Kaloor, 55
Derrida, Jacques, 164
Devadas, M. S., 13
Devika, J., 11, 167
Dhool (film), 102
Dirty Picture, The (film), 31, 37–40, 52, 55–56, 58, 104–6, 143–44
Dirty Picture: Silk Sakkath Maga (film), 55
Dixit, Madhuri, 27–28
Dubai, 93, 121–22, 132–38, 172, 194n87. *See also* Gulf; United Arab Emirates (UAE)
dubbed films, 6, 19–20, 31, 53, 55, 58, 113, 119, 121, 140
dubbing: artists involved in, 76; ban on Hindi language, 191n21; scheduling of, 189n70. *See also* film
dupe, 81, 106, 113–15
Dutta, Madhushree, 65, 140
Dworkin, Andrea, 5
Dyer, Richard, 95

Eastman, Anthony, 52, 55
Edachira, Manju, 27
Eeta (film), 4
Eid al-Fitr, 143
Ek Chhotisi Love Story (film), 190n81
Elayath, K. V. S., 51–52
Eley, Geoff, 10
embodied vulnerability, 87–88
Enforcement Directorate of the Reserve Bank of India, 124
erotic literature, 10, 161, 163
ethical: code of relationality, 7, 86; collaborative approaches to, 26
exploitation, 81–82
extras, 31–32, 34–36
Ezhavas, 1

Facebook, 160–62
failure, 58
Farris, David, 156, 158
feminism, 1, 29, 35–36; anti-pornography, 19, 25; sex- and porn-positive, 25. *See also* women
film, 10; Ambedkarite, 38, 180n30; American exploitation, 8, 20, 128–20, 171; *Amman* (religious), 155; erotic English, 140; Italian exploitation, 129; Kannada industry of, 63, 70, 191n21; Maharashtra industry of, 58; Malayalam industry of, 8, 47, 51–71, 83–85, 90–97, 108–11, 119, 122, 133–35, 149, 152–53, 162, 189n68; Punjab industry of, 58; South Asian (dubbed in Hindi), 140–41; as subversive political tool to resist intolerant attitudes to difference, 6; Tamil industry of, 43, 47, 63, 94, 122, 133, 145, 154, 183n19; Telugu industry of, 47, 63, 70; virtuality of, 144–45. *See also* censorship; cine-workers; dubbing; film journalism; film noir; film subsidies; glamour films; hardcore films; mass media; sex education; silent films; soft-porn films; tinsel town; wait-time economy
Film (film magazine), 9, 14, 44
Film and Television Institute, 70, 131
Film Employees Federation of Kerala (FEFKA), 88, 104
Film Employees Federation of South India (FEFSI), 76
Filmfare (film magazine), 73, 127
Film Federation of India (FFI), 125–26
Film Finance Corporation (FFC), 120, 124
Film Import Contract Registration Committee (IMPEC), 124
filmindia (periodical), 4, 34
film journalism, 36, 107, 170; and career dealers, 43–57; centerfolds in magazines of, 45–46, 95; figure of the starlet in, 58–59, 94–95; Malayalam, 44–46, 57. *See also* film; mass media
Film Mirror (film magazine), 35
film noir, 94. *See also* film
film subsidies, 124, 191n35. *See also* film
Fire (men's magazine), 2, 42–43, 102
Flowers, Amy, 29
forensic gaze, 36, 46
foreplay, 19–20, 104, 149, 156, 159. *See also* sexuality
Forum against Vulgar Posters, 6
Foucault, Michel, 75
Fraser, Nancy, 10
Freitag, Sandria B., 10
Friedland, Sarah, 167

INDEX

Gaines, Jane, 29–30
Gajjala Gurram (film), 55
Ganti, Tejaswini, 27, 77
Geetha (men's magazine), 42
gender: and consumption patterns, 3; equity of, 41; normative roles of, 9, 166; parity, 26; and sexuality, 110. *See also* sexuality
George, K. G., 70
ghost writers, 20
Gill, Sonika, 129
glamour films, 75–86, 131, 170–71; alternative production circuits of, 80–86; directors and technicians who work in, 80. *See also* film; soft-porn films
Goodbye to Kodambakkam (film), 74–75
GoodKnight Films, 52
Gopalakrishnan, Adoor, 120
Gopalakrishnan, K. S., 63, 74, 79–80, 82–85, 94
Gopalan, Lalitha, 159
Gopi, Suresh, 52
Gopinath, Gayatri, 118
Gorfinkel, Elena, 25
gossip, 9, 11–12, 46, 54; columns, 35, 43; "Gossips Out" column, 44
Govil, Nitin, 116, 124
Govindan, Kamala, 185n50
Grewal, Inderpal, 117, 132
Grihalakshmi (women's magazine), 2
Gubar, Susan, 39
Gulf, 2, 50, 93, 116–18, 125, 131–32, 135–36, 138, 150, 162, 171–72; Gulf audience, 28, 121–23, 133–38; Gulf money, 133; Gulf wife, 161; Malayali migrants, 91, 183n13. *See also* Middle East
Gulf Today (newspaper): "Who's Afraid of Shakeela?," 96*fig.*
Gulfukarante Bharya (film), 169, 170*fig.*
Gumrah Jawani (film), 144, 145*fig.*
Gunning, Tom, 22
Gupta, Charu, 4
Gupta, Poonam Das, 58
Gupt Gyan (sex education film), 142, 195n2
Gupt Shastra (film), 130*fig.*

Habermas, Jürgen, 9–10; critics of, 10
Hage, Ghassan, 61
Halo Madras Girl (film), 64
Hamlin, Christopher, 56
Handique, Aideu, 32
hardcore films. *See* pornography
Hardy, Kathryn C., 123
Hariharan, 131
Harvey, David, 65

Hassan, Kamal, 83
Hassan, Sridevi, 83
Herbert, Dan, 122
Higson, Andrew, 118
Hindi cinema, 28, 32, 65, 120–22, 129, 133. *See also* Bollywood
Hindu nationalism, 10
Hindu rituals, 69
Hjort, Mette, 117
Hoek, Lotte, 22
Hollywood, 116, 120, 133
homosexuality, 13. *See also* queer people
Honeymoon Guide (adult magazine), 122
hope labor, 87
Hot Heir (film), 128
Hugs & Kisses Foundation, 162, 196n38
Hussain, P. Zakir, 71
Hyderabad, 43, 65

Import Selection Committee (ISC), 127
Inayathedi (film), 52
India: emergence of cinematic publics in, 4; emergence of consumer economy in, 125; Ministry of Corporate Affairs, 191n20; Ministry of Human Resource Development, 127; Ministry of Information and Broadcasting, 127–28; nineteenth-century colonial, 4; problems regarding the balance of payments in the 1980s for the economy of, 124, 192nn41,42; South, 6, 120, 191n21. *See also* censorship; Chennai; Competition Commission of India; Kerala; Mumbai
India Film Company, 43
Indian Cinema Centenary Celebrations (2013), 120
The Indian Express (newspaper), 14, 93
Indian Film Exporters Association (IFEA), 124
Indian Motion Picture Producers' Association, 34
Indian Motion Pictures Export Corporation (IMPEC), 123
Indian Penal Code, 4
Indian Space Research Organization (ISRO) case, 13
India Times (newspaper), 112
India Today (magazine), 82, 90, 94
Indraganti, Kiranmayi, 27
inequalities, 88
informal economy, 61, 87–88; exchanges in the, 26
internet porn, 3, 92, 149, 164, 167; fragments of soft-porn films in, 139, 149, 157–58, 167; screenshot from website of, 158*fig.*; ubiquity of online streaming of, 136. *See also* pornography; soft-porn films

It Could Happen to You (film), 129
Itha Ivide Vare (film), 187n33
Iyer, Usha, 27

Jabbar, Abdul, 133
Jaikumar, Priya, 62
Janakeeya Kodathi (television show), 108
Janata Party, 5
Janawadi Mahila Samiti, 119
Jan Sanskriti, 5
Janwadi Mahila Samiti, 5
Jayabharati, 187n33
Jeffrey, Craig, 86
Jitendra, 129
Johnson, Eithne, 19
Jordi, 110
Jose, Vazhoor, 181n39
Joseph, Raju, 169
journals, 11
Joy, A. T., 83, 93, 147, 169, 186n20
Joy, K. J., 83
Joymoti (film), 32

Kaagaz Ke Phool (film), 32
Kaamsastra (film), 135
Kadambari (film), 102
Kaif, Katrina, 55
Kairali Arabia, 132
Kairali TV, 11, 132
Kala Kaumudi (film weekly), 82
Kalluvathukkal Kathreena (film), 16–18, 17*fig.*, 97
Kamala (film), 16
kambikathakal, 8, 20, 41, 82, 116
kambipustakam, 81
Kamini (film), 58
kananacinemakal, 81
Kanjirapalli, Jaffar, 104
Kankol, Shivakumar: "A Post-Suicide Note" (poem), 54
Kant, Surya, 31
Kanyaka Talkies (film), 99, 146–47, 149–54; bathing scenes installation used in, 152*fig.*; Silk Smitha image from Lal's installation used in, 151*fig.*
Kaplan, Caren, 117
Kapoor, Ekta, 37
Kapoor, Nina, 6
Kapoor, Raj, 174n15
Kapoor, Randhir, 129
Kapsalis, Terri, 19
Karachi, 122. *See also* Pakistan
Karanjia, B. A., 73

Karimbana (film), 52
Karma News, 164
Karnataka, 21, 67, 84, 94, 112, 121, 156
Karnataka Film Chamber of Commerce, 121
Karwan-e-Hyat (film), 33
Katha Ariyathe (film), 47
Kaviraj, Sudipta, 10
Kerala, 1, 6–11, 15, 30, 62, 67, 74, 78, 83, 90, 94, 108–12, 117, 131–38, 159; co-operative of writers in, 185n50; discussions of obscenity in, 12–13; field of cinema in, 27, 44, 49, 70, 92, 119; literary and cinematic publics of, 73; news cycle of, 166; sex scandals in the public sphere of, 6, 16, 167, 170; sexual frustration among men in, 162; soft-porn wave in, 102; Wayanad district of, 153. *See also* India; Trivandrum
Kerala Film Chamber of Commerce, 99
Kerala State Chalachitra Academy, 82
Kerala State Film Development Corporation (KSFDC), 21, 99
Kerala State Financial Enterprises, 98
Khalifa, Mia, 110
Khamosh (film), 32
Khan, Malaika Arora, 55
Khan, Sana, 55
Khanna, Rajesh, 129
Kiku Films, 83
Kiloyolathumbikal (film), 149
Kinnarathumbikal (film), 97–101, 98*fig.*, 100*fig.*, 104, 110, 149, 187n35
Kipnis, Laura, 19
Kochi, 109, 112
Kochi-Muziris Biennale (2015), 152
Kochu Sita (men's magazine), 42
Kodambakkam, 35, 43–44, 59–75, 90, 97, 113–15, 172; artist's rendition of the map of, 66*fig.*; film labs in, 68, 77; interior of the workshop of a catering unit that serves film crews in, 78*fig.*; Murugan Temple of, 69; origins and development as tinsel town of, 67–71; as remembered space, 71–75; spatiotemporal arrangement of, 86. *See also* Chennai; tinsel town
Koirala, Manisha, 190n81
Kolkata: B-circuit film exhibition in, 139–40; Bhawani Theatre in, 140, 142–43, 142*fig.*; Pradip Cinema in, 140–41, 141*fig.*, 143
Kottarakara, K. P., 51
Kottarakara, Ravi, 120, 122
Kuehn, Kathleen, 87
kulata, 33

Kuliyum Mattu Scenukalam (art installation), 152–53
Kumar, Sanjeev, 129
Kumar, Shanti, 65
Kumar, Udaya, 11
Kumar, Vijeta, 27
Kumararaja, Thiagarajan, 154
Kunchacko, 49
Kunhiraman, Kanayi: *Yakshi* (nude female sculpture), 13
Kutumbam Ena Swargam (film), 4, 5*fig.*
Kuwait, 122

labor practices, 7; alternative, 171; apprenticeship, 60; below-the-line, 60; with film hopefuls, 61, 84; informal, 60; precarity of, 138; of sex work, 189n74; unsafe gendered, 36. *See also* precarity
Laila, 147
Lakshmi, Jyothi, 153
Lal, Mohan, 102
Lal, Priyaranjan, 152–53
Landes, Joan, 10
languages: English, 74, 119; Hindi, 16, 31, 84, 105, 107, 112, 118–19, 143–44, 191n21; Kannada, 16, 43, 55, 67, 84, 105, 121, 185n50; Malayalam, 41, 43, 64, 67–68, 74, 84, 105, 112, 119; Sanskrit, 33, 41; Tamil, 43, 55, 58, 64, 67–68, 74–75, 84, 105; Telugu, 43, 67, 105
Lankesh, Indrajit, 105, 107
Layanam (film), 52–54, 53*fig.*, 99, 185n57
Lee, Keiran, 110
Leone, Sunny (Karenjit Kaur Vohra), 107–10, 109*fig.*, 155
lesbian sex, 23
Locard, Edmond, 56
Lolitha (men's magazine), 42
Lovely (film), 112
low-budget film, 8, 46, 52, 62–63, 70–71, 73, 77, 80–85, 89–90, 97–98, 131
Luthria, Milan, 143
Luv U Alia (film), 107

Maami (film), 101*fig.*
Mackinnon, Catherine, 5
madakarani, 14, 18, 25–27, 31–59, 81, 105, 145, 168–69, 171; actresses cast as, 94–95, 153; screen pleasures of the, 169; theorizing the figure of the, 40–43, 162–64; typecasting as, 49. *See also* soft-porn films
madakathidambu, 51
Madampat, Shajahan, 169–70
Madhuri, 58

Madras. *See* Chennai (also Madras)
Madras Electricity Supply Corporation (MESC), 67
Madras(i) films, 93, 97, 140
Madura Raja (film), 108
Maharashtra, 94, 124
Maharashtra Herald, 119
Mahendra, Balu, 70
Main Aur Tum (film), 129–31
Majumdar, Neepa, 27
Malayalam Chalachitra Parishad, 48
Malayalam Cine Technicians Association (MACTA), 80–81, 88
Malayalanchalachithram (movie and music database), 81
Malaysia, 126
Malik, Veena, 55
Mallapragada, Madhavi, 131
Mammootty, 52, 108
Mangalam (newspaper), 13
Manikyam (film), 187n35
Manimala, Mohan, 82
manipravala sahityam, 41
Manjukalapakshi (film), 97, 187n35
Manjule, Nagraj, 38
Mankekar, Purnima, 28
Manoj, K. R., 149
Manufacturing and Other Companies (Auditor's Report) Order (MAOCARO), 123
manuski, 39
Marar, Kutti Krishna, 12
Maria, 40, 151
marital infidelity, 11
Mark Antony (film), 145
Marunadan Films, 133
mass media, 10; counterfeit, 135; emergence of digital and internet-enabled, 138; transport of illegal, 136. *See also* film; film journalism; media publics; newspapers; photographs; print media; pulp fiction; social media; television; yellow magazines
Master, Thyagarajan, 83
masturbation, 20, 135; female, 23, 156; as replacement for sex, 164. *See also* sexuality
Mathalasa (men's magazine), 42
Mathrubhumi (magazine), 71
Mayer, Vicki, 27
Mazumdar, Ranjani, 40, 63–64
Mazzarella, William, 4
media publics, 9–12, 18, 26, 164–66. *See also* mass media; scandal publics
Mehta, Monika, 20

melodrama, 24–25
Menon, V. B. K., 133
Merryland Studios, 49–50, 70
#MeToo allegations, 168
Middle East, 131–32, 171–72; censorial atmosphere of the, 122. *See also* Gulf migrants, 116–38; Gulf-based Malayali, 91, 93, 118, 132–38, 162, 172, 183n13; Indian workers in the Middle East as, 28, 132–33; in Mumbai, 143. *See also* transnationalism
Miller-Young, Mireille, 25
Mini Fire (men's magazine), 42
Miss Dirty (film), 143
Miss Pamela (film), 52, 105, 106*fig.*
Miss Shakeela (film), 97
Mitchell, W. J. T., 152–53
Mitra, Durba: *Indian Sex Life*, 33
Miyazaki, Hirokazu, 64
Mohan, R., 52
Mohanlal, 52
Motion Picture Export Association of America (MPEA), 124
Movie Times (film magazine), 73
Mudaliar, R. Nadaraja, 43, 67
Mukherjee, Debashree, 60
Mukherjee, Madhuja, 33
mulakkacha, 50
Mules, Warwick, 9
Multimedia Messaging Service (MMS), 112
Mumbai, 51, 64–65, 73–74, 117, 124, 143; B-circuit film exhibition in, 139–40; film production in, 77; New Roshan Theatre in, 140; red-light district of Kamathipura in, 143; Silver Talkies Theatre in, 140, 143–45, 144*fig.*, 146*fig.* *See also* Bombay; India
Muslim identity, 18
Muttuchippi (men's magazine), 42, 121
Muybridge, Eadweard, 151

Naayika (film), 58
Naduvanoor, Shijesh: "Ormayile Nayikamar" (column), 58
Nair, M. T. Vasudevan: *Chitratheruvukal*, 73, 75
Nair, Padmanabhan, 82
Nair, P. A. G.: "What Is the Reason for Excessive Sex-Drive," 102
Nair, Saritha, 166–71, 170*fig.*
Nair, Shashilal, 190n81
Nalla Samayan (film), 34
Nampoothiri, 73
Nana (film magazine), 9, 35, 44–45, 45*fig.*, 48–51, 57, 100, 181n39, 181n45, 181n57

Nash, Jennifer C., 26
nati, 33
National Film Archive of India (NFAI), 93
National Film Development Corporation (NFDC), 28, 73, 117, 123–24, 126, 128
nautch girls, 33
Naya Gupt Gyan (film), 141–42, 142*fig.*
Nazir, Prem, 50–51
neela chitrangal (blue films), 89
Neelakurinji Poothu (film), 104
Neelakuyil (film), 70
Neela Thadakatile Nizhal Pakshikal (film), 89
negotiated anonymity, 83, 92
neoliberal economy, 137, 140
nepotism, 90
New Indian Express, 103*fig.*
newspapers, 11. *See also* mass media
New Theatres Kolkata, 33
New York Times, 47
Nisanth, Deepa, 100–101
Nollywood, 186n16
Non-Resident Indian (NRI) community, 117, 123–32, 137–38, 171, 192n53
nudity, 83, 85; female frontal, 128; use of documentary format to showcase female, 131. *See also* sexuality; women

Obama, President Barack, 110
obituaries, 12, 46–48, 51, 56
obscenity, 4, 12, 13, 36, 55, 100, 102, 110–11, 119, 171
Oman, 122
Om Shanti Om (film), 32
orazchapadangal, 81
Ore Mukham (film), 146
Oru Nadigaiyin Diary (film), 55

Padmarajan, 93
Padmini, Indira, 47–48
Padmini, Polyester, 37
Padmini, Rani, 36, 46–48, 56–57
Paik, Shailaja, 39
painkili, 9, 20, 41, 82, 171, 185n50, 185n52. *See also* pulp fiction
Pakistan, 122, 125
Pakistani *mujra* videos, 28
Pakshiraja Studio, 70
Palekar, Amol, 129
Pamman, 9
Pandian, Anand, 77
Parankimala (film), 47
Parava (film), 146
paricharika, 33

pastoral filmmaking, 85
Patil, Smita, 52
Patita (film), 16
Pati Ya Premi (film), 140
Patreon, 162, 164
Pavada (film), 146–47, 155–56
Pavam Krooran (film), 58
payatti theliyuka, 61
peedhanam, 167
Perilloor Premier League (Malayalam web series), 100
photographs: bedroom, 12, 175n48; from film shoots, 12; nude photo albums, 12; publicity, 72; wedding, 73; with write-up, 44. See also mass media
Pillai, P. Govinda, 21
Pillai, Thakhazhi Sivasankara, 12
Pine, Jason, 85
Pinney, Christopher, 195n16
piracy, 121; shadow economy of smuggling and, 125; video, 122
Play Girls (film), 97, 160
political economy, 183n5; of film production, 61; of waiting, 60
political scandals, 11–13, 16, 23; and sex scandals, 23
Ponnapuramkotta (film), 49–51
Ponnil Kulicha Rathri (film), 93
Pooja Pushpam (film), 48
popular music, 19
pornography, 94; celluloid, 121; hardcore, 18–19, 94; homemade amateur, 142, 158; revenge, 167. See also internet porn; porn stars; soft-porn films
porn stars: agency of, 154–55; as figures of corporeal excess and moral decline, 31, 164; as sexualized women with an unapologetic diva image, 40; transient stardom of, 28; as victims, 154–55. See also pornography; starlets; women
posters, 6; advertising of sex films with, 142–45, 142*fig.*, 146*fig.*; exhibition of soft-porn, 110. See also theaters
pothujanam, 11–12
Prasad, L. V., 73
Prasad, Madhav, 159
Prasad, R. Jay, 98–99, 187n35
Prasad Labs, 23, 68, 77, 127
Prathapachandram, 25
precarity: and body work, 87–115; of production practices, 92–95; of stardom of soft-porn actresses, 95–111. See also labor practices; soft-porn films

print media, 10, 43; English and Hindi, 10; as film magazines, 36; visual and, 23. See also mass media
Private Life (film), 120
production manager, 43, 63, 69, 75–79, 91–92
Profumo affair, 13
progressive literature movement, 12–13
Project Cinema City, 65
projectionists, 22, 24
prostitution, 13, 15–16, 23, 34–35, 50; conflation of film work and, 33, 93–94, 112; illicit relationships and, 12. See also sex workers
Prostitution Prohibition Act, 34
proximate networks, 90, 91
pulp fiction, 10, 12, 41–42, 48, 95, 171; erotic, 116, 137; sensationalism of, 107. See also mass media; *painkili*
Punjab, 94
Purushan Alappuzha, 93
Pushpa: The Rise (film), 118
"Puthumukham" (tabloid column), 46
Pyar Phir Ek Baar (film), 128

Qatar, 122
Qatar Cablevision, 132
queer people, 1–2. See also homosexuality

Radhakrishnan, Biju, 169
Raghu, Bheeman, 83
Raj, Munni, 16
Rajadhyaksha, Ashish, 37
Rajagopal, Arvind, 8, 10
Rajagopal, O.: "Arangozhinja Tharangal" (column), 57
Rajagopalan, Sudha, 123
Rakkilikal (film), 97
Ramankutty, Chunakara, 83
Ramoji Film City (RFC), 65
Ram Teri Ganga Maili (film), 174n15
randam-ezhuthukar, 20
Rangeela (film), 32
Ranjith, Pa, 38
rape, 13, 24, 135; on film, 47–48; and sexual crimes, 106; videos of, 167. See also violence
Rasaleela (film), 97
Rasheeda, Mariam, 13
Rashtradeepika Cinema (film weekly), 58
rathikathakal, 8, 20, 41, 116, 122
Rathilayam (film), 52, 144, 145*fig.*
Rathinirvedam (film), 53, 99, 187n33
Ratna Studio, 70
Raudy Ramu (film), 4

Reshma, 40, 95, 112–13, 142, 142*fig.*, 149, 151, 156–60, 189n74
Reshma Ki Jawani (film), 143, 146*fig.*
resilience, 59
Richard, Mini, 161–63, 163*fig.*, 169–70
Romantic Target (film), 104
Rosapoo (film), 146–47, 149; casting call of, 148*fig.*
Rose, A. M., 147
Roshan, U. C., 147, 187n35
Roshni, 24, 95, 159
Rosy, P. K. (Rajamma), 32
Rowena, Jenny, 27, 38
RRR (film), 118

Sadhana, 153
safe-sex practices, 2; contraceptives, 129. *See also* condoms
Sajini, 95
Sakhi (men's magazine), 42
Samayal Mathiram (sex education television program), 103
Sandhya (men's magazine), 42
Sangharsham (film), 47
Sanjayan (M. R. Nair), 12
Saudi Arabia, 122
savarna, 35, 38–39, 45, 168
Savita Bhabhi (erotic comic series), 102, 188n49
scandal publics, 11, 166–67. *See also* media publics
Screen (film magazine), 73
Screw (adult magazine), 121
Seemanthini (men's magazine), 42
Selvaraj, Mari, 38
sensationalism, 16
Sex and Animals (film), 128–29
sex education, 2–3, 115; films as, 76, 97, 128–31, 130*fig.*, 135; television programs for, 103–4. *See also* film
Sex Education (Netflix show), 104
Sex Education Encyclopedia, The, 121
sex magazines, 12
sexological tracts, 130
sexual harassment, 107, 167
sexuality: exploration of, 2; idealized, 1; imagination of chaste, 10; moralistic tone regarding, 25; need to control women's, 11; normativity of, 9. *See also* foreplay; gender; masturbation; nudity
sex workers, 2, 14, 34, 40, 102, 122, 140, 189n74; confessional accounts of, 43, 108, 136; film roles as, 52; in Gulf massage parlors, 136, 137*fig.*; in red-light district of Mumbai, 143; as "trafficked women," 35. *See also* prostitution

Sexy Girl (film), 5
Shabistan Film Archive project, 156
Shaji Kumar, K. N.: "Malayalathile Classic Rathi Chitrangal" (column), 58
Shajikumar, P. V.: "18+" (short story), 149–50, 153
Shakeela, 3, 27–28, 34–35, 40, 51, 83, 88, 91, 95–115, 122, 147, 151–60, 154*fig.*, 161*fig.*
Shakeela (film), 105–7, 106*fig.*
Shanti, Disco, 37
Sharjah, 121
Sherawat, Mallika, 55
Shivkumar, Rohan, 65
Shivpuri, Om, 129
Shobhanam (film), 97
silent films, 32. *See also* film
Sindhu, 40, 95, 112
Singapore, 126
Singh, Bhrigupati, 16
Singh, Vikram, 127, 131
Sinha, S. N.: *The History of Prostitution*, 33
Sins, Johnny, 110
slut-shaming, 104, 113; online, 149
Smartavicharam, 168
Smitha, Silk, 31, 36–40, 46–48, 52–57, 97, 104–6, 142–45, 151; as cinematic image, 144–45, 151*fig.*
Smitha, Vijayasree, 46–52, 49*fig.*, 56–57
socialism, 124
social media, 109, 112–13, 159–64; Kamakeli page in, 160–61, 161*fig.*; Malayali social media influencers, 161–64; memes of, 160–61; trolling in, 160, 162. *See also* mass media
soft-porn films, 2–10, 52, 73, 81, 83, 90–95, 115, 131, 170–71; alternative production circuits of, 86–96; assignment of "thematic classification" to, 24, 177n96; contemporary B-circuit exhibition of, 140–46, 153, 156; cultural marginality of, 88; as diasporic sociality, 135–38; as digital media, 156–64; directors and technicians who work in, 80, 88–89, 172; as distinct from hardcore pornography, 18; distribution and exhibition of, 29, 149–50, 156; in DVD format, 92, 122, 135–36, 159; female orgasm as the main organizational logic of, 19, 91; feminist history of, 86; fictitious credits in, 27; formal and institutional circuits of, 89–96; impression by an artist of a soft-porn shooting floor, 7*fig.*; indigenous production of, 7; as Madrasi films, 73–74, 140; Malayalam, 3–9, 16, 18–22, 25–29, 33, 41, 62, 90, 116–25, 138–42, 156–66, 171–72; "Midnight Masala" telecasting on cable channels of, 100;

soft-porn films *(continued)*
  narrative importance granted to female characters in, 21–22; as negative form that signals the denigration of moral values and societal norms, 156; in online streaming platforms, 159; political commentary in, 6; popularity among different age groups of male viewers of, 18; popular narratives of the production of, 41, 147, 155–56; re-emergences in cultural objects and public discourse of, 139; resurgence in mainstream Malayalam cinema of, 146–56; waiting for work in, 61–62, 64; "women-centered" narratives in, 111. *See also* cut-pieces; film; glamour films; internet porn; *madakarani*; pornography; precarity; *thundu*
Solar Swapnam (film), 168–69
Sony Betamax, 135
South Indian Chamber of Commerce, 120
Soveksportfil'm, 124, 191n33
Soviet Union, 123, 191n33
Spadikam (film), 52
Speculative capital, 8
Sreedharan, E. V., 82
Sreekala, 44–45
Sreekumar, Bharanikavu, 83, 92
Sreenivasa Cinetone, 67
Sreenivasan, P. K., 70
Srinivas, S. V., 5, 142–43
Srivastava, Sanjay, 8
starlets, 57–61, 83, 92, 94, 113, 149; accounts of the deaths and disappearances of, 61; precarious stardom of, 95, 102. *See also* porn stars
Star of India Glass-Studio, 67
Sthalapuranam (temple history), 67
stock shots, 184n48
Sukran (film), 102
Sundar, Syama: Cartoon, 38–39, 38*fig*.
Sundari Kutty (film), 112
Super Deluxe (film), 146–47, 154–55
Super Good Films, 52, 83
Suryanelli case, 13
Surya TV (satellite channel), 100
svairini, 33
Swapna, 58
Swargam (film), 97

taboo, 23
Tagore, Sharmila, 6
tamasha, 39
Tamil Nadu, 21, 43, 50, 55, 62, 67, 94, 97, 102, 131
Tamil Nadu Exhibition of Films on Television Screen through Video Cassette Recorders and Cable Television Network (Regulation) Act (1984), 192n52
Tatri, Kuriyedattu, 168
television, 10; broadcast of soft-porn films on, 110; diasporic audiences for, 132; internet-distributed, 3; satellite, 6, 136, 155; Tamil, 103. *See also* mass media
Thaniniram (magazine), 11–13, 164
Thaniniram Film Entertainment Magazine (magazine), 11
Thankathoni (film), 97
thatta, 147
thattikoottu padangal, 89, 93
theaters: as all-male spaces, 143, 150; fate of soft-porn, 153; multiplex, 140–41; in the rural hinterlands, 149–50; single-screen, 140, 143. *See also* adult; posters
thirunangai, 107–8
Thitthikkum Iravukal (sex education television program), 103
Thulasidas, 52–53
thundu, 4, 12, 19, 22–24, 50, 58, 93, 98, 127, 129, 150, 156, 159, 161. *See also* soft-porn films
thundu katha, 3
thurannu parachil, 11, 108, 168
Thusharam (film), 47
The Times of India (newspaper), 14, 32–33, 104, 126–27, 135
tinsel town, 62–65, 67–71, 76, 114–15. *See also* film; Kodambakkam
toddy business, 16–17, 50, 181n57
Tower House Studio, 67
trade unionism, 88–89
transnationalism, 116–17; alternative, 123–31; localized, 132; popular imagination of Indian, 131–32, 137. *See also* migrants
Trivandrum, 3, 11, 43, 70, 99, 131–33; S. P. Theatre in, 153–54, 154*fig*. *See also* Kerala
Trump, President Donald, 110
trust, 59; trust-based economy, 26, 85

Udaya Studios, 49–51, 70
United Arab Emirates (UAE), 117, 122, 136; advertisements for massage parlors in the, 136; newspaper advertisements for films from India of the, 134*fig*. *See also* Dubai
United States, 131
Uttama Villain (film), 194n87

Vadakkan Pattukal, 50
Vandichakkaram (film), 37
Vanita (women's magazine), 2

Vasudevan, M. T., 73
Vasudevan, Ravi, 118
Vasudevan, T. E., 99
Velamma (erotic comic series), 102
Vellaripravinte Changathi (film), 58
Venkiteswaran, C. S., 152
veshya, 34, 105
veshyathvam, 34
video, 3, 23–24, 28, 93, 112–13, 121–22, 125, 127, 135–36, 149, 157–58, 163–64, 169, 181. *See also* adult
video cassette recorders (VCRs), 125
Vidler, Anthony, 150
Vigatakumaran (film), 32, 69–70
Vijay, 102
Vijayakumar, Thrikkunnappuzha, 91, 93–94
Vijayanirmala, 50
Vijayasree, 36, 48–52, 56–57, 97
Vijaya Vauhini, 43, 126
Vikram, 102
Vilkanundu Swapnangal (film), 133
Vinayan, 80–81, 112
violence, 2; gendered and sexual, 155–56; images of sex and, 3, 50; sexual, 35, 168, 171, 195n10. *See also* rape
Virgin Lady (film), 140, 141*fig*.
Vishudha Smitha (anthology of poems), 54–55
visibility capital, 115
voyeurism, 12, 41

Waite, Louise, 115
wait-time economy, 60–65, 75–80, 85–86; management of the, 87. *See also* cinematic wait-time; film
Warner, Michael, 10
Whitman, Alden, 47
Wilkinson, Clare M., 27
Williams, Linda, 18–19, 94
women: as actresses paid much less than actors in the Malayalam film industry, 189n68; "derogatory portrayal" in film of, 174n15; forceful exposure by men of, 155; management of catering units from their homes in Kodambakkam by, 68; middle-aged, 102, 161, 164; middle-class (*savarna*), 35, 45, 168; native Malayali, 97; pornography as subordination to patriarchal power for, 5; and sexual and gender normativity, 9, 161; sexual empowerment of, 39, 91, 154–55, 161; sexualized imagination of rustic, 163, 163*fig*. *See also* feminism; nudity; porn stars
women's organizations, 55, 119

Yaamini (film), 97
yellow magazines, 10, 12, 36, 42–43, 102, 171. *See also* mass media
Young Women's Christian Association, 119
YouTube channels, 92, 99

Zacharia, Paul, 52

Founded in 1893,
UNIVERSITY OF CALIFORNIA PRESS
publishes bold, progressive books and journals
on topics in the arts, humanities, social sciences,
and natural sciences—with a focus on social
justice issues—that inspire thought and action
among readers worldwide.

The UC PRESS FOUNDATION
raises funds to uphold the press's vital role
as an independent, nonprofit publisher, and
receives philanthropic support from a wide
range of individuals and institutions—and from
committed readers like you. To learn more, visit
ucpress.edu/supportus.

www.ingramcontent.com/pod-product-compliance
Lightning Source LLC
Chambersburg PA
CBHW070802230426
43665CB00017B/2454